The
Hugh MacDiarmid
Anthology

The Scottish Series

General editor: Alexander Scott

The Scottish Series will include in its range books on every aspect of Scottish literature and social history from the earliest times to the present, including anthologies (both poetry and prose), new editions of Scottish classics, scholarly studies, critical surveys, and collections of essays. These volumes will be designed for the general reader and the serious student alike, and the editors of the various volumes will be recognized authorities in their different fields.

The first publication, in 1972, will be *The Hugh MacDiarmid Anthology*, edited by Michael Grieve (MacDiarmid's son) and Alexander Scott. Issued in honour of the poet's eightieth birthday, this will constitute the most representative selection of his work published to date, illustrating the full scope of Scotland's greatest living writer.

The following volumes are planned for publication in 1973:

A Scottish Ballad Book, edited by David Buchan, Senior Lecturer in English Studies, University of Stirling.

Burns: Critical Essays, edited by Donald Low, Lecturer in English, University of St Andrews.

The 18th Century Scottish Lyric, edited by Thomas Crawford, Senior Lecturer in English, University of Aberdeen.

The general editor of the series, Alexander Scott—the poet, dramatist, critic and biographer—is Head of the Department of Scottish Literature in the University of Glasgow.

The Hugh MacDiarmid Anthology

POEMS IN SCOTS AND ENGLISH

Edited by
Michael Grieve and Alexander Scott

Routledge & Kegan Paul
London and Boston

First published 1972
by Routledge & Kegan Paul Ltd
Broadway House, 68–74 Carter Lane,
London EC4V 5EL and
9 Park Street,
Boston, Mass, 02108, U.S.A.

Printed in Great Britain by
Richard Clay (The Chaucer Press) Ltd
Bungay, Suffolk

Library of Congress Catalog Card Number: 72–83662
ISBN 0 7100 7432 8

Contents

Foreword

This anthology is published in honour of the eightieth birthday of Christopher Murray Grieve ('Hugh MacDiarmid'), and in celebration of the half-century of his great career under that celebrated *nom de plume* (*et de guerre*). It is the first such work to begin to approach something like adequacy in its representation of poems from every period of his production since 'Hugh MacDiarmid' made his bow in *The Scottish Chapbook* magazine on 26 August 1922, a fortnight after the poet's thirtieth birthday.

Although he has since written much remarkable verse in English, MacDiarmid first achieved fame as a poet in Scots. The texts of the Scots poems in these pages follow those of their original book or magazine publication, and this despite the fact that MacDiarmid has recently been persuaded to express a desire that those poems should be re-spelt in accordance with the 'Scots Style Sheet'. (This attempt to standardize the spelling of Scots was composed by members of the Makars' Club—Scottish poets of a younger generation than MacDiarmid—in 1947, more than a decade after he had turned to writing mainly in English.) Although one of the present editors collaborated with the distinguished American scholar, Professor John C. Weston, on the text of his re-spelt edition of MacDiarmid's Scots masterpiece, *A Drunk Man Looks at the Thistle* (University of Massachusetts Press, 1971), we believe that no revised version of the poet's work in Scots can enjoy true authority unless it is made by MacDiarmid himself—and that is a task which he has shown no sign of undertaking.

Ten of the poems given here were not included in MacDiarmid's inaccurately entitled *Collected Poems* (1962 and 1967). We are obliged to Messrs MacGibbon & Kee for permission to include 'On a Raised Beach' and 'Whuchulls' from *A Lap of Honour* (1967).

The head of MacDiarmid on the dust-jacket is from the full-length painting by Aba Bayevsky.

M.G.
A.S.

Hugh MacDiarmid: The Man

Wind-blasted Whalsay, sodden with the peat of forgotten centuries where trees grew and none now stand, was home—a bucket or two of earth in the chilled lapping bitterness of the North Sea; a place where, at midnight, you can read beneath the stars in the *simmer's dim;* and where, in the black thunder of winter, with a shaky moon catching the tumbling fluoresence of warring waves, life became a virgin's ring of uneasy and frustrating self-containment.

Yet it was here, in a fisherman's cottage, abandoned because of death, with the net-mending loft steep-staired above, that he sat—a self-induced Scottish Siberia that allowed no compromise, where mind over matter was the reality, the only salvation; and the loneliness of hardship was contrasted by the bubbling fleshpots of success, where ambition spurred by acclamation turned into reputation and recognition.

The blazing peat fire, surviving in its grey ashes through the hollow of the night to be fanned fresh with the rising sun, patterned his legs to a tartan-red, and great blisters swelled. But nothing matched the white-heat of passionate concentration, the marathon of sleepless nights and days that suddenly ended the sitting around for months indulging in that most deceptive of exercises—thinking.

At such times, conversation was the whispered undertone of necessity, and childhood became a game of patience without the understanding, though the time-machine of words was forever careering madly, powered largely in those early years by the splendours of Scottish history, and its built-in pattern of betrayal and defeat—the fingerprint that detects the unsuccessful.

Fat mackerel, full of oily richness, and cod's roe, like the balls of a bull, fed us—for the islanders, blunt as only a Force Ten can make you, cared for neither. Galvanized buckets, ugly to the feel, stood around filled with seagulls' eggs, obscene in their white-coating of preservative. And the eternal thick black twist, powerful and cool, was a haloed wreath of blue, its smoke thinning to disappearance in the caressing glow of the Aladdin lamp, prim and polished and upright; a light uncannily susceptible to draught, when the mantle crusted black, the edges a creeping red, and the atmosphere in the house whipped and flayed the nerve ends —until once again there was light.

Armed with the long inheritance of a frontier's people, chromosome-encrusted with Border forays, genes menaced by the oozing growth of

England's greed; with the imagination only a genius can occasionally light, and a sense of purpose allied to principle, he took on the smooth, sophisticated, self-congratulatory world of English literature, and established the basis and the fact of the Scottish Renaissance almost single-minded.

But prophets are best remembered dead, and the MacDiarmid message was—and is—far from simple. Not only was the main bulk of his early work in Scots, an almost insuperable, impenetrable barrier to critics and reviewers who had little time to explore the indulgence of individuality in a tongue so strange to their well-trained ears, with its triple-edged meanings and allusions terrifying in their unfamiliarity—especially after taking a degree in English Literature.

Even worse, in English he used words that only the omnivorously erudite would be likely to know; and he scattered quotations, whether from geology or religion, that gained stature by being out of context, and stuck like burrs.

I remember, as the intricate dazzle of Fair Isle patterns grew beneath my mother's needles, the balls of wool bouncing to the kitten's claws, how I eagerly thumbed through the hand-heavy dictionary in an attempt to catch this smoke-hazed figure out—not just at spelling, that would have been too difficult, and there were words I could scarcely sound out, the clutter of their vowels and consonants having fallen from a riddle-shaker.

It was the meanings of the words, their shimmering suggestiveness, the exciting exactness, the image-conjuring. It was a game not to be won; the dictionary and he had established a rare accord of mutual esteem.

There were friends, shooting stars from the south, who travelled sea-sick in wonderment that anyone could exist, let alone live, so far away from the coin-in-slot of civilization, the instant familiarity of people and influence.

Radar had not yet been invented, but his mind blip-blipped its way round the world, extracting information from books and people, the life-line of periodicals and newspapers, which enabled him to build up new patterns of knowledge, and keep the old informations intact.

There were strains, too. The great long poem on *Mature Art* scrunched so hard into a ball of desperate irritation and neglect that it destroyed the carefully built peat fire like a cannon-shot, sending red sparks clouding aloft to grow black on the book spines. Its very tightness, however, saved it from extinction, the outer pages tea-coloured to a crisp as my mother—an eye to the hurricane of creativity—burned her fingers, ignoring the angry torment that urged its abandonment to the nethermost reaches of his own personal hell.

Beneath the card table, sorting tangles of wool, I watched and wondered at the raging quiet of violence, and quaked at the great bang that almost lifted the front door from its hinges. But on an island such as Whalsay there are no places to go; the neighbours few and far; the pubs non-existent.

Whisky came by boat, and when the towering doctor, David Orr, got in his supplies; or the minister, MacKay, decided to prove his strength by tempting the Devil—then white corpuscles turned red and the dawn came and went as the floodgates of conversation fasted them of food. The dead might wait, and the sick groan louder—but in the long year of island life a little time off was grudged by none.

On the only radio set on the island, the news crackled out—war had been declared and the Great War— the war to end all wars—had been relegated to the position of an *hors d'oeuvre*. The old clichés were lovingly dusted, silver-tongued medals of glory. Freedom was the battle-cry and war began to sweep the world. The Treaties and the safety measures were the wastepaper of a generation, the sacrifices had not been enough, and politicians dislodged each other so they could gain ephemeral honour—and make the same mistakes as before.

At the age of fifty, the battlefields of Salonika, where he once had his teeth out with half-a-bottle of whisky as anaesthetic, were not for him. We saw him off from Symbister in the heavy old rowing boat which pulled to the anchored height of the *Earl of Zetland*. In the War Reserve, he was on his way to Glasgow to work in a Clydebank munitions factory. Hands that controlled the mind's pulse now clasped copper bands for shells; and eyes that read words by their tens of millions now searched the blackout streets for some distinguishable feature. Nyctalopia is a poor affliction in a city night-shrouded for war, when even the glow of the moon is cursed as it turns oil-dirty rivers into silvered flarepaths for the restless bomber pilots overhead, the sweat seeping out of them and flak splintering all around.

We sailed in 1942, on the same boat my father had taken, laden with forty tea-chests crammed with manuscripts and books. Whatever happened, whether the Herrenvolk hysteria whipped by Hitler, or the carefully articulated bombast of Churchill triumphed—there would be no going back.

The sweetest memories of childhood sank below the horizon and Whalsay, all love, and sorrow, and longing, became a miniaturized complex circuit imprinted on the memory, an electric light to be switched on though fingers fumble at the switch.

In the creaking rooms of landladies, saggy-breasted and pinched with a stale self-righteousness, who ever-complained about the waste of the light, my father sat up half the night with that compelling energy, and continued to combat the exhaustion of war work by writing and speaking in those endless years of misery.

As the war spluttered to a standstill in Europe, and blasted a launching pad for the Third World War at Hiroshima, the hard days were still with us. Money was uncannily scarce, recognition as slow to come as an acorn sprouting on rock-sheathed soil. Even, for a time, he went back to weekly journalism, forced to a concern about the meaningless trivia of minor court cases, the empty-headed pronouncements of local councillors, the carefully tuned pontification of a sermon, the long ritual of the living life in death; the acceptance of authority from people who employed words like wet concrete in contrast to the individual polish, the harmony of delicate balance.

But like a long-distance writer he carried on, each obstacle yet another experience—and gradually, despite all the difficulties of language, isolation and neglect, the strands of a world reputation began to emerge as positive and enduring.

Mild and gentle, disarmingly polite to strangers (and even to well-known bores), he does not compromise. It is a trait which people pretend to admire. Some do. But it is also embarrassing and difficult, success is so much harder to achieve unless you bend a little, unless you set out to be acceptable in the sense that you are not a living and articulate affront to consciences that stir darkly—and when little is at stake.

There would have been many paths to follow but the dictating pattern of our lives is not so easily escaped. And in the Scotland of today—anxious to be emasculated as penance for some imagined wrong—to remain your own man is even more difficult, more strewn with hazards, than might easily be imagined.

Especially when his contempt today for the 'whole gang of high mucky-mucks, famous fatheads, old wives of both sexes, stuffed shirts, hollow men with headpieces stuffed with straw, bird-wits, lookers-under-beds, trained seals, creeping Jesuses, Scots Wha Ha'evers ... Commercial Calvinists, makers of "noises like a turnip", and all the touts and toadies and lickspittles of the English Ascendancy, and their infernal women-folk, and all their skunkoil skullduggers', is just as decisively searing as the day he wrote these words in *Lucky Poet*.

Courage sparkles with many facets—from the schizophrenia of the spy festering in his long-waiting secrecy for the one moment of justification, to the coolness of the bomb disposal expert, an unknown touch away from eternity, or the brave acceptance of the cancer-ridden, smiling still as they waste to death—or there is the courage that keeps you going when others have long fallen by whatever wayside idol they find themselves opposite when the music stops, when they decide to compromise.

Of course, people like my father are lucky. They are committed, impelled to write, to compose, to dance, to explore—their energies and their talents focus, and they seem to have that sixth sense that occasionally ripples across us all.

In Scotland, too, politically and economically a poor place with a correspondingly low threshold of intellectual awareness and activity, the sheer stretching of the mind has been difficult and often impossible. If people, for reasons innumerable, don't understand what you are driving at, what your aims and intentions are, what you are trying to *do*—then conversation becomes a second-rate affair, a shallow river that passes for communication. To explore the deep, dark holes without the diver's-suit protection of conventional attitudes and responses, takes a courage that cannot be imposed from without, and rarely sustained from within.

He has faults—who has not? Yet one of his gifts is that he throws no shadow. His influence is one of illumination and, at the age of almost eighty, he has gained that state which so many strive for and fail to achieve despite being draped with worldly honours and successes—immortality.

From the weaving town of Langholm, hard by the English border, he has laboured long to produce the 'many splendoured thing' that now survives as his poetic vision. Of course, it is tattered—mountaineers don't exercise in public at 29,000 feet. But he has scaled the heights without becoming an eccentric, a recluse, eaten with egotism, or pompous as to his work, position or reputation. As though he had signed some self-denying ordinance, he has been unsparingly available to all—at home, to universities where the journey has been a tribulation, the fee scarcely worth the fare. For a man who has stood within the entombed history of the Kremlin, walked the Great Wall of China, been in both halves of Berlin, and travelled in almost every European country, lectured in Canada and America, he finds the detail of travel excessively annoying, particularly as movement stops him reading. So far, however, he has always arrived—while others of eminence have resisted outside demands on their time, demanded and gained protection from duty, and been cossetted by publishers so their every word is easily available.

People, meeting him for the first time, and knowing of him through the bare bones of public announcements, or having heard him speak in debate, are commonly amazed by his humility and excessive 'ordinariness'. It is a mask that is occasionally breeched. At a P.E.N. cocktail party (he founded the Scottish branch) he was cornered by two stick-dry ladies who wanted to squeeze every vicarious drop of experience from the encounter of meeting a real, live poet. Well aware that closing time was advancing with awesome speed (pubs in Scotland shut at 9.30 then) he decided the only way to escape was to propose a toast as a farewell salutation—'Ladies, may the skins of your arses never cover a banjo!'

Quite uncharacteristic, if not apocryphal—but reasonably apt. Meaningful survival in Scotland, even in physical terms, is hard in the arts. He has not only survived but flourished—on his own terms. The grit in the oyster now sets the value.

Michael Grieve

MacDiarmid: The Poet

Scotland's greatest living poet, and arguably the very greatest of all the makars who have written in the Scots tradition, Hugh MacDiarmid is also one of the great poets of the world, for he has succeeded in his early aim to 'aye be whaur/Extremes meet', and his work is both national and international, his aim to nourish 'the little white rose of Scotland' co-existing with his resolution 'to bring Scottish literature into closer touch with current European tendencies in technique and ideation'.

Christopher Murray Grieve was born in 1892 in the village of Langholm in Dumfriesshire, within striking distance of the English border. As an inheritor of the fighting spirit of the old Border forayers, he has been a 'bonnie fechter' all his adult life, the representative of a Scottish radicalism seeking to sweep away the conventionality and mediocrity of merely 'received' opinions and attitudes. When he began his literary career in the years immediately following the First World War—which, ostensibly fought on behalf of 'gallant little Serbia' and/or 'gallant little Belgium', had shocked him into concern with his own small country—the Scots tradition was in ruins after more than a century of slavish imitations of Burns by versifiers who were content to sketch only the surface mannerisms of the Scottish scene. The young poet had to achieve nothing less than the restoration of Lowland Scots as a literary language at the same time as he sought to employ it to express the highest reaches of spiritual and intellectual awareness and the deepest levels of emotional and physical experience—matters which had all too seldom found utterance in Scots since the work of the major medieval poets, Henryson, Dunbar and Douglas.

Although he was a native speaker of Scots, Grieve earliest achieved notice as the author of verse in English, and at first he opposed the contemporary movement towards the revival of Scots which the Vernacular Circle of the London Burns Club had begun in 1920. This he regarded as 'a backwater', and when he published the first issue of his literary review, *The Scottish Chapbook*, in August 1922, its slogan was 'Not Traditions—Precedents!' But the current propaganda in favour of Scots led him to investigate it and to experiment with its possibilities. In the course of that experimentation, C. M. Grieve became 'Hugh MacDiarmid', in whose work both traditions and precedents were to play their parts.

Like Stevenson in the nineteenth century and Burns in the eighteenth,

MacDiarmid employed a literary Scots which, while it was based on the speech of his native place, incorporated words which were still alive in the mouths of the people in other parts of Scotland; and he also employed terms which he found enjoying a somewhat dubious immortality in literary and lexicographical sources. Most often, in the lyrics of *Sangschaw* (1925) and *Penny Wheep* (1926), and in his masterpiece, the extended rhapsody *A Drunk Man Looks at the Thistle* (1926), he used occasional archaisms with considerable tact, so weaving them into the texture of spoken Scots that they drew life from their context.

MacDiarmid was the first modern Scots poet whose original verse expressed a post-romantic sensibility; and he was the first to be acutely aware of the contemporary world. The eight short lines of 'The Bonnie Broukit Bairn' contain immensity, for the poem's concern is not confined to a single local parish, as in the fashion of the followers of Burns, but extends to the whole of creation, as the individual stands alone in the darkness, confronting the world around him and the stars above. Again, in 'The Seamless Garment', where MacDiarmid seeks to express his conception of how society should be woven into an integrated and harmonious whole, he uses images derived from the weaving of cloth in a Border textile-mill, the images of a predominantly industrial world, not—as in nearly all earlier Scots verse—those of a community almost entirely rural.

In *Sangschaw* and *Penny Wheep*, the short lyrics possess intensity of passion, audacity of imagery, and original and often profoundly-haunting rhythmical patterns. MacDiarmid had the power to create in a few lines an emotional force of extraordinary strength, and to evoke scenes and situations which, while they are perfectly precise and definite in themselves, nevertheless suggest a whole world of experience behind and beyond them. Yet the latter volume also contains some longer poems on philosophical themes which anticipate much of MacDiarmid's later work, from *A Drunk Man* onwards. No Scottish poet has ever had a finer command of the lyric cry; and none has been less content with it.

In language, the greatest influence on the early MacDiarmid was Jamieson's *Etymological Dictionary of the Scottish Language* (1808), where he found in the Scots vocabulary 'a *vis comica* that has not yet been liberated . . . and in its potential uprising would be no less prodigious, uncontrollable and utterly at variance with conventional morality than was Joyce's tremendous outpouring' in *Ulysses*. In criticism, the major source was Gregory Smith's *Scottish Literature: Character and Influence* (1919), which coined the phrase 'the Caledonian Antisyzygy' for the combination of opposing qualities which Smith held to be a distinctively Scottish characteristic, declaring: 'There is more in the Scottish antithesis of the real and the fantastic than is to be explained by the familiar rules of rhetoric. The sudden jostling of contraries seems to preclude any relationship by literary suggestion. The one invades the other without warning. They are the "polar twins" of the Scottish Muse.'

From Gregory Smith, MacDiarmid derived his view that 'The essence of the genius of our race ... is the reconciliation it effects between the base and the beautiful, recognizing that they are complementary and indispensable to one another', while the dictionary opened his eyes to the way in which the Scots language, embalmed in Jamieson, telescoped 'divers attitudes of mind or shades of temper ... into single words or phrases, investing the whole speech with subtle flavours of irony, commiseration, realism and humour.' This attitude to his medium and to the Scots people who had produced it found its most successfully sustained expression in *A Drunk Man Looks at the Thistle*, the greatest 'poem of some length' in the Scottish verse tradition, and one of the very few achieved extended poems—if not the only one—written in Britain or America since 1900, a work ranging far and wide over time and space, exploring the fundamental mysteries of love and death and human destiny as those are reflected in a Scottish poet's investigation and exploitation of his own creative powers.

In form, the poem—or sequence of poems—is a dramatic monologue, a meditation on Scotland, the world, and universal life as these are viewed through the eyes of an intoxicated reveller who has tumbled into a roadside ditch while plodding his weary way homeward from the pub. As such, it is full of abrupt transitions and sudden changes of mood, those being dictated by the association of ideas in the drunk man's mind as his intoxicated imagination reels and plunges across the universe. Naturally enough, given the central character's predicament, such associations are often incongruous, violent, or ironical, and the poem proceeds by a series of shocks of surprise, as the sublime suggests the ridiculous and the ridiculous the sublime. There is no other Scottish poem which resolves within itself so many of the contradictions of experience, delighting equally in the lovely and the grotesque, the profound and the profane, finding beauty in the terrible and terror in the trumpery.

The work, which astonishes by its appetite for experience, is 'large, and contains multitudes', because it reflects—and is bound together by—the complex character of its protagonist, who is by turns (and sometimes all together) a satirical critic of Scottish life, a wondering spectator of his own situation, a lover of beauty whose senses are alive to the finger-tips, and a speculator on the mysteries of time and fate. MacDiarmid has been described as possessing 'genius of a wild and truculent order', and in *A Drunk Man* the wildness combines with wit,

xix

and the truculence with self-criticism, to produce a poem which is at once a portrait of the author, a vision of the world, and an exploration of the nature of reality. 'A sardonic lover in the routh of contraries', MacDiarmid creates new and striking harmonies from elements of comedy, satire, farce, documentary, lyricism and tragedy, the range and richness of his personality going far towards resolving the contradictions of experience.

How novel and individual an achievement *A Drunk Man* was at the time of its original publication, almost half a century ago, may be in some danger of being overlooked now, when MacDiarmid's success has spurred three generations of younger poets to attempt verse in Scots which seeks to be universal rather than parochial in theme. The departure which MacDiarmid made from the Scots tradition as interpreted during the first two decades of the century was radical. That tradition, still content to follow the folk-song comedy and pathos of Burns and the glamourie of the ballads, still accepting a narrowness of intellectual scope and a limitation of theme to the local concerns of everyday, had been dominant but decadent in Scotland for at least a century. MacDiarmid broke with it; he made 'a new thing', a poem at once popular and profound, a work written mainly in Scots—which he had spoken as a boy in his native village—but which, far from limiting itself to village affairs, ranged over the whole world and all the heavens, tussling and teasing those mysteries which have tormented the minds of men in all ages and in every country, and plundering the literature of the present and the past, of other nations and of his own, to add the treasure of their words to the richness of his own vocabulary. He made Scots what it had not been since medieval times, a tongue capable of expressing the immensities. For behind MacDiarmid, as behind Gregory Smith, stands that other great poet, Coleridge, with his belief in the Imagination as 'the balance or reconciliation of opposite or discordant qualities'. This imaginative power makes *A Drunk Man* a work for the whole world. The drunk man is humanity, and its voice is MacDiarmid's.

The poem remains his supreme achievement in the synthesis of vernacular and literary elements which the French critic Denis Saurat called 'synthetic Scots'. Although MacDiarmid was to continue writing in Scots for most of another decade, and to extend his range of themes, he was never again to weave so many aspects of existence into a living unity. His next volume, *To Circumjack Cencrastus* (1930), an even longer poem-sequence than *A Drunk Man*, contains many passages of sustained intellectual exploration in Scots—and much else besides—but it lacks the unity of form which the device of the drunk man as protagonist enabled MacDiarmid to attain in its predecessor. In later volumes he investigates his early environment and his ancestry, seeking the source of his own inspiration, in verse remarkable on some occasions for its onomatopoeic power and on others for its ability to combine passion with profundity. Yet these poems, fine as a number of them are, represent individual facets of his concerns rather than the complete fusion of every mood of his personality expressed in *A Drunk Man*. Some of this later work in Scots, too, is spoiled by the intrusion of propagandist politics, both of the Scottish nationalist and the marxist varieties. MacDiarmid was always much too much of an individualistic rebel against the nature of things to make himself into a run-of-the-mill party politician, and in the course of the thirties he achieved the distinction of being expelled from the Scottish National Party on account of his communism and from the Communist Party of Great Britain on account of his nationalism, yet in some of his political poems he attempts to express all-too-positive affirmations which seem crude beside the finely-calculated clash of contradictions in his most characteristic work, and where the style is as undistinguished as much of the content. His most successful political poem, 'The Seamless Garment', escapes these strictures by being firmly based on the actualities of Scottish experience.

During this period, however, MacDiarmid was turning more and more towards English, impelled there by his increasing concern with the philosophical implications of the scientific investigation of the universe. After the union of the Crowns in 1603, and throughout the centuries when Scots was increasingly regarded as the language of 'the lower orders', it had lost much of its intellectual vocabulary, and it had never possessed a scientific one—thereby presenting the modern Scottish poet whose interests were directed towards the sciences with a linguistic problem too great for any one man, even a writer of MacDiarmid's superlative talent, to be able to solve alone. Never afraid to attempt the impossible, he wrote some remarkable *tours de force* in Scots on political and scientific themes, but the strain was evidently too great for the effort to be sustained, and the bulk of his later work is composed in an English more immediately suited to his subject-matter.

As a poet in English, MacDiarmid is in direct descent from his boy-hood hero, the poet John Davidson—the subject of one of his most moving, and most concentrated, elegies. Davidson, in the work of his last decade, rejected the religious interpretation of life impressed upon him in childhood by his father, an evangelical minister, and expressed in his epics and tragic dramas a gospel proclaiming that the whole universe is explicable in terms of matter alone. Like his hero, MacDiarmid conceives much of his later work on an epic scale, banishes God from the universe, rejects most—if not all—mysticism, and bends his power towards the expression of what he calls 'a poetry of facts', the facts being of the kind that can be tested by the scientific intelligence. As he writes in his autobiography, *Lucky Poet* (1943): 'I am all for the driving, restless movement of the critical intellect. I want a poetry of fact and first-hand experience and scientific knowledge that is right about every technical detail. What my ideal amounts to is the poetical equivalent of one of nature's annual miracles—the flowering of Daphne Mezereum, the sudden burgeoning of beauty from the bare brown twigs.' The realization of MacDiarmid's ideal, the flowering of poetry from the bare facts, can be seen in such a poem as 'Crystals like Blood', which has the apparent artlessness that conceals the highest art.

Nevertheless, 'Crystals like Blood', in its brevity, expresses only one aspect of existence, and—generally speaking—MacDiarmid in his later work wishes to express the whole of it, to collect and arrange such a tremendous assembly of facts that 'their fineness and profundity of organization ... is the condition of a variety great enough/To express all the world's.' Small wonder that, elsewhere, he describes the kind of poetry he seeks to create as 'such poems as might be written in eternal life'—for it would seem that only the God who has been expelled from MacDiarmid's universe could experience and express the simultaneous synthesis of all knowledge which is the poet's aim. The range of reference in the later poems is wider than that in any other modern poetry in English, but it is still scarcely wide enough for MacDiarmid to qualify as the exemplar of Rilke's dictum that 'the poet must know everything', and nothing less than such a totality of knowledge would appear to be able to achieve MacDiarmid's purpose.

Even as things are, however, the weight of his erudition—whether earned or borrowed—threatens not infrequently to crush the poetry and bury its emotional impetus under an accumulation of technical details. What MacDiarmid calls 'The terrific and sustained impact/Of intellect upon passion and passion upon intellect', which the later work seeks to express, is sometimes replaced by a kind of passionless recollection, or—even less satisfactorily—by a painstaking catalogue of scientific references which appear to have been culled from text-books. His manner of expression, too, often seems perfunctory, as if he were so intent on what he has to say as to have only a lesser interest in how it gets said. However, the above criticisms are only interim judgments, for all of MacDiarmid's late poems, even the bulky *In Memoriam James Joyce*, are eventually intended to be seen as parts of a mammoth 'work in progress', *Mature Art*, and it may be that in the perspective of the complete epic—should it ever take form as such—the more prosaic passages will find their own level and play their part in the total effect, whatever that may turn out to be. Certainly, on the occasions when MacDiarmid's own passions are directly involved, the rhythms of the verse quicken and cohere, and the recital of facts becomes charged with a potent energy whose effect is all the more powerful for the complete absence of any element which approaches conventional poeticizing.

Hugh MacDiarmid has the widest scope of any Scottish poet, intellectually, emotionally, and in command of verse forms, and to try to sum up his achievement in a few thousand words is a vain attempt 'to put an ocean in a mutchkin'. But the greatness of his work speaks for itself.

Alexander Scott

Department of Scottish Literature,
University of Glasgow

From *Sangschaw* (1925)

The Bonnie Broukit Bairn

(For Peggy)

Mars is braw in crammasy,
Venus in a green silk goun,
The auld mune shak's her gowden feathers,
Their starry talk's a wheen o' blethers,
Nane for thee a thochtie sparin',
Earth, thou bonnie broukit bairn!
—*But greet, an' in your tears ye'll droun*
The haill clanjamfrie!

The Watergaw

Ae weet forenicht i' the yow-trummle
I saw yon antrin thing,
A watergaw wi' its chitterin' licht
Ayont the on-ding;
An' I thocht o' the last wild look ye gied
Afore ye deed!

There was nae reek i' the laverock's hoose
That nicht—an' nane i' mine;
But I hae thocht o' that foolish licht
Ever sin' syne;
An' I think that mebbe at last I ken
What your look meant then.

---

broukit, neglected   bairn, child   braw, handsome   crammasy, crimson
wheen o' blethers, pack of nonsense   greet, weep   clanjamfrie, collection

watergaw, indistinct rainbow   forenicht, early evening
yow-trummle, cold weather after sheep-shearing   antrin, rare
chitterin', shivering   on-ding, onset (of rain)   reek, smoke
laverock, lark   sin' syne, since then

Au Clair de la Lune

(For W.B.)

> . . . *She's yellow*
> *An' yawps like a peany.*
>
> Anon.

> *They mix ye up wi' loony fowk,*
> *Wha are o' stars the mense,*
> *The madness that ye bring to me,*
> *I wadna change't for sense.*
>
> W.B.

I

Prelude to Moon Music

Earth's littered wi' larochs o' Empires,
Muckle nations are dust.
Time'll meissle it awa', it seems,
An' smell nae must.

But wheest!—Whatna music is this,
While the win's haud their breath?
—*The Moon has a wunnerfu' finger*
For the back-lill o' Death!

---

loony fowk, mad people   mense, ornament

larochs, fragments   meissle, crumble   must, bad smell   wheest, hush
back-lill, thumb-hole on bagpipe chanter

II

Moonstruck

When the warl's couped soon' as a peerie
That licht-lookin' craw o' a body, the moon,
Sits on the fower cross-win's
Peerin' a' roon'.

She's seen me—she's seen me—an' straucht
Loupit clean on the quick o' my hert.
The quhither o' cauld gowd's fairly
Gi'en me a stert.

An' the roarin' o' oceans noo'
Is peerieweerie to me:
Thunner's a tinklin' bell: an' Time
Whuds like a flee.

III

The Man in the Moon

Oh, lad, I fear that yon's the sea
Where they fished for you and me,
And there, from whence we both were ta'en,
You and I shall drown again.
                                        A. E. Housman

The moonbeams kelter i' the lift,
An' Earth, the bare auld stane,
Glitters beneath the seas o' Space,
White as a mammoth's bane.

---

couped, tilted   soon', sound   peerie, spinning top   craw, crow
loupit, leapt   quhither, beam   peerieweerie, dwindled to a thread of sound
whuds, flits   flee, fly

kelter, undulate   lift, sky

5

An', lifted owre the gowden wave,
Peers a dumfoun'ered Thocht,
Wi' keethin' sicht o' a' there is,
An' bodily sicht o' nocht.

IV

The Huntress and her Dogs

Her luchts o' yellow hair
Flee oot ayont the storm,
Wi' mony a bonny flaught
The colour o' Cairngorm.

Oot owre the thunner-wa'
She haiks her shinin' breists,
While th' oceans to her heels
Slink in like bidden beasts.

So sall Earth's howlin' mobs
Drap, lown, ahint the sang
That frae the chaos o' Thocht
In triumph braks or lang.

Crowdieknowe

Oh to be at Crowdieknowe
When the last trumpet blaws,
An' see the deid come loupin' owre
The auld grey wa's.

---

keethin' sicht, glimpse, as of salmon ripple

luchts, locks   flaught, gleam   haiks, trails   lown, silent   or, ere

Crowdieknowe, graveyard   loupin', leaping

Muckle men wi' tousled beards,
I grat as a bairn
'll scramble frae the croodit clay
Wi' feck o' swearin'.

An' glower at God an' a' his gang
O' angels i' the lift
—Thae trashy bleezin' French-like folk
Wha gar'd them shift!

Fain the weemun-folk'll seek
To mak' them haud their row
—*Fegs, God's no blate gin he stirs up*
The men o' Crowdieknowe!

The Innumerable Christ

Other stars may have their Bethlehem, and their Calvary too.
Professor J. Y. Simpson

Wha kens on whatna Bethlehems
Earth twinkles like a star the nicht,
An' whatna shepherds lift their heids
     In its unearthly licht?

'Yont a' the stars oor een can see
An' farther than their lichts can fly,
I' mony an unco warl' the nicht
     The fatefu' bairnies cry.

I' mony an unco warl' the nicht
The lift gaes black as pitch at noon,
An' sideways on their chests the heids
     O' endless Christs roll doon.

---

grat, wept   bairn, child   feck, plenty   lift, sky   thae, those
bleezin', blazing   gar'd, made   fegs, an exclamation   blate, backward
gin, if

kens, knows   whatna, whichever   'yont, beyond   een, eyes   unco, strange

An' when the earth's as cauld's the mune
An' a' its folk are lang syne deid,
On coontless stars the Babe maun cry
    An' the Crucified maun bleed.

The Eemis Stane

I' the how-dumb-deid o' the cauld hairst nicht
The warl' like an eemis stane
Wags i' the lift;
An' my eerie memories fa'
Like a yowdendrift.

Like a yowdendrift so's I couldna read
The words cut oot i' the stane
Had the fug o' fame
An' history's hazelraw
No' yirdit thaim.

---

lang syne, long since

eemis, unsteady   how-dumb-deid, dead silent depth
cauld hairst nicht, cold harvest night   yowdendrift, blizzard   fug, moss
hazelraw, lichen   yirdit, buried   thaim, them

From *Penny Wheep* (1926)

Wheesht, Wheesht

Wheesht, wheesht, my foolish hert,
For weel ye ken
I widna ha'e ye stert
Auld ploys again.

It's guid to see her lie
Sae snod an' cool,
A' lust o' lovin' by—
Wheesht, wheesht, ye fule!

Sea-Serpent

(From 'A Sea-Suite')

The soul grows clotted by contagion,
Imbodies, and imbrutes till she quite lose
The divine property of her first being.

Milton

It fits the universe man can ken
As a man's soul fits his body;
And the spirit o' God gaed dirlin' through't
In stound upon stound o' pride
Draughtin' his thick-comin' notions o' life
As fast as they flashed in owre'm
When there was sea and licht and little beside.

His joy in his wark gied it lint-white lines
Brichter than lichtnin's there.
Like starry keethins its fer-aff coils
Quhile the nearer rings
Ran like a raw o' siller girds

---

wheesht, hush   auld ploys, old games   guid, good   sae snod, so tidy
fule, fool

dirlin' through't, throbbing through it   stound, pang   owre'm, over him
keethins, ripples   fer-aff, far off   siller girds, silver hoops

On the wan-shoggin' tap o' the waters
And soupled awa' like wings.

Round the cantles o' space Leviathan flickered
Like Borealis in flicht
Or eelied thro' the poorin' deeps o' the sea
Like a ca' o' whales and was tint to sicht,
But aye in its endless ups-and-doons
As it dwined to gleids or walloped in rings
God like a Jonah whirled in its kite
But blithe as a loon in the swings.

Syne it gethered in on itsel' again
And lowed like the plans o' Heaven,
A michty puzzle o' flames that mirrored
The ends o' the thocht
—For aince He had hit upon Life itsel'
Hoo c'u'd the mere mak'in o' lives
Keep gien'm the thrills He socht?

And the serpent's turned like a wud sin' syne
That canna be seen for the trees
Or's tint as the mid-day sun is tint
In the glory o' its rays,
And God has forgotten, it seems,
In the moniplied maze o' the forms
The a'efauld form o' the maze.

Whiles a blindin' movement tak's in my life
As a quick tide swallows a sea.
I feel like a star on a starry nicht,
A'e note in a symphony,
And ken that the serpent is movin' still,
A movement that a'thing shares,
Yet it seems as tho' it twines in a nicht
When God neither kens nor cares.

---

wan-shoggin', pale swinging   soupled, accelerated
cantles, summits   eelied, vanished   ca' o' whales, school of whales
tint, lost   aye, always   dwined, dwindled   gleids, sparks   kite, stomach
loon, boy   syne, then   lowed, blazed   aince, once   hoo c'u'd, how could
gien'm, giving Him   wud, wood   sin' syne, since then
moniplied, manifold   a'efauld, singled   a'e, one   a'thing, everything

But mebbe yet the hert o' a man
When it feels the twist in its quick
O' the link that binds it to ilka life,
A'e stab in the nerves o' the stars,
'll raise a cry that'll fetch God back
To the hert o' His wark again?
—Though Nature and Man ha'e cried in vain
Rent in unendin' wars!

Or does the serpent dern wi' a mortal wound
Unseen in its unseen side,
And are the surges that still come owre us
Like the thraws o' a stricken man
—Wi' the pooer to inform undeemis lives
Wi' the single movement o' life nae mair,
But ebbin' fast—and ebbin' for aye—
Tho' we skinkle ahint like pools in the san'?

O Thou that we'd fain be ane wi' again
Frae the weary lapses o' self set free,
Be to oor lives as life is to Daith,
And lift and licht us eternally.
Frae the howe o' the sea to the heich o' the lift,
To the licht as licht to the darkness is,
Spring fresh and fair frae the spirit o' God
Like the a'e first thocht that He kent was His.

Loup again in His brain, O Nerve,
Like a trumpet-stang,
Lichtnin-clear as when first owre Chaos
Your shape you flang
—And swee his mind till the mapamound,
And meanin' o' ilka man,
Brenn as then wi' the instant pooer
O' an only plan!

---

ilka, every   dern, hide   owre, over   thraws, convulsions
undeemis, countless   skinkle ahint, shine behind   howe, valley
heich, height   loup, leap   trumpet-stang, trumpet-blast
flang, flung   swee, sway   till, to   mapamound, earth's surface
brenn, burn

Focherty

Duncan Gibb o' Focherty's
A giant to the likes o' me,
His face is like a roarin' fire
For love o' the barley-bree.

He gangs through this and the neebrin' shire
Like a muckle rootless tree
—And here's a caber for Daith to toss
That'll gi'e his spauld a swee!

His gain was aye a wee'r man's loss
And he took my lass frae me,
And wi' mony a quean besides
He's ta'en his liberty.

I've had nae chance wi' the likes o' him
And he's tramped me underfit
—Blaefaced afore the throne o' God
He'll get his fairin' yet.

He'll be like a bull in the sale-ring there,
And I'll lauch lood to see,
Till he looks up and canna mak' oot
Whether it's God—or me!

Scunner

Your body derns
In its graces again
As the dreich grun' does
In the gowden grain,
And oot o' the daith
O' pride you rise
Wi' beauty yet
For a hauf-disguise.

barley-bree, whisky   gangs, goes   neebrin', neighbouring
spauld, backbone   swee, jerk   wee'r, lesser   quean, lass
blaefaced, livid with fear   fairin', deserts

scunner, disgust   derns, hides   dreich, drab

14

The skinklan' stars
Are but distant dirt
Tho' fer owre near
You are still—whiles—girt
Wi' the bonnie licht
You bood ha'e tint
—And I lo'e Love
Wi' a scunner in't.

Empty Vessel

I met ayont the cairney
A lass wi' tousie hair
Singin' till a bairnie
That was nae langer there.

Wunds wi' warlds to swing
Dinna sing sae sweet,
The licht that bends owre a' thing
Is less ta'en up wi't.

Gairmscoile

Aulder than mammoth or than mastodon
Deep i' the herts o' a' men lurk scaut-heid
Skrymmorie monsters few daur look upon.
Brides sometimes catch their wild een, scansin' reid,
Beekin' abune the herts they thocht to lo'e
And horror-stricken ken that i' themselves
A like beast stan's, and lookin' love thro' and thro'
Meets the reid een wi' een like seevun hells.

---

skinklan', gleaming   fer owre, far too   bood, should   lo'e, love   in't, in it

ayont, beyond   cairney, small cairn

scaut-heid, disfigured   skrymmorie, frightful and terrific   daur, dare
scansin', glinting   reid, red   beekin', exposing themselves   abune, above

... Nearer the twa beasts draw, and, couplin', brak
The bubbles o' twa sauls and the haill warld gangs black.

Yet wha has heard the beasts' wild matin'-call
To ither music syne can gi'e nae ear.
The nameless lo'enotes haud him in a thrall.
Forgot are guid and ill, and joy and fear.
... My bluid sall thraw a dark hood owre my een
And I sall venture deep into the hills
Whaur, scaddows on the skyline, can be seen
—Twinin' the sun's brent broo wi' plaited horns
As gin they crooned it wi' a croon o' thorns—
The beasts in wha's wild cries a' Scotland's destiny thrills.

The lo'es o' single herts are strays: but there
The herds that draw the generations are,
And whasae hears them roarin', evermair
Is yin wi' a' that gangs to mak' or mar
The spirit o' the race, and leads it still
Whither it can be led, 'yont a' desire and will.

I

Wergeland, I mind o' thee—for thy bluid tae
Kent the rouch dirl o' an auld Scots strain,
—A dour dark burn that has its ain wild say
Thro' a' the thrang bricht babble o' Earth's flood.
Behold, thwart my ramballiach life again,
What thrawn and roothewn dreams, royat and rude,
Reek forth—a foray dowless herts condemn—
While chance wi rungs o' sang or silence renshels them.

(A foray frae the past—and future tae
Sin Time's a blindness we'll thraw aff some day!)

---

haill, whole   scaddows, shadows   brent broo, wrinkled brow   yin, one

tae, too, also   rouch dirl, rough rattle   burn, stream   ain, own
thrang bricht, busy bright   thwart, across   ramballiach, tempestuous
thrawn, stubborn, perverse   royat, unmanageable   dowless, feeble
rungs, cudgels   renshels, beats

. . . On the rumgunshoch sides o' hills forgotten
Life bears beasts rowtin' that it deemed extinct,
And, sudden, on the hapless cities linked
In canny civilisation's canty dance
Poor herds o' heich-skeich monsters, misbegotten,
. . . Streets clear afore the scarmoch advance:
Frae every winnock skimmerin' een keek oot
To see what sic camsteerie cast-offs are aboot.
Cast-offs?—But wha mak's life a means to ony end?
This sterves and that stuff's fu', scraps this and succours that?
The best survive there's nane but fules contend.
Na! Ilka daith is but a santit need.
. . . Lo! what bricht flames o' beauty are lit at
The unco' een o' lives that Life thocht deid
Till winnock efter winnock kindles wi' a sense
O' gain and glee—as gin a mair intense
Starn nor the sun had risen in wha's licht
Mankind and beasts anew, wi' gusto, see their plicht.

Mony's the auld hauf-human cry I ken
Fa's like a revelation on the herts o' men
As tho' the graves were split and the first man
Grippit the latest wi' a freendly han'
. . . And there's forgotten shibboleths o' the Scots
Ha'e keys to senses lockit to us yet
—Coorse words that shamble thro' oor minds like stots,
Syne turn on's muckle een wi' doonsin' emerauds lit.

I hear nae 'hee-haw' but I mind the day
A'e donkey strunted doon a palm-strewn way
As Chesterton has sung; nae wee click-clack
O' hoofs but to my hert at aince comes back
Jammes' Prayer to Gang to Heaven wi' the Asses;
And shambles-ward nae cattle-beast e'er passes
But I mind hoo the saft een o' the kine
Lichted Christ's craidle wi' their canny shine.

---

rumgunshoch, rough   rowtin', roaring   canny, careful   canty, happy
heich-skeich, crazy   scarmoch, tumultuous   winnock, window
skimmerin', glittering   keek, peep   sic, such   camsteerie, disorderly
fu', full   santit, swallowed up in sand   unco' een, strange eyes
coorse, coarse   stots, bullocks   doonsin' emerauds, dazzling emeralds
strunted, walked with dignity

Hee-Haw! Click-Clack! And Cock-a-doodle-doo!
—Wull Gabriel in Esperanto cry
Or a' the warld's undeemis jargons try?
It's soon', no' sense, that faddoms the herts o' men,
And by my sangs the rouch auld Scots I ken
E'en herts that ha'e nae Scots'll dirl rich thro'
As nocht else could—for here's a language rings
Wi' datchie sesames, and names for nameless things.

II

Wergeland, my warld as thine 'ca' canny' cries,
And daurna lippen to auld Scotland's virr.
Ah, weel ye kent—as Carlyle quo' likewise—
Maist folk are thowless fules wha downa stir,
Crouse sumphs that hate nane 'bies wha'd wauken them.
To them my Pegasus tae's a crocodile.
Whummelt I tak' a bobquaw for the lift.
Insteed o' sangs my mou' drites eerned phlegm.
. . . Natheless like thee I stalk on mile by mile,
Howk'n up deid stumps o' thocht, and saw'in my eident gift.
Ablachs, and scrats, and dorbels o' a' kinds
Aye'd drob me wi' their puir eel-droonin' minds,
Wee drochlin' craturs drutling their bit thochts
The dorty bodies! Feech! Nae Sassunuch drings
'll daunton me.—Tak' ye sic things for poets?
Cock-lairds and drotes depert Parnassus noo.

---

undeemis, countless   datchie, secret

ca' canny, be careful   lippen, trust   virr, stamina, force   thowless, useless
downa, unable   crouse sumphs, conceited blockheads   'bies, except
whummelt, overturned   bobquaw, bog   drites, drips   eerned, clotted
howk'n, digging   eident, busy   ablachs, dwarfs   scrats, hermaphrodites
dorbels, eyesores   drob, prick   puir eel-droonin', poor ludicrously vain
drochlin' craturs drutling, puny creatures piddling   bit thochts, slight thoughts
dorty bodies, petted persons   feech, expression of disgust
Sassunuch drings, English wretches   daunton, intimidate
cock-lairds, empty braggarts   drotes, uppish yeomen   depert, divide

A'e flash o' wit the lot to drodlich dings.
Rae, Martin, Sutherland—the dowless crew,
I'll twine the dow'd sheaves o' their toom-ear'd corn,
Bind them wi' pity and dally them wi' scorn.

Lang ha'e they posed as men o' letters here,
Dounhaddin' the Doric and keepin't i' the draiks,
Drivellin' and druntin', wi' mony a datchie sneer
. . . But soon we'll end the haill eggtaggle, fegs!
. . . The auld volcanoes rummle 'neath their feet,
And a' their shoddy lives 'll soon be drush,
Danders o' Hell! They feel th' unwelcome heat,
The deltit craturs, and their sauls are slush,
For we ha'e faith in Scotland's hidden poo'ers,
The present's theirs, but a' the past and future's oors.

---

drodlich, a useless mass   dings, beats   dowless, feeble   dow'd, faded
toom-ear'd, empty eared
dally, stick used in binding sheaves to push in ends of rope
dounhaddin', holding down   the Doric, the Scots vernacular
i' the draiks, in a slovenly, neglected condition   druntin', whining
eggtaggle, act of wasting time in bad company   drush, refuse
danders, cinders   deltit, pampered   sauls, souls

A Drunk Man Looks at the Thistle
(1926)

A Drunk Man Looks at the Thistle

I amna' fou' sae muckle as tired—deid dune.
It's gey and hard wark' coupin' gless for gless
Wi' Cruivie and Gilsanquhar and the like,
And I'm no' juist as bauld as aince I wes.

The elbuck fankles in the coorse o' time,
The sheckle's no' sae souple, and the thrapple
Grows deef and dour: nae langer up and doun
Gleg as a squirrel speils the Adam's apple.

Forbye, the stuffie's no' the real Mackay,
The sun's sel' aince, as sune as ye began it,
Riz in your vera saul: but what keeks in
Noo is in truth the vilest 'saxpenny planet'.

And as the worth's gane doun the cost has risen.
Yin canna throw the cockles o' yin's hert
Wi'oot ha'en' cauld feet noo, jalousin' what
The wife'll say (I dinna blame her fur't).

It's robbin' Peter to pey Paul at least . . .
And a' that's Scotch aboot it is the name,
Like a' thing else ca'd Scottish nooadays
—A' destitute o' speerit juist the same.

(To prove my saul is Scots I maun begin
Wi' what's still deemed Scots and the folk expect,
And spire up syne by visible degrees
To heichts whereo' the fules ha'e never recked.

But aince I get them there I'll whummle them
And souse the craturs in the nether deeps,
—For it's nae choice, and ony man s'ud wish
To dree the goat's weird tae as weel's the sheep's!)

---

fou', drunk   deid dune, exhausted   gey, extremely   coupin', upending
aince, once   elbuck fankles, elbow becomes clumsy   sheckle, wrist
thrapple, gullet   deef, unimpressionable   gleg, lively   speils, climbs
forbye, besides   keeks, peeps   jalousin', suspecting   spire, soar
whummle, overturn   craturs, creatures   dree, endure
weird tae, fate also

Heifetz in tartan, and Sir Harry Lauder!
Whaur's Isadora Duncan dancin' noo?
Is Mary Garden in Chicago still
And Duncan Grant in Paris—and me fou'?

Sic transit gloria Scotia—a' the floo'ers
O' the Forest are wede awa'. (A blin' bird's nest
Is aiblins biggin' in the thistle tho'? . . .
And better blin' if'ts brood is like the rest!)

You canna gang to a Burns supper even
Wi'oot some wizened scrunt o' a knock-knee
Chinee turns roon to say, 'Him Haggis—velly goot!'
And ten to wan the piper is a Cockney.

No' wan in fifty kens a wurd Burns wrote
But misapplied is a'body's property,
And gin there was his like alive the day
They'd be the last a kennin' haund to gie—

Croose London Scotties wi' their braw shirt fronts
And a' their fancy freen's, rejoicin'
That similah gatherings in Timbuctoo,
Bagdad—and Hell, nae doot—are voicin'

Burns' sentiments o' universal love,
In pidgin' English or in wild-fowl Scots,
And toastin' ane wha's nocht to them but an
Excuse for faitherin' Genius wi' *their* thochts.

A' *they've* to say was aften said afore
A lad was born in Kyle to blaw aboot.
What unco fate mak's *him* the dumpin'-grun'
For a' the sloppy rubbish they jaw oot?

Mair nonsense has been uttered in his name
Than in ony's barrin' liberty and Christ.
If this keeps spreedin' as the drink declines,
Syne turns to tea, wae's me for the *Zeitgeist!*

---

wede awa', vanished   aiblins biggin', perhaps building   scrunt, mite
kennin', knowing   croose, conceited   braw, fine   jaw, splash

Rabbie, wad'st thou wert here—the warld hath need,
And Scotland mair sae, o' the likes o' thee!
The whisky that aince moved your lyre's become
A laxative for a' loquacity.

O gin they'd stegh their guts and haud their wheesht
I'd thole it, for 'a man's a man,' I ken,
But though the feck ha'e plenty o' the 'a' that,'
They're nocht but zoologically men.

I'm haverin', Rabbie, but ye understaun'
It gets my dander up to see your star
A bauble in Babel, banged like a saxpence
'Twixt Burbank's Baedeker and Bleistein's cigar.

There's nane sae ignorant but think they can
Expatiate on *you*, if on nae ither.
The sumphs ha'e ta'en you at your wurd, and, fegs!
The foziest o' them claims to be a—Brither!

Syne 'Here's the cheenge'—the star o' Rabbie Burns.
Sma' cheenge, 'Twinkle, Twinkle.' The memory slips
As G. K. Chesterton heaves up to gi'e
'The Immortal Memory' in a huge eclipse,

Or somebody else as famous if less fat.
You left the like in Embro' in a scunner
To booze wi' thieveless cronies sic as me.
I'se warrant you'd shy clear o' a' the hunner

Odd Burns' Clubs tae, or ninety-nine o' them,
And haud your birthday in a different kip
Whaur your name isna' ta'en in vain—as Christ
Gied a' Jerusalem's Pharisees the slip,

—Christ wha'd ha'e been Chief Rabbi gin he'd lik't!—
Wi' publicans and sinners to foregather,
But, losh! the publicans noo are Pharisees,
And I'm no' shair o' maist the sinners either.

---

stegh, stuff   haud their wheesht, be quiet   thole, endure   feck, majority
haverin', rambling   dander, temper   sumphs, fools   fegs, faith
foziest, most stupid   scunner, disgust   thieveless, powerless
kip, house of ill fame   shair, sure

But that's aside the point! I've got fair waun'ert.
It's no' that I'm sae fou' as juist deid dune,
And dinna ken as muckle's whaur I am
Or hoo I've come to sprawl here 'neth the mune.

That's it! It isna me that's fou' at a',
But the fu' mune, the doited jade, that's led
Me fer agley, or 'mogrified the warld.
—For a' I ken I'm safe in my ain bed.

Jean! Jean! Gin *she's* no' here it's no' *oor* bed,
Or else I'm dreamin' deep and canna wauken,
But it's a fell queer dream if this is no'
A real hillside—and thae things thistles and bracken!

It's hard wark haud'n by a thocht worth ha'en'
And harder speakin't, and no' for ilka man;
Maist Thocht's like whisky—a thoosan' under proof,
And a sair price is pitten on't even than.

As Kirks wi' Christianity ha'e dune,
Burns' Clubs wi' Burns—wi' a'thing it's the same,
The core o' ocht is only for the few,
Scorned by the mony, thrang wi'ts empty name.

And a' the names in History mean nocht
To maist folk but 'ideas o' their ain,'
The vera opposite o' onything
The Deid 'ud awn gin they cam' back again.

A greater Christ, a greater Burns, may come.
The maist they'll dae is to gi'e bigger pegs
To folly and conceit to hank their rubbish on.
They'll cheenge folks' talk but no their natures, fegs!

I maun feed frae the common trough ana'
Whaur a' the lees o' hope are jumbled up;
While centuries like pigs are slorpin' owre't
Sall my wee 'oor be cryin': 'Let pass this cup?'

---

waun'ert, confused   doited, foolish   fer agley, far astray
fell, exceedingly   ocht, anything   thrang, busy   hank, fasten
slorpin' owre't, slobbering over it

In wi' your gruntle then, puir wheengin' saul,
Lap up the ugsome aidle wi' the lave,
What gin it's your ain vomit that you swill
And frae Life's gantin' and unfaddomed grave?

I doot I'm geylies mixed, like Life itsel',
But I was never ane that thocht to pit
An ocean in a mutchkin. As the haill's
Mair than the pairt sae I than reason yet.

I dinna haud the warld's end in my heid
As maist folk think they dae; nor filter truth
In fishy gills through which its tides may poor
For ony *animalculae* forsooth.

I lauch to see my crazy little brain
—And ither folks'—tak'n itsel' seriously,
And in a sudden lowe o' fun my saul
Blinks dozent as the owl I ken't to be.

I'll ha'e nae hauf-way hoose, but aye be whaur
Extremes meet—it's the only way I ken
To dodge the curst conceit o' bein' richt
That damns the vast majority o' men.

I'll bury nae heid like an ostrich's,
Nor yet believe my een and naething else.
My senses may advise me, but I'll be
Mysel' nae maitter what they tell's . . .

I ha'e nae doot some foreign philosopher
Has wrocht a system oot to justify
A' this: but I'm a Scot wha blin'ly follows
Auld Scottish instincts, and I winna try.

For I've nae faith in ocht I can explain,
And stert whaur the philosophers leave aff,
Content to glimpse its loops I dinna ettle
To land the sea serpent's sel' wi' ony gaff.

---

gruntle, snout   puir wheengin' saul, poor complaining soul
ugsome aidle, repulsive slop   lave, remainder   gantin', yawning
doot, suspect   geylies, pretty well   haill's, whole is   poor, pour
lauch, laugh   lowe, blaze   dozent, stupid   ken't, know it   een, eyes
ettle, aspire

Like staundin' water in a pocket o'
Impervious clay I pray I'll never be,
Cut aff and self-sufficient, but let reenge
Heichts o' the lift and benmaist deeps o' sea.

Water! Water! There was owre muckle o't
In yonder whisky, sae I'm in deep water
(And gin I could wun hame I'd be in het,
For even Jean maun natter, natter, natter) . . .

And in the toon that I belang tae
—What tho'ts Montrose or Nazareth?—
Helplessly the folk continue
To lead their livin' death! . . .

*At darknin' hings abune the howff
A weet and wild and eisenin' air.
Spring's spirit wi' its waesome sough
Rules owre the drucken stramash there.

And heich abune the vennel's pokiness,
Whaur a' the white-weshed cottons lie;
The Inn's sign blinters in the mochiness,
And lood and shrill the bairnies cry.

The hauflins 'yont the burgh boonds
Gang ilka nicht, and a' the same,
Their bonnets cocked; their bluid that stounds
Is playin' at a fine auld game.

And on the lochan there, hauf-herted
Wee screams and creakin' oar-locks soon',
And in the lift, heich, hauf-averted,
The mune looks owre the yirdly roon'.

---

lift, sky   benmaist, inmost   het, hot   natter, nag
hings abune, hangs above   howff, tavern   eisenin', lustful
waesome sough, woeful sigh   drucken stramash, drunken uproar
vennel's pokiness, lane's congestion   blinters, gleams
mochiness, moist air   bairnies, children   hauflins 'yont, lads beyond
ilka, every   stounds, throbs   lochan, small lake   yirdly, earthly

* From the Russian of Alexander Blok.

28

And ilka evenin', derf and serious
(Jean ettles nocht o' this, puir lass),
In liquor, raw yet still mysterious,
A'e freend's aye mirrored in my glass.

Ahint the sheenin' coonter gruff
Thrang barmen ding the tumblers doun
'In vino veritas' cry rough
And reid-een'd fules that in it droon.

But ilka evenin' fey and fremt
(Is it a dream nae wauk'nin' proves?)
As to a trystin'-place undreamt,
A silken leddy darkly moves.

Slow gangs she by the drunken anes,
And lanely by the winnock sits;
Frae'r robes, atour the sunken anes,
A rooky dwamin' perfume flits.

Her gleamin' silks, the taperin'
O' her ringed fingers, and her feathers
Move dimly like a dream wi'in,
While endless faith aboot them gethers.

I seek, in this captivity,
To pierce the veils that darklin' fa'
—See white clints slidin' to the sea,
And hear the horns o' Elfland blaw.

I ha'e dark secrets' turns and twists,
A sun is gi'en to me to haud,
The whisky in my bluid insists,
And spiers my benmaist history, lad.

And owre my brain the flitterin'
O' the dim feathers gangs aince mair,
And, faddomless, the dark blue glitterin'
O' twa een in the ocean there.

---

derf, taciturn   ettles, suspects   a'e freend's aye, one friend is always
ahint, behind   sheenin' coonter, shining counter   thrang, busy   ding, dash
fey, fated   fremt, lonely   winnock, window   frae'r, from her
atour, around   rooky dwamin', misty swooning   clints, cliffs   haud, hold
spiers, inquires of   benmaist, inmost

My soul stores up this wealth unspent,
The key is safe and nane's but mine.
You're richt, auld drunk impenitent,
I ken it tae—the truth's in wine!

The munelicht's like a lookin'-glass,
The thistle's like mysel',
But whaur ye've gane, my bonnie lass,
Is mair than I can tell.

Were you a vision o' mysel',
Transmuted by the mellow liquor?
Neist time I glisk you in a glass,
I'se warrant I'll mak' siccar.

A man's a clean contrairy sicht
Turned this way in-ootside,
And, fegs, I feel like Dr. Jekyll
Tak'n guid tent o' Mr. Hyde . . .

Gurly thistle—hic—you canna
Daunton me wi' your shaggy mien,
I'm sair—hic—needin' a shave,
That's plainly to be seen.

But what aboot it—hic—aboot it?
Mony a man's been that afore.
It's no' a fact that in his lugs
A wund like this need roar! . . .

★I hae forekent ye! O I hae forekent.
The years forecast your face afore they went.
A licht I canna thole is in the lift.
I bide in silence your slow-comin' pace.
The ends o' space are bricht: at last—oh swift!
While terror clings to me—an unkent face!

Ill-faith stirs in me as she comes at last,
The features lang forekent . . . are unforecast.

---

neist, next   glisk, glimpse   mak' siccar, make sure
tak'n guid tent, paying close attention to   gurly, savage   daunton, frighten
sair, badly   lugs, ears   forekent, foreknown   thole, endure   lift, sky

★ Freely adapted from the Russian of Alexander Blok.

O it gangs hard wi' me, I am forespent.
Deid dreams ha'e beaten me and a face unkent
And generations that I thocht unborn
Hail the strange Goddess frae my hert's-hert torn! . . .

Or dost thou mak' a thistle o' me, wumman? But for thee
I were as happy as the munelicht, withoot care,
But thocht o' thee—o' thy contempt and ire—
Turns hauf the warld into the youky thistle there,

Feedin' on the munelicht and transformin' it
To this wanrestfu' growth that winna let me be.
The munelicht is the freedom that I'd ha'e
But for this cursèd Conscience thou hast set in me.

It is morality, the knowledge o' Guid and Ill,
Fear, shame, pity, like a will and wilyart growth,
That kills a' else wi'in its reach and craves
Nae less at last than a' the warld to gi'e it scouth.

The need to wark, the need to think, the need to be,
And a' thing that twists Life into a certain shape
And interferes wi' perfect liberty—
These feed this Frankenstein that nae man can escape.

For ilka thing a man can be or think or dae
Aye leaves a million mair unbeen, unthocht, undune,
Till his puir warped performance is,
To a' that micht ha' been, a thistle to the mune.

It is Mortality itsel'—the mortal coil,
Mockin' Perfection, Man afore the Throne o' God
He yet has bigged himsel', Man torn in twa
And glorious in the lift and grisly on the sod! . . .

There's nocht sae sober as a man blin' drunk.
I maun ha'e got an unco bellyfu'
To jaw like this—and yet what I am sayin'
Is a' the apter, aiblins, to be true.

---

youky, itchy   wanrestfu', restless   will, uncertain   wilyart, uncertain
scouth, scope   bigged, built   unco, unusual

This munelicht's fell like whisky noo I see't
—Am I a thingum mebbe that is kept
Preserved in spirits in a muckle bottle
Lang centuries efter sin' wi' Jean I slept?

—Mounted on a hillside, wi' the thistles
And bracken for verisimilitude,
Like a stuffed bird on metal like a brainch,
Or a seal on a stump o' rock-like wood?

Or am I juist a figure in a scene
O' Scottish life A.D. one-nine-two-five?
The haill thing kelters like a theatre claith
Till I micht fancy that I was alive!

I dinna ken and nae man ever can.
I micht be in my ain bed efter a'.
The haill damned thing's a dream for ocht we ken,
—The Warld and Life and Daith, Heaven, Hell ana'.

We maun juist tak' things as we find them then,
And mak' a kirk or mill o' them as we can,
—And yet I feel this muckle thistle's staun'in'
Atween me and the mune as pairt o' a Plan.

It isna there—nor me—by accident.
We're brocht thegither for a certain reason,
Ev'n gin it's naething mair than juist to gi'e
My jaded soul a necessary *frisson*.

I never saw afore a thistle quite
Sae intimately, or at sic an 'oor.
There's something in the fickle licht that gi'es
A different life to't and an unco poo'er.

*'Rootit on gressless peaks, whaur its erect
And jaggy leafs, austerly cauld and dumb,
Haud the slow scaly serpent in respect,
The Gothic thistle, whaur the insect's hum
Soon's fer aff, lifts abune the rock it scorns
Its rigid virtue for the Heavens to see.
The too'ering boulders gaird it. And the bee
Mak's honey frae the roses on its thorns.'*

---

kelters, ripples   a kirk or mill, the best or worse

* From the Belgian poet, George Ramaekers.

But that's a Belgian refugee, of coorse.
This Freudian complex has somehoo slunken
Frae Scotland's soul—the Scots aboulia—
Whilst a' its *terra nullius* is *betrunken*.

And a' the country roon' aboot it noo
Lies clapt and shrunken syne like somebody wha
Has lang o' seven devils been possessed;
Then when he turns a corner tines them a',

Or like a body that has tint its soul,
Perched like a monkey on its heedless kist,
Or like a sea that peacefu' fa's again
When frae its deeps an octopus is fished.

I canna feel it has to dae wi' me
Mair than a composite diagram o'
Cross-sections o' my forbears' organs
—And mine—'ud bring a kind o' freen'ly glow.

And yet like bindweed through my clay it's run,
And a' my folks'—it's queer to see't unroll.
My ain soul looks me in the face, as 'twere,
And mair than my ain soul—my nation's soul!

And sall a Belgian pit it into words
And sing a sang to't syne, and no' a Scot?
Oors is a wilder thistle, and Ramaekers
Canna bear aff the gree—avaunt the thocht!

To meddle wi' the thistle and to pluck
The figs frae't is *my* metier, I think.
Awak', my muse, and gin you're in puir fettle,
We aye can blame it on th' inferior drink.

T. S. Eliot—it's a Scottish name—
Afore he wrote 'The Waste Land' s'ud ha'e come
To Scotland here. He wad ha'e written
A better poem syne—like this, by gum!

Type o' the Wissenschaftsfeindlichkeit,
Begriffsmüdigkeit that has gar't
Men try Morphologies der Weltgeschichte,
And mad Expressionismus syne in Art.

clapt, pressed down   tines, loses   tint, lost   kist, chest

33

*A shameless thing, for ilka vileness able,
It is deid grey as dust, the dust o' a man.
I perish o' a nearness I canna win awa' frae,
Its deidly coils aboot my buik are thrawn.

A shaggy poulp, embracin' me and stingin',
And as a serpent cauld agen' my hert.
Its scales are poisoned shafts that jag me to the quick
—And waur than them's my scunner's fearfu' smert!

O that its prickles were a knife indeed,
But it is thowless, flabby, dowf, and numb.
Sae sluggishly it drains my benmaist life
A dozent dragon, dreidfu', deef, and dumb.

In mum obscurity it twines its obstinate rings
And hings caressin'ly, its purpose whole;
And this deid thing, whale-white obscenity,
This horror that I writhe in—is my soul!

Is it the munelicht or a leprosy
That spreids aboot me; and a thistle
Or my ain skeleton through wha's bare banes
A fiendish wund's begood to whistle?

The devil's lauchter has a *hwll* like this.
My face has flown open like a lid
—And gibberin' on the hillside there
Is a' humanity sae lang has hid! . . .

My harns are seaweed—when the tide is in
They swall like blethers and in comfort float,
But when the tide is oot they lie like gealed
And runkled auld bluid-vessels in a knot!

The munelicht ebbs and flows and wi't my thocht,
Noo' movin' mellow and noo lourd and rough.
I ken what I am like in Life and Daith,
But Life and Daith for nae man are enough . . .

---

buik, body   thrawn, twisted   agen', against   waur, worse   scunner, disgust
thowless, impotent   dowf, inert   begood, begun   harns, brains
blethers, bladders   gealed, congealed   runkled auld, wrinkled old   lourd, heavy

* Adapted from the Russian of Zinaida Hippius.

And O! to think that there are members o'
St. Andrew's Societies sleepin' soon',
Wha to the papers wrote afore they bedded
On regimental buttons or buckled shoon,

Or use o' England whaur the U.K.'s meent,
Or this or that anent the Blue Saltire,
Recruitin', pedigrees, and Gude kens what,
Filled wi' a proper patriotic fire!

Wad I were them—they've chosen a better pairt,
The couthie craturs, than the ane I've ta'en,
Tyauvin' wi' this root-hewn Scottis soul;
A fer, fer better pairt—except for men.

Nae doot they're sober, as a Scot ne'er was,
Each tethered to a punctual-snorin' missus,
Whilst I, puir fule, owre continents unkent
And wine-dark oceans waunder like Ulysses . . .

*The Mune sits on my bed the nicht unsocht,
And mak's my soul obedient to her will;
And in the dumb-deid, still as dreams are still,
Her pupils narraw to bricht threids that thrill
Aboot the sensuous windin's o' her thocht.

But ilka windin' has its coonter-pairt
—The opposite 'thoot which it couldna be—
In some wild kink or queer perversity
O' this great thistle, green wi' jealousy,
That breenges 'twixt the munelicht and my hert . . .

Plant, what are you then? Your leafs
Mind me o' the pipes' lood drone
—And a' your purple tops
Are the pirly-wirly notes
That gang staggerin' owre them as they groan.

---

anent, concerning   Blue Saltire, Scottish Flag   Gude kens, God knows
couthie craturs, smug creatures   tyauvin', struggling
dumb-deid, middle of the night   breenges, moves impetuously
pirly-wirly notes, grace notes   gang, go   owre, over

* Suggested by the German of Else Lasker-Schüler.

Or your leafs are alligators
That ha'e gobbled owre a haill
Company o' Heilant sodgers,
And left naethin' but the toories
O' their Balmoral bonnets to tell the tale.

Or a muckle bellows blawin'
Wi' the sperks a' whizzin' oot;
Or green tides sweeshin'
'Neth heich-skeich stars,
Or centuries fleein' doun a water-chute.

Grinnin' gargoyle by a saint,
Mephistopheles in Heaven,
Skeleton at a tea-meetin',
Missin' link—or creakin'
Hinge atween the deid and livin' . . .

(I kent a Terrier in a sham fecht aince,
Wha louped a dyke and landed on a thistle.
He'd naething on ava aneth his kilt.
Schönberg has nae notation for his whistle.) . . .

(Gin you're surprised a village drunk
Foreign references s'ud fool in,
You ha'ena the respect you s'ud
For oor guid Scottish schoolin'.

For we've the maist unlikely folk
Aye braggin' o' oor lear,
And, tho' I'm drunk, for Scotland's sake
I tak my barrowsteel here!

Yet Europe's faur eneuch for me,
Puir fule, when bairns ken mair
O' th' ither warld than I o' this
—But that's no' here nor there!) . . .

Guid sakes, I'm in a dreidfu' state.
I'll ha'e nae inklin' sune
Gin I'm the drinker or the drink,
The thistle or the mune.

---

toories, pom-poms   heich-skeich, irresponsible   Terrier, Territorial soldier
fecht, fight   louped a dyke, jumped a wall   ava aneth, at all beneath
lear, learning   tak' my barrowsteel, co-operate   faur eneuch, far enough

I'm geylies feart I couldna tell
Gin I su'd lay me doon
The difference betwixt the warld
And my ain heid gaen' roon'! . . .

Drums in the Walligate, pipes in the air,
Come and hear the cryin' o' the Fair.

A' as it used to be, when I was a loon
On Common-Ridin' Day in the Muckle Toon.

The bearer twirls the Bannock-and-Saut-Herrin',
The Croon o' Roses through the lift is farin',

The aucht-fit thistle wallops on hie;
In heather besoms a' the hills gang by.

But noo it's a' the fish o' the sea
Nailed on the roond o' the Earth to me.

Beauty and Love that are bobbin' there;
Syne the breengin' growth that alane I bear;

And Scotland followin' on ahint
For threepenny bits spleet-new frae the mint.

Drums in the Walligate, pipes in the air,
The wallopin' thistle is ill to bear.

But I'll dance the nicht wi' the stars o' Heaven
In the Mairket Place as shair's I'm livin'.

Easy to carry roses or herrin',
And the lave may weel their threepenny bits earn.

Devil the star! It's Jean I'll ha'e
Again as she was on her weddin' day . . .

Nerves in stounds o' delight,
Muscles in pride o' power,
Bluid as wi' roses dight
Life's toppin' pinnacles owre,
The thistle yet'll unite
Man and the Infinite!

---

geylies feart, very much afraid   loon, boy   Muckle Toon, Langholm
aucht-fit, eight-foot   wallops on hie, dances on high   besoms, brooms
breengin', bursting   ahint, behind   spleet-new, brand new
dight, coloured

Swippert and swith wi' virr
In the howes o' man's hert
Forever its muckle roots stir
Like a Leviathan astert,
Till'ts coils like a thistle's leafs
Sweep space wi' levin sheafs.

Frae laichest deeps o' the ocean
It rises in flight upon flight,
And 'yont its uttermaist motion
Can still set roses alight,
As else unreachable height
Fa's under its triumphin' sight.

Here is the root that feeds
The shank wi' the blindin' wings
Dwinin' abuneheid to gleids
Like stars in their keethin' rings,
And blooms in sunrise and sunset
Inowre Eternity's yett.

Lay haud o' my hert and feel
Fountains ootloupin' the starns
Or see the Universe reel
Set gaen' by my eident harns,
Or test the strength o' my spauld
The wecht o' a' thing to hauld!

—The howes o' Man's hert are bare,
The Dragon's left them for good,
There's nocht but naethingness there,
The hole whaur the Thistle stood,
That rootless and radiant flies
A Phoenix in Paradise! . . .

---

swippert, active   swith wi' virr, quick with vigour   howes, hollows
astert, on the move   levin, lightning   laichest, lowest   shank, stem
dwinin' abuneheid to gleids, dwindling overhead to sparks
keethin' rings, rings on water made by fish   inowre, over   yett, gate
starns, stars   eident harns, eager brains   spauld, shoulder
wecht o' a' thing to hauld, weight of everything to hold

Masoch and Sade
Turned into ane
Havoc ha'e made
O' my a'e brain.

Weel, gin it's Sade
Let it be said
They've made me mad
—That'll da'e instead.

But it's no' instead
In Scots, but insteed.
—The life they've led
In my puir heid.

But aince I've seen
In the thistle here
A' that they've been
I'll aiblins wun clear.

Thistleless fule,
You'll ha'e nocht left
But the hole frae which
Life's struggle is reft! . . .

Reason ser's nae end but pleasure,
Truth's no' an end but a means
To a wider knowledge o' life
And a keener interest in't.

We wha are poets and artists
Move frae inklin' to inklin',
And live for oor antrin lichtnin's
In the haingles atweenwhiles,

Laich as the feck o' mankind
Whence we breenge in unkennable shapes
—*Crockats up, hair kaimed to the lift,*
And no' to cree legs wi'! . . .

---

a'e, single   gin, if   aiblins wun, perhaps get   reft, torn   ser's, serves
in't, in it   antrin lichtnin's, rare lightnings
haingles atweenwhiles, states of boredom inbetween   laich, low
feck, majority   crockats up, proud   hair kaimed to the lift, on the go
no' to cree legs wi', not safe to be meddled with

We're ootward boond frae Scotland.
Guid-bye, fare-ye-weel; guid-bye, fare-ye-weel.
—A' the Scots that ever wur
Gang ootward in a creel.

We're ootward boond frae Scotland.
Guid-bye, fare-ye-weel; guid-bye, fare-ye-weel.
The cross-tap is a monkey-tree
That nane o' us can spiel.

We've never seen the Captain,
But the first mate is a Jew.
We've shipped aboord Eternity.
Adieu, kind freends, adieu! . . .

In the creel or on the gell
O' oor coutribat and ganien.
What gin ithers see or hear
Naething but a gowkstorm?

Gin you stop the galliard
To teach them hoo to dance,
There comes in Corbaudie
And turns their gammons up! . . .

You vegetable cat's melody!
Your *Concert Miaulant* is
A triumph o' discord shairly,
And suits my fancy fairly
—I'm shair that Scott'll agree
He canna vie wi' this . . .

Said my body to my mind,
'I've been startled whiles to find,
When Jean has been in bed wi' me,
A kind o' Christianity!'

To my body said my mind,
'But your benmaist thocht you'll find
Was "Bother what I think I feel
—Jean kens the set o' my bluid owre weel,

---

wur, were   creel, state of confusion   cross-tap, mizen-mast   spiel, climb
gell, go   coutribat, struggle   ganien, boasting talk
gowkstorm, foolish fuss   galliard, dance   Corbaudie, Difficulty
gammons, hoofs   Scott, F. G. Scott, the composer

And lauchs to see me in the creel
O' my courage-bag confined."' . . .

I wish I kent the physical basis
O' a' life's seemin' airs and graces.

It's queer the thochts a kittled cull
Can lowse or splairgin' glit annul.

Man's spreit is wi' his ingangs twined
In ways that he can ne'er unwind.

A wumman whiles a bawaw gi'es
That clean abaws him gin he sees.

Or wi' a movement o' a leg
Shows'm his mind is juist a geg.

I'se warrant Jean 'ud no' be lang
In findin' whence this thistle sprang.

Mebbe it's juist because I'm no'
Beddit wi' her that gars it grow! . . .

A luvin' wumman is a licht*
That shows a man his waefu' plicht,
Bleezin' steady on ilka bane,
Wrigglin' sinnen an' twinin' vein,
Or fleerin' quick an' gane again,
And the mair scunnersome the sicht
The mair for love and licht he's fain
Till clear and chitterin' and nesh
Move a' the miseries o' his flesh . . .

O lass, wha see'est me
As I daur hardly see,
I marvel that your bonny een
Are as they hadna' seen.

---

courage-bag, scrotum   kittled cull, tickled testicle   lowse, loosen
splairgin' glit, splattering slime   spreit, spirit   ingangs, entrails
bawaw, scornful glance   abaws, abashes   geg, deception   gars, makes
waefu', woeful   bleezin', blazing   bane, bone   sinnen, sinew
twinin', twisting   fleerin', flaring   scunnersome, disgusting
chitterin', shivering   nesh, alertly, aware

* Suggested by the French of Edmond Rocher.

Through a' my self-respect
They see the truth abject
—*Gin you could pierce their blindin' licht*
You'd see a fouler sicht! . . .

O wha's the bride that cairries the bunch
O' thistles blinterin' white?
Her cuckold bridegroom little dreids
What he sall ken this nicht.

For closer than gudeman can come
And closer to'r than hersel',
Wha didna need her maidenheid
Has wrocht his purpose fell.

O wha's been here afore me, lass,
And hoo did he get in?
—*A man that deed or I was born*
This evil thing has din.

And left, as it were on a corpse,
Your maidenheid to me?
—*Nae lass, gudeman, sin' Time began*
'S hed ony mair to gi'e.

But I can gi'e ye kindness, lad,
And a pair o' willin' hands,
And you sall ha'e my briests like stars,
My limbs like willow wands,

And on my lips ye'll heed nae mair,
And in my hair forget,
The seed o' a' the men that in
My virgin womb ha'e met . . .

Millions o' wimmen bring forth in pain
Millions o' bairns that are no' worth ha'en.

Wull ever a wumman be big again
Wi's muckle's a Christ? Yech, there's nae sayin'.

Gin that's the best that you ha'e comin',
Fegs but I'm sorry for you, wumman!

---

blinterin', gleaming   gudeman, husband   to'r, to her   deed or, died ere
din, done

Yet a'e thing's certain.—Your faith is great.
Whatever happens, you'll no' be blate! . . .

Mary lay in jizzen
As it were claith o' gowd,
But it's in orra duds
Ilka ither bairntime's row'd.

Christ had never toothick,
Christ was never seeck,
But Man's a fiky bairn
Wi' bellythraw, ripples, and worm-i'-the-cheek! . . .

Dae what ye wull ye canna parry
This skeleton-at-the-feast that through the starry
Maze o' the warld's intoxicatin' soiree
Claughts ye, as micht at an affrontit quean
A bastard wean!

Prood mune, ye needna thring your shouder there,
And at your puir get like a snawstorm stare,
It's yours—there's nae denyin't—and I'm shair
You'd no' enjoy the evenin' much the less
Gin you'd but openly confess!

Dod! It's an eaten and a spewed-like thing,
Fell like a little-bodie's changeling,
And it's nae credit t'ye that you s'ud bring
The like to life—yet, gi'en a mither's love,
—Hee, hee!—wha kens hoo't micht improve? . . .

Or is this Heaven, this yalla licht,
And I the aft'rins o' the Earth,
Or sic's in this wanchancy time
May weel fin' sudden birth?

---

blate, bashful   jizzen, childbed   claith o' gowd, cloth of gold
orra duds, shabby clothes
ilka ither bairntime's row'd, every other woman's lying in is rolled
seeck, sick   fiky bairn, troublesome child   bellythraw, colic
ripples, diarrhoea   worm-i'-the-cheek, toothache   claughts, clutches
quean, young woman   wean, child
thring your shouder, shrug your shoulder   puir get, poor offspring
spewed-like, vomit-like   little-bodie's, fairy's   hoo't, how it
aft'rins, off-scourings   sic's, such as   wanchancy, unfortunate

The roots that wi' the worms compete
Hauf-publish me upon the air.
The struggle that divides me still
Is seen fu' plainly there.

The thistle's shank scarce holes the grun',
My grave'll spare nae mair I doot.
—*The crack's fu' wide; the shank's fu' strang;*
A' that I was is oot.

My knots o' nerves that struggled sair
Are weel reflected in the herb;
My crookit instincts were like this,
As sterile and acerb.

My self-tormented spirit took
The shape repeated in the thistle;
Sma' beauty jouked my rawny banes
And maze o' gristle.

I seek nae peety, Paraclete,
And, fegs, I think the joke is rich
—*Pairt soul, pairt skeleton's come up;*
They kentna which was which! . . .

Thou Daith in which my life
Sae vain a thing can seem,
Frae whatna source d'ye borrow
Your devastatin' gleam?

Nae doot that hidden sun
'Ud look fu' wae ana',
Gin I could see it in the licht
That frae the Earth you draw! . . .

Shudderin' thistle, gi'e owre, gi'e owre!
A'body's gi'en in to the facts o' life;
The impossible truth'll triumph at last,
And mock your strife.

---

shank, stem   jouked, avoided   rawny, prominent   kentna, did not know
whatna, what kind of   fu' wae ana', extremely sad as well

Your sallow leafs can never thraw,
Wi' a' their oorie shakin',
Ae doot into the hert o' life
That it may be mistak'n . . .

O Scotland is
THE barren fig.
Up, carles, up
And roond it jig.

Auld Moses took
A dry stick and
Instantly it
Floo'ered in his hand.

Pu' Scotland up,
And wha can say
It winna bud
And blossom tae.

A miracle's
Oor only chance.
Up, carles, up
And let us dance!

Puir Burns, wha's bouquet like a shot kail blaws
—Will this rouch sicht no' gi'e the orchids pause?
The Gairdens o' the Muses may be braw,
But nane like oors can breenge and eat ana'!

And owre the kailyaird-wa' Dunbar they've flung,
And a' their countrymen that e'er ha'e sung
For ither than ploomen's lugs or to enrichen
Plots on Parnassus set apairt for kitchen.

Ploomen and ploomen's wives—shades o' the Manse
May weel be at the heid o' sic a dance,
As through the polish't ha's o' Europe leads
The rout o' bagpipes, haggis, and sheep's heids!

---

oorie, weird   carles, fellows   shot kail, sprouted cabbage   rouch, rough
kailyaird-wa', kitchen-garden wall   ha's, halls

The vandal Scot! Frae Branksome's deidly barrow
I struggle yet to free a'e winsome marrow,
To show what Scotland micht ha'e hed instead
O' this preposterous Presbyterian breed.

(Gin Glesca folk are tired o' Hengler,
And still need breid and circuses, there's Spengler,
Or gin ye s'ud need mair than ane to teach ye,
Then learn frae Dostoevski and frae Nietzsche.

And let the lesson be—to be yersel's,
Ye needna fash gin it's to be ocht else.
To be yersel's—and to mak' that worth bein',
Nae harder job to mortals has been gi'en.

To save your souls fu' mony o' ye are fain,
But de'il a dizzen to mak' it worth the daein'.
I widna gi'e five meenits wi' Dunbar
For a' the millions o' ye as ye are).

I micht ha'e been contentit wi' the Rose
Gin I'd had ony reason to suppose
That what the English dae can e'er mak' guid
For what Scots dinna—and first and foremaist should.

I micht ha'e been contentit—gin the feck
O' my ain folk had grovelled wi' less respec',
But their obsequious devotion
Made it for me a criminal emotion.

I micht ha'e been contentit—ere I saw
That there were fields on which it couldna draw,
(While strang-er roots ran under't) and a'e threid
O't drew frae Scotland a' that it could need,

And left the maist o' Scotland fallow
(Save for the patch on which the kail-blades wallow),
And saw hoo ither countries' genius drew
Elements like mine that in a rose ne'er grew . . .

Branksome, Flodden   marrow, mate   fash, trouble   fu' mony, a great many
de'il a dizzen, not a dozen

Gin the threid haud'n us to the rose were snapt,
There's no' a'e petal o't that 'ud be clapt.
A' Scotland gi'es gangs but to jags or stalk,
The bloom is English—and 'ud ken nae lack! . . .

O drumlie clood o' crudity and cant,
Obliteratin' as the Easter rouk
That rows up frae the howes and droons the heichs,
And turns the country to a faceless spook.

Like blurry shapes o' landmarks in the haar
The bonny idiosyncratic place-names loom,
Clues to the vieve and maikless life that's lain
Happit for centuries in an alien gloom . . .

Eneuch! For noo I'm in the mood,
Scotland, responsive to my thoughts,
Lichts mile by mile, as my ain nerves
Frae Maidenkirk to John o' Groats!

What are prophets and priests and kings,
What's ocht to the people o' Scotland?
Speak—and Cruivie'll goam at you,
Gilsanquhar jalouse you're dottlin!

And Edinburgh and Glasgow
Are like ploomen in a pub.
They want to hear o' naething
But their ain foul hubbub . . .

The fules are richt; an extra thocht
Is neither here nor there.
Oor lives may differ as they like
—The self-same fate we share.

And whiles I wish I'd nae mair sense
Than Cruivie and Gilsanquhar,
And envy their rude health and curse
My gnawin' canker.

---

clapt, shrunken   drumlie, dreary   rouk, mist   howes, hollows   haar, mist
vieve, vivid   maikless, matchless   happit, covered   goam, gape stupidly
jalouse, imagine   dottlin, going crazy

Guid sakes, ye dinna need to pass
Ony exam. to dee
—Daith canna tell a common flech
Frae a performin' flea! . . .

It sets you weel to slaver
To let sic gaadies fa'
—*The mune's the muckle white whale*
I seek in vain to kaa!

The Earth's my mastless samyn,
The thistle my ruined sail.
—Le'e go as you maun in the end,
And droon in your plumm o' ale! . . .

Clear keltie aff an' fill again
Withoot corneigh bein' cryit,
The drink's aye best that follows a drink.
Clear keltie aff and try it.

Be't whisky gill or penny wheep,
Or ony ither lotion,
We 'bood to ha'e a thimblefu' first,
And syne we'll toom an ocean! . . .

'To Luna at the Craidle-and-Coffin
To sof'n her hert if owt can sof'n:—

Auld bag o' tricks, ye needna come
And think to stap me in your womb.

You needna fash to rax and strain.
Carline, I'll *no* be born again

In ony brat you can produce.
Carline, gi'e owre—O what's the use?

You pay nae heed but plop me in,
Syne shove me oot, and winna be din,

---

flech, flea   slaver, slobber   gaadies fa', howlers fall   kaa, drive
samyn, deck   plumm, deep pool   keltie, bumper   corneigh, enough
whisky gill, dram of whisky   penny wheep, light beer   'bood, intend
toom, empty   owt, anything   stap, stuff   fash, trouble   rax, stretch
Carline, Hag   brat, child   winna be din, won't be finished

—Owre and owre, the same auld trick,
Cratur withoot climacteric! . . .

'Noo Cutty Sark's tint that ana,
And dances in her skin—Ha! Ha!

I canna ride awa' like Tam,
But e'en maun bide juist whaur I am.

I canna ride—and gin I could,
I'd sune be sorry I hedna stood,

For less than a' there is to see
'll never be owre muckle for me.

Cutty, gin you've mair to strip,
Aff wi't, lass—and let it rip!' . . .

Ilka pleesure I can ha'e
Ends like a dram ta'en yesterday.

And tho' to ha'e it I am lorn
—What better 'ud I be the morn? . . .

My belly on the gantrees there,
The spigot frae my cullage,
And wow but how the fizzin' yill
In spilth increased the ullage!

I was an anxious barrel, lad,
When first they tapped my bung.
They whistled me up, yet thro' the lift
My freaths like rainbows swung.

Waesucks, a pride for ony bar,
The boast o' barleyhood,
Like Noah's Ark abune the faem
Maun float, a gantin' cude,

For I was thrawn fu' cock owre sune,
And wi' a single jaw
I made the pub a blindin' swelth,
And how'd the warld awa'! . . .

---

lorn, longing   the morn, tomorrow   gantrees, wooden stand for barrels
cullage, genitals   yill, ale   ullage, deficiency of the contents
freaths, plumes of foam   waesucks, alas   gantin' cude, gaping barrel
thrawn fu' cock owre sune, thrown full cock (completely on) too soon
jaw, spurt   swelth, whiarlpool   how'd, washed

What forest worn to the back-hauf's this,
What Eden brocht doon to a bean-swaup?
The thistle's to earth as the man
In the mune's to the mune, puir chap.

The haill warld's barkin' and fleein',
And this is its echo and aiker,
A soond that arrears in my lug
Herrin'-banein' back to its maker,

A swaw like a flaw in a jewel
Or *nadryv*★ jaloused in a man,
Or Creation unbiggit again
To the draucht wi' which it began . . .

Abordage o' this toom houk's nae mowse.
It munks and's ill to lay haud o',
As gin a man ettled to ride
On the shoulders o' his ain shadow.

I canna biel't; tho' steekin' an e'e
Tither's munkie wi' munebeam for knool in't,
For there's nae sta'-tree and the brute's awa'
Wi' me kinkin' like foudrie ahint . . .

Sae Eternity'll buff nor stye
For Time, and shies at a touch, man;
Yet aye in a belth o' Thocht
Comes alist like the Fleein' Dutchman . . .

---

back-hauf, completely out   bean-swaup, bean-husk
barkin' and fleein', on the verge of ruin   aiker, movement of water (by fish)
arrears, goes backwards   herrin'-banein', herring boning
swaw, ripple   jaloused, suspected   unbiggit, unbuilt   draucht, draught
abordage, embarking   toom houk, empty hulk   nae mowse, no joke
munks, swings away   canna biel't, cannot secure it
steekin' an e'e, hooking one eye   tither's munkie, the other is a rope-loop
knool, peg   sta'-tree, tethering pole   kinkin', twisting
foundrie ahint, lightning behind   buff nor stye, pay no attention
belth, sudden swirl   comes alist, recovers

★ Tragical crack (Dostoevski's term).

As the worms'll breed in my corpse until
It's like a rice-puddin', the thistle
Has made an eel-ark o' the lift
Whaur elvers like skirl-in-the-pan sizzle,

Like a thunder-plump on the sunlicht,
Or the slounge o' daith on my dreams,
Or as to a fair forfochen man
A breedin' wife's beddiness seems,

Saragossa Sea, St. Vitus' Dance,
A *cafard* in a brain's despite,
Or lunacy that thinks a' else
Is loony—and is dootless richt! . . .

Gin my thochts that circle like hobby-horses
'Udna loosen to nightmares I'd sleep;
For nocht but a chowed core's left whaur Jerusalem lay
Like aipples in a heap! . . .

It's a queer thing to tryst wi' a wumman
When the boss o' her body's gane,
And her banes in the wund as she comes
Dirl like a raff o' rain.

It's a queer thing to tryst wi' a wumman
When her ghaist frae abuneheid keeks,
And you see in the licht o't that a'
You ha'e o'r's the cleiks . . .

What forest worn to the backhauf's this,
What Eden brocht doon to a beanswaup?
—A' the ferlies o' natur' spring frae the earth,
And into't again maun drap.

Animals, vegetables, what are they a'
But as thochts that a man has ha'en?
And Earth sall be like a toom skull syne.
—Whaur'll its thochts be then? . . .

---

eel-ark, breeding ground for eels   elvers, young eels
skirl-in-the-pan, fried oatmeal   slounge, sudden splash
fair forfochen, completely exhausted   beddiness, sexual importunity
boss o' her body, front part of her torso   dirl, rattle   raff, flurry
abuneheid keeks, overhead peers
ha'e o'r's the cleiks, have of her is the merest shadow   ferlies, marvels

The munelicht is my knowledge o' mysel',
Mysel' the thistle in the munelicht seen,
And hauf my shape has fund itsel' in thee
And hauf my knowledge in your piercin' een.

E'en as the munelicht's borrowed frae the sun,
I ha'e my knowledge o' mysel' frae thee,
And much that nane but thee can e'er mak' clear,
Save my licht's frae the source, is dark to me.

Your acid tongue, vieve lauchter, and hawk's een,
And bluid that drobs like hail to quicken me,
Can turn the mid-day black or midnicht bricht,
Lowse me frae licht or eke frae darkness free.

Bite into me forever mair and lift
Me clear o' chaos in a great relief
Till, like this thistle in the munelicht growin',
I brak in roses owre a hedge o' grief . . .

I am like Burns, and ony wench
Can ser' me for a time.
Licht's in them a'—in some a sun,
In some the merest skime.

I'm no' like Burns, and weel I ken,
Tho' ony wench can ser',
It's no' through mony but through yin
That ony man wuns fer . . .

I weddit thee frae fause love, lass,
To free thee and to free mysel';
But man and wumman tied for life
True can be and truth can tell.

Pit ony couple in a knot
They canna lowse and needna try,
And mair o' love at last they'll ken
—If ocht!—than joy'll alane descry.

For them as for the beasts, my wife,
A's fer frae dune when pleesure's owre,
And coontless difficulties gar
Ilk hert discover a' its power.

---

vieve, vivid   drobs, pricks   eke, else   skime, gleam   wuns fer, gets far
fause, false

I dinna say that bairns alane
Are true love's task—a sairer task
Is aiblins to create oorsels
As we can be—it's that I ask.

Create oorsels, syne bairns, syne race.
Sae on the cod I see't in you
Wi' Maidenkirk to John o' Groats
The bosom that you draw me to.

And nae Scot wi' a wumman lies,
But I am he and ken as 'twere
A stage I've passed as he maun pass't,
Gin he grows up, his way wi' her! . . .

A'thing wi' which a man
Can intromit's a wumman,
And can, and s'ud, become
As intimate and human.

And Jean's nae mair my wife
Than whisky is at times,
Or munelicht or a thistle
Or kittle thochts or rhymes.

He's no' a man ava',
And lacks a proper pride,
Gin less than a' the warld
Can ser' him for a bride! . . .

Use, then, my lust for whisky and for thee,
Your function but to be and let me be
And see and let me see.

If in a lesser licht I grope my way,
Or use't for ends that need your different ray
Whelm't in superior day.

Then aye increase and ne'er withdraw your licht.
—Gin it shows either o's in hideous plicht,
What gain to turn't to nicht?

cod, pillow   Maidenkirk to John o' Groats, all of Scotland   intromit, meddle
kittle, exciting

Whisky mak's Heaven or Hell and whiles mells baith,
Disease is but the privy torch o' Daith,
—But sex reveals life, faith!

I need them a' and maun be aye at strife.
Daith and ayont are nocht but pairts o' life.
—Then be life's licht, my wife! . . .

Love often wuns free
In lust to be strangled,
Or love, o' lust free,
In law's sairly tangled.

And it's ill to tell whether
Law or lust is to blame
When love's chokit up
—It comes a' to the same.

In this sorry growth
Whatna beauty is tint
That freed o't micht find
A waur fate than is in't? . . .

Yank oot your orra boughs, my hert!

God gied man speech and speech created thocht,
He gied man speech but to the Scots gied nocht
Barrin' this clytach that they've never brocht
To onything but sic a Blottie O
As some bairn's copybook micht show,

A spook o' soond that frae the unkent grave
In which oor nation lies loups up to wave
Sic leprous chuns as tatties have
That cellar-boond send spindles gropin'
Towards ony hole that's open,

Like waesome fingers in the dark that think
They still may widen the ane and only chink
That e'er has gi'en mankind a blink
O' Hope—tho' ev'n in that puir licht
They s'ud ha'e seen their hopeless plicht.

---

mells baith, mixes both	orra, worthless	barrin', except	clytach, nonsense
Blottie O, a school game	loups, leaps	chuns, sprouts	tatties, potatoes
waesome, woeful			

This puir relation o' my topplin' mood,
This country cousin, streak o' churl-bluid,
This hopeless airgh 'twixt a' we can and should,
This Past that like Astarte's sting I feel,
This arrow in Achilles' heel.

Yank oot your orra boughs, my hert!

Mebbe we're in a vicious circle cast,
Mebbe there's limits we can ne'er get past,
Mebbe we're sentrices that at the last
Are flung aside, and no' the pillars and props
O' Heaven foraye as in oor hopes.

Oor growth at least nae steady progress shows,
Genius in mankind like an antrin rose
Abune a jungly waste o' effort grows,
But to Man's purpose it mak's little odds,
And seems irrelevant to God's . . .

Eneuch? Then here you are. Here's the haill story.
Life's connached shapes too'er up in croons o' glory,
Perpetuatin', natheless, in their gory
Colour the endless sacrifice and pain
That to their makin's gane.

The roses like the saints in Heaven treid
Triumphant owre the agonies o' their breed,
And wag fu' mony a celestial heid
Abune the thorter-ills o' leaf and prick
In which they ken the feck maun stick.

Yank oot your orra boughs, my hert!

A mongrel growth, jumble o' disproportions,
Whirlin' in its incredible contortions,
Or wad-be client that an auld whore shuns,
Wardin' her wizened orange o' a bosom
Frae importunities sae gruesome,

Or new diversion o' the hormones
Mair fond o' procreation than the Mormons,
And fetchin' like a devastatin' storm on's
A' the uncouth dilemmas o' oor natur'
Objectified in vegetable maitter.

---

airgh, gap   sentrices, scaffolding   foraye, forever   antrin, rare
connached, spoiled   treid, tread   thorter-ills, paralytic seizures

Yank oot your orra boughs, my hert!
And heed nae mair the foolish cries that beg
You slice nae mair to aff or pu' to leg,
You skitin' duffer that gars a'body fleg,
—What tho' you ding the haill warld oot o' joint
Wi' a skier to cover-point!
Yank oot your orra boughs, my hert!
There *was* a danger—and it's weel I see't—
Had brocht ye like Mallarmé to defeat:—
'Mon doute, amas de nuit ancienne s'achève
En maint rameau subtil, qui, demeuré les vrais
Bois même, prouve, hélas! que bien seul je m'offrais
Pour triomphe la faute idéale des roses.'★
Yank oot your orra boughs, my hert! . . .
I love to muse upon the skill that gangs
To mak' the simplest thing that Earth displays,
The eident life that ilka atom thrangs,
And uses it in the appointit ways,
And a' the endless brain that nocht escapes
That myriad moves them to inimitable shapes.

Nor to their customed form or ony ither
New to Creation, by man's cleverest mind,
A' needfu' particles first brocht thegither,
Could they wi' timeless labour be combined.
There's nocht that Science yet's begood to see
In hauf its deemless detail or its destiny.

Oor een gi'e answers based on pairt-seen facts
That beg a' questions, to ebb minds' content,
But hoo a'e feature or the neist attracts,
Wi' millions mair unseen, wha kens what's meant
By human brains and to what ends may tell
—For naething's seen or kent that's near a thing itsel'!

---

skitin', capering   gars, makes   fleg, afraid   ding, knock
eident, eager   thrangs, crowds   begood, begun   deemless, countless

★ The line which precedes these in Mallarmé's poem is 'Aimai-je un rêve?' and
Wilfrid Thorley translates the passage thus:

'Loved I Love's counterfeit?
My doubts, begotten of the long night's heat,
Dislimn the woodland till my triumph shows
As the flawed shadow of a frustrate rose.'

Let whasae vaunts his knowledge then and syne
Sets up a God and kens *His* purpose tae
Tell me what's gart a'e strain o' maitter twine
In sic an extraordinary way,
And what God's purpose wi' the Thistle is
—I'll aiblins ken what he and his God's worth by this.

I've watched it lang and hard until I ha'e
A certain symp'thy wi' its orra ways
And pride in its success, as weel I may,
In growin' exactly as its instinct says,
Save in sae fer as thwarts o' weather or grun'
Or man or ither foes ha'e'ts aims perchance fordone.

But I can form nae notion o' the spirit
That gars it tak' the difficult shape it does,
Nor judge the merit yet or the demerit
O' this detail or that sae fer as it goes
T' advance the cause that gied it sic a guise
As maun ha'e pleased its Maker wi' a gey surprise.

The craft that hit upon the reishlin' stalk,
Wi'ts gausty leafs and a' its datchie jags,
And spired it syne in seely flooers to brak
Like sudden lauchter owre its fousome rags
Jouks me, sardonic lover, in the routh
O' contrairies that jostle in this dumfoondrin' growth.

What strength 't'ud need to pit its roses oot,
Or double them in number or in size,
He canna tell wha canna plumb the root,
And learn what's gar't its present state arise,
And what the limits are that ha'e been put
To change in thistles, and why—and what a change 'ud boot...

I saw a rose come loupin' oot*
Frae a camsteerie plant.
O wha'd ha'e thocht yon puir stock had
Sic an inhabitant?

---

whasae, whosoever   twine, unite   thwarts, obstructions   grun', ground
reishlin', rustling   gausty, ghastly   datchie, sly   spired, made it soar
seely, innocent   fousome, disgusting   jouks, dodges   routh, plenty
boot, profit   camsteerie, perverse

* The General Strike (May 1926).

For centuries it ran to waste,
Wi' pin-heid flooers at times.
O'ts hidden hert o' beauty they
Were but the merest skimes.

Yet while it ran to wud and thorns,
The feckless growth was seekin'
Some airt to cheenge its life until
A' in a rose was beekin'.

'Is there nae way in which my life
Can mair to flooerin' come,
And bring its waste on shank and jags
Doon to a minimum?

'It's hard to struggle as I maun
For scrunts o' blooms like mine,
While blossom covers ither plants
As by a knack divine.

'What hinders me unless I lack
Some needfu' discipline?
—I wis I'll bring my orra life
To beauty or I'm din!'

Sae ran the thocht that hid ahint
The thistle's ugsome guise,
'I'll brak' the habit o' my life
A worthier to devise.

'My nobler instincts sall nae mair
This contrair shape be gi'en.
I sall nae mair consent to live
A life no' fit to be seen.'

Sae ran the thocht that hid ahint
The thistle's ugsome guise,
Till a' at aince a rose loupt oot
—I watched it wi' surprise.

A rose loupt oot and grew, until
It was ten times the size
O' ony rose the thistle afore
Hed heistit to the skies.

---

wud, would   airt, way   beekin', showing   scrunts, stunted things
wis, know   ugsome, ugly   hed heistit, had hoisted

And still it grew till a' the buss
Was hidden in its flame.
I never saw sae braw a floo'er
As yon thrawn stock became.

And still it grew until it seemed
The haill braid earth had turned
A reid reid rose that in the lift
Like a ball o' fire burned.

The waefu' clay was fire aince mair,
As Earth had been resumed
Into God's mind, frae which sae lang
To grugous state 'twas doomed.

Syne the rose shrivelled suddenly
As a balloon is burst;
The thistle was a ghaistly stick,
As gin it had been curst.

Was it the ancient vicious sway
Imposed itsel' again,
Or nerve owre weak for new emprise
That made the effort vain,

A coward strain in that lorn growth
That wrocht the sorry trick?
—The thistle like a rocket soared
And cam' doon like the stick.

Like grieshuckle the roses glint,
The leafs like farles hing,
As roond a hopeless sacrifice
Earth draws its barren ring.

The dream o' beauty's dernin' yet
Ahint the ugsome shape.
—Vain dream that in a pinheid here
And there can e'er escape!

The vices that defeat the dream
Are in the plant itsel',
And till they're purged its virtues maun
In pain and misery dwell.

---

buss, bush   thrawn, obstinate   grugous, ugly   grieshuckle, embers
farles, ash filaments   dernin', hiding

Let Deils rejoice to see the waste,
The fond hope brocht to nocht.
The thistle in their een is as
A favourite lust they've wrocht.

The orderin' o' the thistle means
Nae richtin' o't to them.
Its loss they ca' a law, its thorns
A fule's fit diadem.

And still the idiot nails itsel'
To its ain crucifix,
While here a rose and there a rose
Jaups oot abune the pricks.

Like connoisseurs the Deils gang roond
And praise its attitude,
Till on the Cross the silly Christ
To fidge fu' fain's begood!

Like connoisseurs the Deils gang roond
Wi' ready platitude.
It's no' sae dear as vinegar,
And every bit as good!

The bitter taste is on my tongue,
I chowl my chafts, and pray
'Let God forsake me noo and no'
Staund connoisseur-like tae!' . . .

The language that but sparely flooers
And maistly gangs to weed;
The thocht o' Christ and Calvary
Aye liddenin' in my heid;
And a' the dour provincial thocht
That merks the Scottish breed
—These are the thistle's characters,
To argie there's nae need.
Hoo weel my verse embodies
The thistle you can read!
—But will a Scotsman never
Frae this vile growth be freed? . . .

Deils, Devils   jaups, splashes   fidge fu' fain's begood, has begun to move eagerly
chowl my chafts, distort my jaws   liddenin', moving to and fro

O ilka man alive is like
A quart that's squeezed into a pint
(A maist unScottish-like affair!)
Or like the little maid that showed
Me into a still sma'er room.

What use to let a sunrise fade
To ha'e anither like't the morn,
Or let a generation pass
That ane nae better may succeed,
Or wi' a' Time's machinery
Keep naething new aneth the sun,
Or change things oot o' kennin' that
They may be a' the mair the same?

The thistle in the wund dissolves
In lichtnin's as shook foil gi'es way
In sudden splendours, or the flesh
As Daith lets slip the infinite soul;
And syne it's like a sunrise tint
In grey o' day, or love and life,
That in a cloody blash o' sperm
Undae the warld to big't again,
Or like a pickled foetus that
Nae man feels ocht in common wi'
—But micht as easily ha' been!
Or like a corpse a soul set free
Scunners to think it tenanted
—And little recks that but for it
It never micht ha' been at a',
Like love frae lust and God frae man!

The wasted seam that dries like stairch
And pooders aff, that micht ha' been
A warld o' men and syne o' Gods;
The grey that haunts the vievest green;
The wrang side o' the noblest scene
We ne'er can whummle to oor een,
As 'twere the hinderpairts o' God
His face aye turned the opposite road,

---

blash, spurt   big't, build it   scunners, feels disgusted   seam, semen
stairch, starch   vievest, most vivid   whummle, overturn

Or's neth the flooers the drumlie clods
Frae which they come at sicna odds,
As a' Earth's magic frae a spirt,
In shame and secrecy, o' dirt!

Then shak' nae mair in silly life,
Nor stand impossible as Daith,
Incredible as a'thing is
Inside or oot owre closely scanned.
As mithers aften think the warld
O' bairns that ha'e nae end or object,
Or lovers think their sweethearts made
Yince-yirn—wha haena waled the lave,
Maikless—when they are naebody,
Or men o' ilka sort and kind
Are prood o' thochts they ca' their ain,
That nameless millions had afore
And nameless millions yet'll ha'e,
And that were never worth the ha'en,
Or Cruivie's 'latest' story or
Gilsanquhar's vows to sign the pledge,
Or's if I thocht maist whisky *was*,
Or failed to coont the cheenge I got,
Sae wad I be gin I rejoiced,
Or didna ken my place, in thee.

O stranglin' rictus, sterile spasm,
Thou stricture in the groins o' licht,
Thou ootrie gangrel frae the wilds
O' chaos fenced frae Eden yet
By the unsplinterable wa'
O' munebeams like a bleeze o' swords!

Nae chance lunge cuts the Gordion knot,
Nor sall the belly find relief
In wha's entangled moniplies
Creation like a stoppage jams,
Or in whose loins the mapamound

---

drumlie, dull   sicna, such great   yince-yirn, especially
waled the lave, tried the rest   maikless, matchless
ootrie gangrel, outré wanderer   wha's, whose   moniplies, intestines
mapamound, map of the world

Runkles in strawns o' bubos whaur
The generations gravel.
The soond o' water winnin' free,
The sicht o' licht that braks the rouk,
The thocht o' every thwart owrecome
Are in my ears and een and brain,
In whom the bluid is spilt in stour,
In whom a' licht in darkness fails,
In whom the mystery o' life
Is to a wretched weed bewrayed.

But let my soul increase in me,
God dwarfed to enter my puir thocht
Expand to his true size again,
And protoplasm's look befit
The nature o' its destiny,
And seed and sequence be nae mair
Incongruous to ane anither,
And liquor packed impossibly
Mak' pint-pot an eternal well,
And art be relevant to life,
And poets mair than dominies yet,
And ends nae langer tint in means,
Nor forests hidden by their trees,
Nor men be sacrificed alive
In foonds o' fates designed for them,
Nor mansions o' the soul stand toom
Their owners in their cellars trapped,
Nor a' a people's genius be
A rumple-fyke in Heaven's doup.
While Calvinism uses her
To breed a minister or twa!

A black leaf owre a white leaf twirls,
A grey leaf flauchters in atween,
Sae ply my thochts aboot the stem
O' loppert slime frae which they spring.

---

runkles, wrinkles   strawns o' bubos, chains of swellings
gravel, collect in confusion   rouk, mist   thwart, hindrance   stour, dust
bewrayed, distorted   dominies, school masters   foonds, foundations
toom, empty   rumple-fyke, anus-itch   doup, backside   flauchters, flutters
loppert, coagulated

The thistle like a snawstorm drives,
Or like a flicht o' swallows lifts,
Or like a swarm o' midges hings,
A plague o' moths, a starry sky,
But's naething but a thistle yet,
And still the puzzle stands unsolved.
Beauty and ugliness alike,
And life and daith and God and man,
Are aspects o't but nane can tell
The secret that I'd fain find oot
O' this bricht hive, this sorry weed,
The tree that fills the universe,
Or like a reistit herrin' crines.

Gin I was sober I micht think
It was like something drunk men see!

The necromancy in my bluid
Through a' the gamut cheenges me
O' dwarf and giant, foul and fair,
But winna let me be mysel'
—My mither's womb that reins me still
Until I tae can prick the witch
And 'Wumman' cry wi' Christ at last,
'Then what hast thou to do wi' me?'

The tug-o'-war is in me still,
The dog-hank o' the flesh and soul,
Faither in Heaven, what gar'd ye tak'
A village slut to mither me,
Your mongrel o' the fire and clay?
The trollop and the Deity share
My writhen form as tho' I were
A picture o' the time they had
When Licht rejoiced to file itsel'
And Earth upshuddered like a star.

A drucken hizzie gane to bed
Wi' three-in-ane and ane-in-three.

---

reistit, dried   crines, shrivels   dog-hank, dog-knot (during mating)
gar'd, made   file, defile   drucken hizzie, drunken hussie

O fain I'd drink until I saw
Scotland a ferlie o' delicht,
And fain bide drunk nor ha'e't recede
Into a shrivelled thistle syne,
As when a sperklin' tide rins oot,
And leaves a wreath o' rubbish there!

Wull a' the seas gang dry at last
(As dry as I am gettin' noo),
Or wull they aye come back again,
Seilfu' as my neist drink to me,
Or as the sunlicht to the mune,
Or as the bonny sangs o' men,
Wha're but puir craturs in themsels,
And save when genius mak's them drunk,
As donnert as their audiences,
—As dreams that mak' a tramp a king,
A madman sane to his ain mind,
Or what a Scotsman thinks himsel',
Tho' naethin' but a thistle kyths.

The mair I drink the thirstier yet,
And whiles when I'm alowe wi' booze,
I'm like God's sel' and clad in fire,
And ha'e a Pentecost like this.
O wad that I could aye be fou',
And no' come back as aye I maun
To naething but a fule that nane
'Ud credit wi' sic thochts as thae,
A fule that kens they're empty dreams!

Yet but fer drink and drink's effects,
The yeast o' God that barms in us,
We micht as weel no' be alive.
It maitters not what drink is ta'en,
The barley bree, ambition, love,
Or Guid or Evil workin' in's,
Sae lang's we feel like souls set free
Frae mortal coils and speak in tongues

---

ferlie o' delicht, marvel of delight   nor ha'e't, nor have it   seilfu', blissful
donnert, stupid   kyths, appears   alowe, ablaze   barms, ferments
barley bree, whisky

We dinna ken and never wull,
And find a merit in oorsels,
In Cruivies and Gilsanquhars tae,
And see the thistle as ocht but that!

For wha o's ha'e the thistle's poo'er
To see we're worthless and believe 't?

A'thing that ony man can be's
A mockery o' his soul at last.
The mair it shows't the better, and
I'd suner be a tramp than king,
Lest in the pride o' place and poo'er
I e'er forgot my waesomeness.
Sae to debauchery and dirt,
And to disease and daith I turn,
Sin' otherwise my seemin' worth
'Ud block my view o' what is what,
And blin' me to the irony
O' bein a grocer 'neth the sun,
A lawyer gin Justice ope'd her een,
A pedant like an ant promoted,
A parson buttonholin' God,
Or ony cratur o' the Earth
Sma'-bookt to John Smith, High Street, Perth,
Or sic like vulgar gaffe o' life
Sub speciem aeternitatis—
Nae void can fleg me hauf as much
As bein' mysel', whate'er I am,
Or, waur, bein' onybody else.

The nervous thistle's shiverin' like
A horse's skin aneth a cleg,
Or Northern Lichts or lustres o'
A soul that Daith has fastened on,
Or mornin' efter the nicht afore.

Shudderin' thistle, gi'e owre, gi'e owre . . .

---

waesomeness, woefulness   sma'-bookt, shrunken   sic like, such similar
fleg, frighten   waur, worse   cleg, gadfly

Grey sand is churnin' in my lugs
The munelicht flets, and gantin' there
The grave o' a' mankind's laid bare
—On Hell itsel' the drawback rugs!

Nae man can ken his hert until
The tide o' life uncovers it,
And horror-struck he sees a pit
Returnin' life can never fill! . . .

Thou art the facts in ilka airt
That breenge into infinity,
Criss-crossed wi' coontless ither facts
Nae man can follow, and o' which
He is himsel' a helpless pairt,
Held in their tangle as he were
A stick-nest in Ygdrasil!

The less man sees the mair he is
Content wi't, but the mair he sees
The mair he kens hoo little o'
A' that there is he'll ever see,
And hoo it mak's confusion aye
The waur confoondit till at last
His brain inside his heid is like
Ariadne wi' an empty pirn,
Or like a birlin' reel frae which
A whale has rived the line awa.'

What better's a forhooied nest
Than skasloch scattered owre the grun'?

O hard it is for man to ken
He's no creation's goal nor yet
A benefitter by't at last—
A means to ends he'll never ken,
And as to michtier elements
The slaughtered brutes he eats to him
Or forms o' life owre sma' to see
Wi' which his heedless body swarms,
And a' man's thocht nae mair to them

---

flets, flits   gantin', yawning   drawback rugs, obstruction pulls
ilka airt, every way   breenge, spring   pirn, bobbin   birlin', whirling
rived, torn   forhooied, abandoned   skasloch, loose straw

Than ony moosewob to a man,
His Heaven to them the blinterin' o'
A snail-trail on their closet wa'!

For what's an atom o' a twig
That tak's a billion to an inch
To a' the routh o' shoots that mak'
The bygrowth o' the Earth aboot
The michty trunk o' Space that spreids
Ramel o' licht that ha'e nae end,
—The trunk wi' centuries for rings,
Comets for fruit, November shooers
For leafs that in its Autumns fa'
—And Man at maist o' sic a twig
Ane o' the coontless atoms is!

My sinnens and my veins are but
As muckle o' a single shoot
Wha's fibre I can ne'er unwaft
O' my wife's flesh and mither's flesh
And a' the flesh o' humankind,
And revelled thrums o' beasts and plants
As gangs to mak' twixt birth and daith
A'e sliver for a microscope;
And a' the life o' Earth to be
Can never lift frae underneath
The shank o' which oor destiny's pairt
As heich's to stand forenenst the trunk
Stupendous as a windlestrae!

I'm under nae delusions, fegs!
The whuppin' sooker at wha's tip
Oor little point o' view appears,
A midget coom o' continents
Wi' blebs o' oceans set, sends up
The braith o' daith as weel as life,
And we maun braird anither tip
Oot owre us ere we wither tae,

---

moosewob, spider's web   blinterin', glistening
routh, plenty   ramel, branches   sinnens, sinews   unwaft, unweave
revelled thrums, ravelled threads   forenenst, in relation to
windlestrae, straw   whuppin' sooker, whipping sucker of a tree
coom, comb   blebs, drops   braird, sprout

68

And join the sentrice skeleton
As coral insects big their reefs.

What is the tree? As fer as Man's
Concerned it disna maitter
Gin but a giant thistle 'tis
That spreids eternal mischief there,
As I'm inclined to think.
Ruthless it sends its solid growth
Through mair than he can e'er conceive,
And braks his warlds abreid and rives
His Heavens to tatters on its horns.

The nature or the purpose o't
He needna fash to spier, for he
Is destined to be sune owre grown
And hidden wi' the parent wud
The spreidin' boughs in darkness hap,
And a' its future life'll be
Ootwith'm as he's ootwith his banes.

Juist as man's skeleton has left
Its ancient ape-like shape ahint,
Sae states o' mind in turn gi'e way
To different states, and quickly seem
Impossible to later men,
And Man's mind in its final shape,
Or lang'll seem a monkey's spook,
And, strewth, to me the vera thocht
O' Thocht already's fell like that!
Yet still the cracklin' thorns persist
In fitba' match and peepy show,
To antic hay a dog-fecht's mair
Than Jacob v. the Angel
And through a cylinder o' wombs,
A star reflected in a dub,
I see as 'twere my ain wild harns
The ripple o' Eve's moniplies.

---

sentrice, scaffold-like   abreid, asunder   rives, tears   fash to spier, trouble to ask
wud, would   hap, cover   or lang, ere long   peepy show, cinema
antic hay, grotesque dance   dub, puddle   harns, brains   moniplies, intestines

And faith! yestreen in Cruivie's een
Life rocked at midnicht in a tree,
And in Gilsanquhar's glower I saw
The taps o' waves 'neth which the warld
Ga'ed rowin' like a jeelyfish,
And whiles I canna look at Jean
For fear I'd seen the sunlicht turn
Worm-like into the glaur again!

A black leaf owre a white leaf twirls,
My liver's shadow on my soul,
And clots o' bluid loup oot frae stems
That back into the jungle rin,
Or in the waters underneath
Kelter like seaweed, while I hear
Abune the thunder o' the flood,
The voice that aince commanded licht
Sing 'Scots Wha Ha'e' and hyne awa'
Like Cruivie up a different glen,
And leave me like a mixture o'
A wee Scotch nicht and Judgment Day,
The bile, the Bible, and the *Scotsman*,
Poetry and pigs—Infernal Thistle,
Damnition haggis I've spewed up,
And syne return to like twa dogs!
Blin' Proteus wi' leafs or hands
Or flippers ditherin' in the lift
—Thou Samson in a warld that has
Nae pillars but your cheengin' shapes
That dung doon, rise in ither airts
Like windblawn reek frae smoo'drin' ess!
—Hoo lang maun I gi'e aff your forms
O' plants and beasts and men and Gods
And like a doited Atlas bear
This steeple o' fish, this eemis warld,
Or, maniac heid wi' snakes for hair,
A Maenad, ape Aphrodite,
And scunner the Eternal sea?

glaur, primal ooze   kelter, undulate   hyne awa', far away
dung doon, dashed down   ither airts, other ways
windblawn reek frae smoo'drin ess, windblown smoke from smouldering ashes
doited, mad   eemis, ill-poised   scunner, disgust

Man needna fash and even noo
The cells that mak' a'e sliver wi'm,
The threidy knit he's woven wi',
'Ud fain destroy what sicht he has
O' this puir transitory stage,
Yet tho' he kens the fragment is
O' little worth he e'er can view,
Jalousin' it's a cheatrie weed,
He tyauves wi' a' his micht and main
To keep his sicht despite his kind
Conspirin' as their nature is
'Gainst ocht wi' better sicht than theirs.

What gars him strive? He canna tell—
It may be nocht but cussedness.
—At best he hopes for little mair
Than his suspicions to confirm,
To mock the sicht he hains sae weel
At last wi' a' he sees wi' it,
Yet, thistle or no' whate'er its end,
Aiblins the force that mak's it grow
And lets him see a kennin' mair
Than ither folk and fend his sicht
Agen their jealous plots awhile
'll use the poo'ers it seems to waste,
This purpose ser'd, in ither ways,
That may be better worth the bein'
—Or sae he dreams, syne mocks his dream
Till Life grows sheer awa' frae him,
And bratts o' darkness plug his een.

It may be nocht but cussedness,
But I'm content gin a' my thocht
Can dae nae mair than let me see,
Free frae desire o' happiness,
The foolish faiths o' ither men
In breedin', industry, and War,

---

fash, trouble   wi'm, with him   threidy knit, thready knot
jalousin', suspecting   cheatrie, fraudulent   tyauves, struggles   hains, preserves
kennin', little bit   fend, defend   bratts, scum

Religion, Science, or ocht else
Gang smash—when I ha'e nane mysel',
Or better gin I share them tae,
Or mind at least a time I did!

Aye, this is Calvary—to bear
Your Cross wi'in you frae the seed,
And feel it grow by slow degrees
Until it rends your flesh apairt,
And turn, and see your fellow-men
In similar case but sufferin' less
Thro' bein' mair wudden frae the stert! . . .

I'm fu' o' a stickit God.
THAT's what's the maitter wi' me,
Jean has stuck sic a fork in the wa'
That I row in agonie.

Mary never let dab.
SHE was a canny wumman.
She hedna a gaw in Joseph at a'
But, wow, this secund comin'! . . .

Narodbogonosets★ are my folk tae,
But in a sma' way nooadays—
A faitherly God wi' a lang white beard,
Or painted Jesus in a haze
O' blue and gowd, a gird aboot his heid
Or some sic thing. It's been a sair come-doon,
And the trade's nocht to what it was.
Unnatural practices are the cause.
Baith bairns and God'll be obsolete soon
(The twaesome gang thegither), and forsooth
Scotland turn Eliot's waste—the Land o' Drouth.

But even as the stane the builders rejec'
Becomes the corner-stane, the time may be
When Scotland sall find oot its destiny,
And yield the *vse-chelovek.*†

---

stickit, frustrated   row, roll   let dab, let on   canny, cautious
gaw, hold   seecund, second   gird, hoop   Drouth, Drought

★ God-bearers.
† The All-Man or Pan-Human.

—At a' events, owre Europe flaught atween,
My whim (and mair than whim) it pleases
To seek the haund o' Russia as a freen'
In workin' oot mankind's great synthesis . . .

Melville★ (a Scot) kent weel hoo Christ's
Corrupted into creeds malign,
Begotten strife's pernicious brood
That claims for patron Him Divine.
(The Kirk in Scotland still I cry
Crooks whaur it canna crucify!)

Christ, bleedin' like the thistle's roses,
He saw—as I in similar case—
Maistly, in beauty and in fear,
'Ud 'paralyse the nobler race,
Smite or suspend, perplex, deter,
And, tortured, prove the torturer.'

And never mair a Scot sall tryst,
Abies on Calvary, wi' Christ,
Unless, mebbe, a poem like this'll
Exteriorise things in a thistle,
And gi'e him in this form forlorn
What Melville socht in vain frae Hawthorne . . .

Spirit o' strife, destroy in turn
Syne this fule's Paradise, syne that;
In thee's in Calvaries that owrecome
Daith efter Daith let me be caught,

Or in the human form that hauds
Us in its ignominious thrall,
While on brute needs oor souls attend
Until disease and daith end all,

Or in the grey deluded brain,
Reflectin' in anither field
The torments o' its parent flesh
In thocht-preventin' thocht concealed,

flaught, abased   abies, except

★ Herman Melville.

Or still in curst impossible mould,
Last thistle-shape men think to tak',
The soul, frae flesh and thocht set free,
On Heaven's strait if unseen rack.

There may be heicher forms in which
We can nae mair oor plicht define,
Because the agonies involved
'll bring us their ain anodyne.

Yet still we suffer and still sall,
Altho', puir fules, we mayna ken 't
As lang as like the thistle we
In coil and in recoil are pent.

And ferrer than mankind can look
Ghast shapes that free but to transfix
Twine rose-crooned in their agonies,
And strive agen the endless pricks.

The dooble play that bigs and braks
In endless victory and defeat
Is in your spikes and roses shown,
And a' my soul is haggar'd wi't . . .

Be like the thistle, O my soul,
Heedless o' praise and quick to tak' affront,
And growin' like a mockery o' a'
Maist life can want or thole,
And manifest forevermair
Contempt o' ilka goal.

O' ilka goal—save ane alane;
To be yoursel', whatever that may be,
And as contemptuous o' that,
Kennin' nocht's worth the ha'en,
But certainty that nocht can be,
And hoo that certainty to gain.

For this you still maun grow and grope
In the abyss wi' ever-deepenin' roots
That croon your scunner wi' the grue
O' hopeless hope

bigs, builds   thole, endure   scunner, disgust   grue, revulsion

—And gin the abyss is bottomless,
Your growth'll never stop! . . .

What earthquake chitters oot
In the Thistle's oorie shape,
What gleids o' central fire
In its reid heids escape,
And whatna coonter forces
In growth and ingrowth graip
In an eternal clinch
In this ootcuissen form
That winna be outcast,
But triumphs at the last
(Owre a' abies itsel'
As fer as we can tell,
Sin' frae the Eden o' the world
Ilka man in turn is hurled,
And ilka gairden rins to waste
That was ever to his taste?)

O keep the Thistle 'yont the wa'
Owre which your skeletons you'll thraw.

I, in the Thistle's land,
As you★ in Russia where
Struggle in giant form
Proceeds for evermair,
In my sma' measure 'bood
Address a similar task,
And for a share o' your
Appallin' genius ask.

Wha built in revelations
What maist men in reserves
(And only men confound!)
A better gift deserves
Frae ane wha like hissel
(As ant-heap unto mountain)
Needs big his life upon
The everloupin' fountain

chitters, trembles   oorie, weird   gleids, sparks   whatna, what kind of
graip, grip   ootcuissen, outcast   'bood, intend to

★ Dostoevski.

That frae the Dark ascends
Whaur Life begins, Thocht ends
—A better gift deserves
Than thae wheen yatterin' nerves!

For mine's the clearest insicht
O' man's facility
For constant self-deception,
And hoo his mind can be
But as a floatin' iceberg
That hides aneth the sea
Its bulk: and hoo frae depths
O' an unfaddomed flood
Tensions o' nerves arise
And humours o' the blood
—Keethin's nane can trace
To their original place.

Hoo mony men to mak' a man
It tak's he kens wha kens Life's plan.

But there are flegsome deeps
Whaur the soul o' Scotland sleeps
That I to bottom need
To wauk Guid kens what deid,
Play at stertle-a-stobie,
Wi' nation's dust for hobby,
Or wi' God's sel' commerce
For the makin' o' a verse.

'Melville, sea-compelling man,
Before whose wand Leviathan
Rose hoary-white upon the Deep,'★
What thou hast sown I fain 'ud reap
O' knowledge 'yont the human mind
In keepin' wi' oor Scottish kind,
And, thanks to thee, may aiblins reach
To what this Russian has to teach,

thae wheen yatterin', these few chattering keethin's, appearances
flegsome, frightening what deid, which corpses
stertle-a-stobie, chasing dust puffs

★ Quoted from Robert Buchanan.

Closer than ony ither Scot,
Closer to me than my ain thocht,
Closer than my ain braith to me,
As close as to the Deity
Approachable in whom appears
This Christ o' the neist thoosand years.

As frae your baggit wife
You turned whenever able,
And often when you werena,
Unto the gamin' table,
And opened wide to ruin
Your benmaist hert, aye brewin'
A horror o' whatever
Seemed likely to deliver
You frae the senseless strife
In which alane is life,
—As Burns in Edinburgh
Breenged arse-owre-heid thoro'
A' *it* could be the spur o'
To pleuch his sauted furrow,
And turned frae a' men honour
To what could only scunner
Wha thinks that common-sense
Can e'er be but a fence
To keep a soul worth ha'en
Frae what it s'ud be daein'
—Sae I in turn maun gie
My soul to misery,
Daidle disease
Upon my knees,
And welcome madness
Wi' exceedin' gladness
—Aye, open wide my hert
To a' the thistle's smert.

And a' the hopes o' men
Sall be like wiles then

---

baggit, big bellied   benmaist, inmost
breenged arse-owre-heid thoro', burst regardless through   pleuch, plough
sauted, salted   daidle, dandle

To gar my soul betray
Its only richtfu' way,
Or as a couthie wife
That seeks nae mair frae life
Than domesticity
E'en wi' the likes o' me—
As gin I could be carin'
For her or for her bairn
When on my road I'm farin'
—O I can spend a nicht
In ony man's Delicht
Or wi' ony wumman born
—But aye be aff the morn!

In a' the inklin's cryptic,
Then, o' an epileptic,
I ha'e been stood in you
And droukit in their grue
Till I can see richt through
Ilk weakness o' my frame
And ilka dernin' shame,
And can employ the same
To jouk the curse o' fame,
Lowsed frae the dominion
O' popular opinion,
And risen at last abune
The thistle like a mune
That looks serenely doon
On what queer things there are
In an inferior star
That couldna be, or see,
Themsel's, except in me.

Wi' burnt-oot hert and poxy face
I sall illumine a' the place,
And there is ne'er a fount o' grace
That isna in a similar case.

---

couthie, comfortable   droukit, drenched   grue, revulsion   dernin', hiding
jouk, dodge   lowsed, freed

Let a' the thistle's growth
Be as a process, then,
My spirit's gane richt through,
And needna threid again,
Tho' in it sall be haud'n
For aye the feck o' men
Wha's queer contortions there
As memories I ken,
As memories o' my ain
O' mony an ancient pain.
But sin' wha'll e'er wun free
Maun tak' like coorse to me,
A fillip I wad gi'e
Their eccentricity,
And leave the lave to dree
Their weirdless destiny.

It's no' withoot regret
That I maun follow yet
The road that led me past
Humanity sae fast,
Yet scarce can gi'e a fate
That is at last mair fit
To them wha tak' that gait
Than theirs wha winna ha'e't,
Seein' that nae man can get
By ony airt or wile,
A destiny quite worth while
As fer as he can tell
—Or even you yoursel'!

And O! I canna thole
Aye yabblin' o' my soul,
And fain I wad be free
O' my eternal me,
Nor fare mysel' alane
—Withoot that tae be gane,
And this, I ha'e nae doot,
This road'll bring aboot.

dree, endure   weirdless, purposeless   gait, way
winna ha'e't, will not have it   airt, way   thole, endure   yabblin', gabbling

79

The munelicht that owre clear defines
The thistle's shrill cantankerous lines
E'en noo whiles insubstantialises
Its grisly form and 'stead devises
A maze o' licht, a siller-frame,
As 'twere God's dream frae which it came,
Ne'er into bein' coorsened yet,
The essence lowin' pure in it,
As tho' the fire owrecam' the clay,
And left its wraith in endless day.

These are the moments when a' sense
Like mist is vanished and intense,
Magic emerges frae the dense
Body o' bein' and beeks immense
As, like a ghinn oot o' a bottle,
Daith rises frae's when oor lives crottle.

These are the moments when my sang
Clears its white feet frae oot amang
My broken thocht, and moves as free
As souls frae bodies when they dee.
There's naething left o' me ava'
Save a' I'd hoped micht whiles befa'.

Sic sang to men is little worth.
It has nae message for the earth.
Men see their warld turned tapsalteerie,
Drookit in a licht owre eerie,
Or sent birlin' like a peerie—
Syne it turns a' they've kent till then
To shapes they can nae langer ken.

Men canna look on nakit licht.
It flings them back wi' darkened sicht,
And een that canna look at it,
Maun draw earth closer roond them yet
Or, their sicht tint, find nocht instead
That answers to their waefu' need.

---

lowin', blazing   owrecam', overcame   beeks, shows   crottle, crumble
ava', at all   tapsalteerie, topsy-turvy   drookit, drenched   birlin', spinning
peerie, top   tint, lost

And yet this essence frae the clay
In dooble form aye braks away,
For, in addition to the licht,
There is an e'er-increasin' nicht,
A nicht that is the bigger, and
Gangs roond licht like an airn band
That noo and then mair tichtly grips,
And snuffs it in a black eclipse,
But rings it maistly as a brough
The mune, till it's juist bricht enough—
O wull I never lowse a licht
I canna dowse again in spite,
Or dull to haud within my sicht?

The thistle canna vanish quite.
Inside a' licht its shape maun glint,
A spirit wi' a skeleton in't.

The world, the flesh, 'll bide in us
As in the fire the unburnt buss,
Or as frae sire to son we gang
And coontless corpses in us thrang.

And e'en the glory that descends
I kenna whence on *me* depends,
And shapes itsel' to what is left
Whaur I o' me ha'e me bereft,
And still the form is mine, altho'
A force to which I ne'er could grow
Is movin' in't as 'twere a sea
That lang syne drooned the last o' me
—That drooned afore the warld began
A' that could ever come frae Man.

And as at sicna times am I,
I wad ha'e Scotland to my eye
Until I saw a timeless flame
Tak' Auchtermuchty for a name,
And kent that Ecclefechan stood
As pairt o' an eternal mood.

---

airn, iron   brough, halo   lowse, loosen   buss, bush   thrang, throng
kenna, don't know   lang syne, long ago   sicna, such

Ahint the glory comes the nicht
As Maori to London's ruins,
And I'm amused to see the plicht
O' Licht as't in the black tide droons,
Yet even in the brain o' Chaos
For Scotland I wad hain a place,
And let Tighnabruaich still
Be pairt and paircel o' its will,
And Culloden, black as Hell,
A knowledge it has o' itsel'.

Thou, Dostoevski, understood,
Wha had your ain land in your bluid,
And into it as in a mould
The passion o' your bein' rolled,
Inherited in turn frae Heaven
Or sources fer abune it even.

Sae God retracts in endless stage
Through angel, devil, age on age,
Until at last his infinite natur'
Walks on earth a human cratur'
(Or less than human as to my een
The people are in Aiberdeen);
Sae man returns in endless growth
Till God in him again has scouth.

For sic a loup towards widsom's croon
Hoo fer a man maun base him doon,
Hoo plunge aboot in Chaos ere
He finds his needfu' fittin' there,
The matrix oot o' which sublime
Serenity sall soar in time!

Ha'e I the cruelty I need,
Contempt and syne contempt o' that,
And still contempt in endless meed
That I may never yet be caught
In ony satisfaction, or
Bird-lime that winna let me soar?

hain, preserve   scouth, scope   fittin', footing

Is Scotland big enough to be
A symbol o' that force in me,
In wha's divine inebriety
A sicht abune contempt I'll see?

For a' that's Scottish is in me,
As a' things Russian were in thee,
And I in turn 'ud be an action
To pit in a concrete abstraction
My country's contrair qualities,
And mak' a unity o' these
Till my love owre its history dwells,
As owretone to a peal o' bells.

And in this heicher stratosphere
As bairn at giant at thee I peer . . .

O Jean, in whom my spirit sees,
Clearer than through whisky or disease,
Its dernin' nature, wad the searchin' licht
Oor union raises poor'd owre me the nicht.

I'm faced wi' aspects o' mysel'
At last wha's portent nocht can tell,
Save that sheer licht o' life that when we're joint
Loups through me like a fire a' else t' aroint.

Clear my lourd flesh, and let me move
In the peculiar licht o' love,
As aiblins in Eternity men may
When their swack souls nae mair are clogged wi' clay.

Be thou the licht in which I stand
Entire, in thistle-shape, as planned,
And no' hauf-hidden and hauf-seen as here
In munelicht, whisky, and in fleshly fear,

In fear to look owre closely at
The grisly form in which I'm caught,
In sic a reelin' and imperfect licht
Sprung frae incongruous elements the nicht!

dernin', hidden   the nicht, tonight   t' aroint, to expel   lourd, heavy
swack, supple

But wer't by thou they were shone on,
Then wad I ha'e nae dreid to con
The ugsome problems shapin' in my soul,
Or gin I hed—certes, nae fear you'd thole!

Be in this fibre like an eye,
And ilka turn and twist descry,
Hoo here a leaf, a spine, a rose—or as
The purpose o' the poo'er that brings 't to pass.

Syne liberate me frae this tree,
As wha had there imprisoned me,
The end achieved—or show me at the least
Mair meanin' in't, and hope o' bein' released.

I tae ha'e heard Eternity drip water
(Aye water, water!), drap by drap
On the a'e nerve, like lichtnin', I've become,
And heard God passin' wi' a bobby's feet
Ootby in the lang coffin o' the street
—Seen stang by chitterin' knottit stang loup oot
Uncrushed by th' echoes o' the thunderin' boot,
Till a' the dizzy lint-white lines o' torture made
A monstrous thistle in the space aboot me,
A symbol o' the puzzle o' man's soul
—And in my agony been pridefu' I could still
Tine nae least quiver or twist, watch ilka point
Like a white-het bodkin ripe my inmaist hert,
And aye wi' clearer pain that brocht nae anodyne,
But rose for ever to a fer crescendo
Like eagles that ootsoar wi' skinklan' wings
The thieveless sun they blin'
          —And pridefu' still
That 'yont the sherp wings o' the eagles fleein'
Aboot the dowless pole o' Space,
Like leafs aboot a thistle-shank, my bluid
Could still thraw roses up
          —And up!

---

ugsome, horrible   certes, certainly   thole, tolerate
tae, also   stang, paroxysm   chitterin', shivering   tine, lose   het, hot
ripe, search   skinklan', shining   thieveless, dull   dowless, imponderable

O rootless thistle through the warld that's pairt o' you,
Gin you'd withstand the agonies still to come,
You maun send roots doon to the deeps unkent,
Fer deeper than it's possible for ocht to gang,
Savin' the human soul,
Deeper than God himsel' has knowledge o',
Whaur lichtnin's canna probe that cleave the warld,
Whaur only in the entire dark there's founts o' strength
Eternity's poisoned draps can never file,
And muckle roots thicken, deef to bobbies' feet.

A mony-brainchin' candelabra fills
The lift and's lowin' wi' the stars;
The Octopus Creation is wallopin'
In coontless faddoms o' a nameless sea.
I am the candelabra, and burn
My endless candles to an Unkent God.
I am the mind and meanin' o' the octopus
That thraws its empty airms through a' th' Inane.

And a' the bizzin' suns ha'e bigged
Their kaims upon the surface o' the sea.
My lips may feast for ever, but my guts
Ken naething o' the Food o' Gods.

'Let there be Licht,' said God, and there was
A little: but He lacked the poo'er
To licht up mair than pairt o' space at aince,
And there is lots o' darkness that's the same
As gin He'd never spoken
      —Mair darkness than there's licht,
And dwarfin't to a candle-flame,
A spalin' candle that'll sune gang oot.
—Darkness comes closer to us than the licht,
And is oor natural element. We peer oot frae't
Like cat's een bleezin' in a goustrous nicht
(Whaur there is nocht to find but stars
That look like ither cats' een),
Like cat's een, and there is nocht to find
Savin' we turn them in upon oorsels;
Cats canna.

file, defile   deef, deaf   bizzin', buzzing   bigged, built   kaims, honey-combs
spalin', guttering   goustrous, frightful

Darkness is wi' us a' the time, and Licht
But veesits pairt o' us, the wee-est pairt
Frae time to time on a short day atween twa nichts.
Nae licht is thrawn on *them* by ony licht.
Licht thraws nae licht upon itsel';
But in the darkness them wha's een
Nae fleetin' lichts ha'e dazzled and deceived
Find qualities o' licht, keener than ony licht,
Keen and abidin'
That show the nicht unto itsel',
And syne the licht,
That queer extension o' the dark,
That seems a separate and a different thing,
And, seemin' sae, has lang confused the dark,
And set it at cross-purposes wi' itsel'.

O little Life
In which Daith guises and deceives itsel',
Joy that mak's Grief a Janus,
Hope that is Despair's fause-face,
And Guid and Ill that are the same,
Save as the chance licht fa's!

And yet the licht is there,
Whether frae within or frae withoot.
The conscious Dark can use it, dazzled nor deceived.
The licht is there, and th' instinct for it,
Pairt o' the Dark and o' the need to guise,
To deceive and be deceived,
But let us then be undeceived
When we deceive,
When we deceive oorsels.
Let us enjoy deceit, this instinct in us.
Licht cheenges naething,
And gin there is a God wha made the licht
We are adapted to receive,
He cheenged naething.
And hesna kythed Hissel!
Save in this licht that fa's whaur the Auld Nicht was,

---

kythed Hissel, revealed Himself

Showin' naething that the Darkness didna hide,
And gin it shows a pairt o' that
Confoondin' mair than it confides
Ev'n in that.

The epileptic thistle twitches
(A trick o' wund or mune or een—or whisky).
A brain laid bare,
A nervous system,
The skeleton wi' which men labour
And bring to life in Daith
—I, risen frae the deid, ha'e seen
My deid man's eunuch offspring.
—The licht frae bare banes whitening evermair,
Frae twitchin' nerves thrawn aff,
Frae nakit thocht,
Works in the Darkness like a fell disease,
A hungry acid and a cancer,
Disease o' Daith-in-Life and Life-in-Daith.

O for a root in some untroubled soil,
Some cauld soil 'yont this fevered warld,
That 'ud draw darkness frae a virgin source,
And send it slow and easefu' through my veins,
Release the tension o' my grisly leafs,
Withdraw my endless spikes,
Move coonter to the force in me that hauds
Me raxed and rigid and ridiculous
        —And let my roses drap
Like punctured ba's that at a Fair
Fa' frae the loupin' jet!
        —Water again! . . .

Omsk and the Calton turn again to dust,
The suns and stars fizz out with little fuss,
The bobby booms away and seems to bust,
And leaves the world to darkness and to us.

The circles of our hungry thought
Swing savagely from pole to pole.
Death and the Raven drift above
The graves of Sweeney's body and soul.

raxed, stretched

My name is Norval. On the Grampian Hills
It is forgotten, and deserves to be.
So are the Grampian Hills and all the people
Who ever heard of either them or me.

What's in a name? From pole to pole
Our interlinked mentality spins.
I know that you are Deosil, and suppose
That therefore I am Widdershins.

Do you reverse? Shall us? Then let's.
Cyclone and Anti?—how absurd!
She should know better at her age.
Auntie's an ass, upon my word.

This is the sort of thing they teach
The Scottish children in the school.
Poetry, patriotism, manners—
No wonder I am such a fool . . .

Hoo can I graipple wi' the thistle syne,
Be intricate as it and up to a' its moves?
A' airts its sheenin' points are loupin' 'yont me,
Quhile still the firmament it proves.

And syne it's like a wab in which the warld
Squats like a spider, quhile the mune and me
Are taigled in an endless corner o't
Tyauvin' fecklessly . . .

The wan leafs shak' atour us like the snaw.
Here is the cavaburd in which Earth's tint.
There's naebody but Oblivion and us,
Puir gangrel buddies, waunderin' hameless in't.

The stars are larochs o' auld cottages,
And a' Time's glen is fu' o' blinnin' stew.
Nae freen'ly lozen skimmers: and the wund
Rises and separates even me and you.★

---

quhile, while   taigled, tangled   tyauvin', struggling   atour, around
cavaburd, snowstorm   tint, lost   ganrel buddies, vagrant persons
larochs, ruined sites   blinnin' stew, blinding dust
freen'ly lozen skimmers, friendly window glimmers

★ Dostoevski.

I ken nae Russian and you ken nae Scots.
We canna tell oor voices frae the wund.
The snaw is seekin' everywhere: oor herts
At last like roofless ingles it has f'und,

And gethers there in drift on endless drift,
Oor broken herts that it can never fill;
And still—its leafs like snaw, its growth like wund—
The thistle rises and forever will! . . .

The thistle rises and forever will,
Getherin' the generations under't.
This is the monument o' a' they were,
And a' they hoped and wondered.

The barren tree, dry leafs and cracklin' thorns,
This is the mind o' a' humanity,
—The empty intellect that left to grow
'll let nocht ither be.

Lo! It has choked the sunlicht's gowden grain,
And strangled syne the white hairst o' the mune.
Thocht that mak's a' the food o' nocht but Thocht
Is reishlin' grey abune . . .

O fitly frae oor cancerous soil
May this heraldic horror rise!
The Presbyterian thistle flourishes,
And its ain roses crucifies . . .

No' Edinburgh Castle or the fields
O' Bannockburn or Flodden
Are dernin' wi' the miskent soul
Scotland sae lang has hod'n.

It hauds nae pew in ony kirk,
The soul Christ cam' to save;
Nae R.S.A.'s ha'e pentit it,
F.S.A.'s fund its grave.

Is it alive or deid? I show
My hert—wha will can see.
The secret clyre in Scotland's life
Has brust and reams through me,

hairst, harvest   reishlin', rustling   dernin', hiding   hod'n, hidden
clyre, diseased gland   brust, burst   reams, foams

A whummlin' sea in which is heard
The clunk o' nameless banes;
A grisly thistle dirlin' shrill
Abune the broken stanes.

Westminster Abbey nor the Fleet,
Nor England's Constitution, but
In a' the michty city there,
You mind a'e fleggit slut,

As Tolstoi o' Lucerne alane
Minded a'e beggar minstrel seen!
The woundit side draws a' the warld.
Barbarians ha'e lizards' een.

Glesca's a gless whaur Magdalene's
Discovered in a million crimes.
Christ comes again—wheesht, whatna bairn
In backlands cries betimes?

Hard faces prate o' their success,
And pickle-makers awn the hills.
There is nae life in a' the land
But this infernal Thistle kills . . .

    Nae mair I see
    As aince I saw
    Mysel' in the thistle
    Harth and haw!

Nel suo profondo vidi che s'interna
Legato con amore in un volume
(Or else by Hate, fu' aft the better Love)
Ciò che per l'universo si squaderna.

Sustanzia ed accidenti, e lor costume,
Quasi conflati insieme fer tal modo.
(The michty thistle in wha's boonds I rove)
Ché ciò ch'io dico è un semplice lume.★

---

whummlin', overwhelming   dirlin', vibrating   mind, remember
a'e fleggit, one frightened   wheesht, hush   whatna, whatever
backlands, slum tenements   awn, own   harth, lean   haw, hollow

★Wicksteed's translation of Dante's Italian (Paradiso, canto xxxiii, 85–90) is as
follows: 'Within its depths I saw ingathered, bound by love in one volume, the
scattered leaves of all the universe; substance and accidents and their relations, as
though together fused, after such fashion that what I tell of is one simple flame.'

And kent and was creation
In a' its coontless forms,
Or glitterin' in raw sunlicht,
Or dark wi' hurrying storms.

But what's the voice
That sings in me noo?
—A'e hauf o' me tellin'
The tither it's fou!

It's the voice o' the Sooth
That's held owre lang
My Viking North
Wi' its siren sang . . .

Fier comme un Ecossais.

If a' that I can be's nae mair
Than what mankind's been yet, I'll no'
Begink the instincts thistlewise
That dern—and canna show.

Damned threids and thrums and skinny shapes
O' a' that micht, and su'd, ha' been
—Life onyhow at ony price!—
In sic I'll no' be seen!

Fier comme un Ecossais.

The wee reliefs we ha'e in booze,
Or wun at times in carnal states,
May hide frae us but canna cheenge
The silly horrors o' oor fates.

Fier—comme un Ecossais!

There's muckle in the root,
That never can wun oot,
Or't owre what is 'ud sweep
Like a thunderstorm owre sheep.

But shadows whiles upcreep,
And heavy tremors leap. . . .
C'wa', Daith, again, sned Life's vain shoot,
And your ain coonsel keep! . . .

---

a'e hauf, one half   begink, cheat   dert, hide   thrums, loose ends
sned, lop off

Time like a bien wife,
Truth like a dog's gane—
The bien wife's gane to the aumrie
To get the puir dog a bane.

Opens the aumrie door,
And lo! the skeleton's there,
And the gude dog, Truth, has gotten
Banes for evermair . . .

Maun I tae perish in the keel o' Heaven,
And is this fratt upon the air the ply
O' cross-brath'd cordage that in gloffs and gowls
Brak's up the vision o' the warld's bricht gy?

Ship's tackle and an eemis cairn o' fraucht
Darker than clamourin' veins are roond me yet,
A plait o' shadows thicker than the flesh,
A fank o' tows that binds me hand and fit.

What gin the gorded fullyery on hie
And a' the fanerels o' the michty ship
Gi'e back mair licht than fa's upon them ev'n
Gin sic black ingangs haud us in their grip?

Grugous thistle, to my een
Your widdifow ramel evince,
Sibness to snakes wha's coils
Rin coonter airts at yince,
And fain I'd follow each
Gin you the trick'll teach.

Blin' root to bleezin' rose,
Through a' the whirligig
O' shanks and leafs and jags
What sends ye sic a rig?
Bramble yokin' earth and heaven,
Till they're baith stramulyert driven!

bien, complacent   aumrie, cupboard   fratt, fretwork
cross-brath'd, cross-braided   gloffs and gowls, dark and light   gy, spectacle
eemis cairn o' fraucht, unsteady stone-pile of cargo   plait, pleat
fank o' tows, coil of rope   fit, foot
gorded fullyery on hie, frosted foliage on high   fanerels, loose, flapping things
ingangs haud, deficiencies hold   grugous, ugly
widdifow ramel, perverse branches   sibness, relation   yince, once
stramulyert, aghast

Roses to lure the lift
And roots to wile the clay
And wuppit brainches syne
To claught them 'midyards tae
Till you've the precious pair
Like hang'd men dancin' there,

Wi' mony a seely prickle
You'll fleg a sunburst oot,
Or kittle earthquakes up
Wi' an amusin' root,
While, kilted in your tippet,
They still can mak' their rippit . . .

And let me pit in guid set terms
My quarrel wi' th' owre sonsy rose,
That roond aboot its devotees
A fair fat cast o' aureole throws
That blinds them, in its mirlygoes,
To the necessity o' foes.

Upon their King and System I
Glower as on things that whiles in pairt
I may admire (at least for them),
But wi' nae claim upon my hert,
While a' their pleasure and their pride
Ootside me lies—and there maun bide.

Ootside me lies—and mair than that,
For I stand still for forces which
Were subjugated to mak' way
For England's poo'er, and to enrich
The kinds o' English, and o' Scots,
The least congenial to my thoughts.

Hauf his soul a Scot maun use
Indulgin' in illusions,
And hauf in gettin rid o' them
And comin' to conclusions

---

wuppit, binding   claught, clutch   'midyards, together in the middle
seely, happy   fleg, frighten   kittle, tickle   kilted in your tippet, hung in a noose
mak' their rippit, raise a rumpus
th' owre sonsy rose, the too contented English rose   mirlygoes, dazzle
bide, remain

Wi' the demoralisin' dearth
O' onything worth while on Earth . . .

I'm weary o' the rose as o' my brain,
And for a deeper knowledge I am fain
Than frae this noddin' object I can gain.

Beauty is a'e thing, but it tines anither
(For, fegs, they never can be f'und thegither),
And 'twixt the twa it's no' for me to swither.

As frae the grun' sae thocht frae men springs oot,
A ferlie that tells little o' its source, I doot,
And has nae vera fundamental root.

And cauld agen my hert are laid
The words o' Plato when he said,
'God o' geometry is made.'

Frae my ain mind I fa' away,
That never yet was feared to say
What turned the souls o' men to clay,

Nor cared gin truth frae me ootsprung
In ne'er a leed o' ony tongue
That ever in a heid was hung.

I ken hoo much oor life is fated
Aince its first cell is animated,
The fount frae which the flesh is jetted.

I ken hoo lourd the body lies
Upon the spirit when it flies
And fain abune its stars 'ud rise.

And see I noo a great wheel move,
And a' the notions that I love
Drap into stented groove and groove?

It maitters not my mind the day,
Nocht maitters that I strive to dae,
—For the wheel moves on in its ain way.

---

swither, hesitate   ferlie, marvel   cauld agen, cold against
ne'er a leed, never a language   lourd, heavy   stented, appointed

94

I sall be moved as it decides
To look at Life frae ither sides;
Rejoice, rebel, its turn abides.

And as I see the great wheel spin
There flees a licht frae't lang and thin
That Earth is like a snaw-ba' in.

(To the uncanny thocht I clutch
—The nature o' man's soul is such
That it can ne'er wi' life tine touch.

Man's mind is in God's image made,
And in its wildest dreams arrayed
In pairt o' Truth is still displayed.)

Then suddenly I see as weel
As me spun roon' within the wheel,
The helpless forms o' God and Deil.

And on a birlin' edge I see
Wee Scotland squattin' like a flea,
And dizzy wi' the speed, and me!

I've often thrawn the warld frae me,
Into the Pool o' Space, to see
The Circles o' Infinity.

Or like a flat stone gar'd it skite,
A Morse code message writ in licht
That yet I couldna read aricht

The skippin' sparks, the ripples, rit
Like skritches o' a grain o' grit
'Neth Juggernaut in which I sit.

Twenty-six thoosand years it tak's
Afore a'e single roond it mak's,
And syne it melts as it were wax.

The Phœnix guise 'tll rise in syne
Is mair than Euclid or Einstein
Can dream o' or's in dreams o' mine.

---

snaw-ba', snowball   tine, lose   birlin', spinning   skite, skip   rit, scrape
skritches, scratches

Upon the huge circumference are
As neebor points the Heavenly War
That dung doun Lucifer sae far,

And that upheaval in which I
Sodgered 'neth the Grecian sky
And in Italy and Marseilles,

And there isna room for men
Wha the haill o' history ken
To pit a pin twixt then and then.

Whaur are Bannockburn and Flodden?
—O' a'e grain like facets hod'n,
Little wars (twixt that which God in

Focht and won, and that which He
Took baith sides in hopelessly),
Less than God or I can see.

By whatna cry o' mine oot-topped
Sall be a' men ha'e sung and hoped
When to a'e note they're telescoped?

And Jesus and a nameless ape
Collide and share the selfsame shape
That nocht terrestrial can escape?

But less than this nae man need try.
He'd better be content to eye
The wheel in silence whirlin' by.

Nae verse is worth a ha'et until
It can join issue wi' the Will
That raised the Wheel and spins it still,

But a' the music that mankind
'S made yet is to the Earth confined,
Poo'erless to reach the general mind,

Poo'erless to reach the neist star e'en,
That as a pairt o'ts sel' is seen,
And only men can tell between.

Yet I exult oor sang has yet
To grow wings that'll cairry it
Ayont its native speck o' grit,

dung doun, dashed down   sodgered, soldiered
hod'n, held   focht, fought   ha'et, whit   e'en, even

And I exult to find in me
The thocht that this can ever be,
A hope still for humanity.

For gin the sun and mune at last
Are as a neebor's lintel passed,
The wheel'll tine its stature fast,

And birl in time inside oor heids
Till we can thraw oot conscious gleids
That draw an answer to oor needs,

Or if nae answer still we find
Brichten till a' thing is defined
In the huge licht-beams o' oor kind,

And if we still can find nae trace
Ahint the Wheel o' ony Face,
There'll be a glory in the place,

And we may aiblins swing content
Upon the wheel in which we're pent
In adequate enlightenment.

Nae ither thocht can mitigate
The horror o' the endless Fate
A'thing 's whirled in predestinate.

O whiles I'd fain be blin' to it,
As men wha through the ages sit,
And never move frae aff the bit,

Wha hear a Burns or Shakespeare sing,
Yet still their ain bit jingles string,
As they were worth the fashioning.

Whatever Scotland is to me,
Be it aye pairt o' a' men see
O' Earth and o' Eternity

Wha winna hide their heids in't till
It seems the haill o' Space to fill,
As t'were an unsurmounted hill.

---

gleids, sparks   a'thing, everything   the bit, the same place

He canna Scotland see wha yet
Canna see the Infinite,
And Scotland in true scale to it.

Nor blame I muckle, wham atour
Earth's countries blaw, a pickle stour,
To sort wha's grains they ha'e nae poo'er.

E'en stars are seen thegither in
A'e skime o' licht as grey as tin
Flyin' on the wheel as t'were a pin.

Syne ither systems ray on ray
Skinkle past in quick array
While it is still the self-same day,

A'e day o' a' the million days
Through which the soul o' man can gaze
Upon the wheel's incessant blaze,

Upon the wheel's incessant blaze
As it were on a single place
That twinklin' filled the howe o' space.

A'e point is a' that it can be,
I wis nae man 'll ever see
The rest o' the rotundity.

Impersonality sall blaw
Through me as 'twere a bluffert o' snaw
To scour me o' my sense o' awe,

A bluffert o' snaw, the licht that flees
Within the Wheel, and Freedom gi'es
Frae Dust and Daith and a' Disease,

—The drumlie doom that only weighs
On them wha ha'ena seen their place
Yet in creation's lichtnin' race,

In the movement that includes
As a tide's resistless floods
A' their movements and their moods,—

---

wham atour, them who around   pickle stour, a dust of small particles
a'e skime, a single glimmer   skinkle, twinkle   howe, void   wis, know
bluffert, blast   drumlie, troubled

Until disinterested we,
O' a' oor auld delusions free,
Lowe in the wheel's serenity

As conscious items in the licht,
And keen to keep it clear and bricht
In which the haill machine is dight,

The licht nae man has ever seen
Till he has felt that he's been gi'en
The stars themsels insteed o' een,

And often wi' the sun has glowered
At the white mune until it cowered,
As when by new thocht auld's o'erpowered.

Oor universe is like an e'e
Turned in, man's benmaist hert to see,
And swamped in subjectivity.

But whether it can use its sicht
To bring what lies withoot to licht
To answer's still ayont my micht.

But when that inturned look has brocht
To licht what still in vain it's socht
Ootward maun be the bent o' thocht.

And organs may develop syne
Responsive to the need divine
O' single-minded humankin'.

The function, as it seems to me,
O' Poetry is to bring to be
At lang, lang last that unity . . .

But wae's me on the weary wheel!
Higgledy-piggledy in't we reel,
And little it cares hoo we may feel.

Twenty-six thoosand years 'tll tak'
For it to threid the Zodiac
—A single roond o' the wheel to mak'!

owe, flame   dight, arrayed   benmaist, inmost

Lately it turned—I saw mysel'
In sic a company doomed to mell.
I micht ha'e been in Dante's Hell.

It shows hoo little the best o' men
E'en o' themsels at times can ken,
—I sune saw *that* when I gaed ben.

The lesser wheel within the big
That moves as merry as a grig,
Wi' mankind in its whirligig

And hasna turned a'e circle yet
Tho' as it turns we slide in it,
And needs maun tak' the place we get,

I felt it turn, and syne I saw
John Knox and Clavers in my raw,
And Mary Queen o' Scots ana',

And Rabbie Burns and Weelum Wallace,
And Carlyle lookin' unco gallus,
And Harry Lauder (to enthrall us).

And as I looked I saw them a',
A' the Scots baith big and sma',
That e'er the braith o' life did draw.

'Mercy o' Gode, I canna thole
Wi' sic an orra mob to roll.'
—'Wheesht! It's for the guid o' your soul.'

'But what's the meanin', what's the sense?'
   —'Men shift but by experience.
'Twixt Scots there is nae difference.

They canna learn, sae canna move,
But stick for aye to their auld groove
—The only race in History who've

Bidden in the same category
Frae stert to present o' their story,
And deem their ignorance their glory.

Mell, mix   grig, lively child   unco gallus, extremely reckless   thole, stand
orra, disreputable

The mair they differ, mair the same.
The wheel can whummle a' but them,
—They ca' their obstinacy "Hame,"

And "Puir Auld Scotland" bleat wi' pride,
And wi' their minds made up to bide
A thorn in a' the wide world's side.

There ha'e been Scots wha ha'e ha'en thochts,
They're strewn through maist o' the various lots
—Sic traitors are nae langer Scots!'

'But in this huge ineducable
Heterogeneous hotch and rabble,
Why am *I* condemned to squabble?'

'*A Scottish poet maun assume*
The burden o' his people's doom,
And dee to brak' their livin' tomb.

Mony ha'e tried, but a' ha'e failed.
Their sacrifice has nocht availed.
Upon the thistle they're impaled.

You maun choose but gin ye'd see
Anither category ye
Maun tine your nationality.'

And I look at a' the random
Band the wheel leaves whaur it fand 'em
                              'Auch to Hell,
I'll tak' it to avizandum.' . . .

O wae's me on the weary wheel,
And fain I'd understand them!

And blessin' on the weary wheel
Whaurever it may land them! . . .

But aince Jean kens what I've been through
The nicht, I dinna doot it,
She'll ope her airms in welcome true,
And clack nae mair aboot it . . .

whummle, overturn   hotch, swarm   dee, die
tak' it to avizandum, under judicial advisement   clack, talk

   ★   ★   ★   ★   ★

The stars like thistle's roses floo'er
The sterile growth o' Space ootour,
That clad in bitter blasts spreids oot
Frae me, the sustenance o' its root.

O fain I'd keep my hert entire,
Fain hain the licht o' my desire,
But ech! the shinin' streams ascend,
And leave me empty at the end.

For aince it's toomed my hert and brain,
The thistle needs maun fa' again.
—But a' its growth 'll never fill
The hole it's turned my life intill! . . .

Yet ha'e I Silence left, the croon o' a'.

No' her, wha on the hills langsyne I saw
Liftin' a foreheid o' perpetual snaw.

No' her, wha in the how-dumb-deid o' nicht
Kyths, like Eternity in Time's despite.

No' her, withooten shape, wha's name is Daith,
No' Him, unkennable abies to faith

—God whom, gin e'er He saw a man, 'ud be
E'en mair dumfooner'd at the sicht than he.

—But Him, whom nocht in man or Deity,
Or Daith or Dreid or Laneliness can touch,
Wha's deed owre often and has seen owre much.

O I ha'e Silence left,

                —'And weel ye micht,'
Sae Jean'll say, 'efter sic a nicht!'

---

ootour, out over   hain, preserve   toomed, emptied   langsyne, long ago
how-dumb-deid, uttermost depths of midnight   kyths, appears
abies, except   dumfooner'd, dumbfoundered

From *To Circumjack Cencrastus*
(1930)

Lourd on My Hert

Lourd on my hert as winter lies
The state that Scotland's in the day.
Spring to the North has aye come slow
But noo dour winter's like to stay
      For guid,
      And no' for guid!

O wae's me on the weary days
When it is scarce grey licht at noon;
It maun be a' the stupid folk
Diffusin' their dullness roon and roon
      Like soot
      That keeps the sunlicht oot.

Nae wonder if I think I see
A lichter shadow than the neist
I'm fain to cry: 'The dawn, the dawn!
I see it brakin' in the East.'
      But ah
      —It's juist mair snaw!

Frae Anither Window in Thrums

Here in the hauf licht waitin' till the clock
Chops: while the winnock
Hauds me as a serpent hauds a rabbit
Afore it's time to grab it
—A serpent faded to a shadow
In the stelled een its een ha'e haud o'

Here in the daurk, while like a frozen
Scurl on Life's plumm the lozen
Skimmers—or goams in upon me
Wan as Dostoevski

---

lourd, heavy   dour, hard, grim   guid, good

hauf licht, half-light   chops, strikes   winnock, window   stelled, fixed
ha'e haud o', have hold of   scurl, scab   plumm, deep pool in a river
lozen, window-pane   skimmers, shimmers   goams, gazes stupidly

Glowered through a wudden dream to find
Stavrogin in the corners o' his mind,

—Or I haud it, a 'prentice snake, and gar
Heaven dwine to a haunfu' haar
Or am like cheengeless deeps aneth
Tho' ice or sunshine, life or death,
Chequer the tap; or like Stavrogin
Joukin' his author wi' a still subtler grin . . .

And yet I canna for the life o' me see
That I'd write better poetry
If like the feck o' Scots insteed
I read the books they read
And drew my thochts o' God and Man
Frae Neil Munro and Annie Swan!

Fu' weel I ken I would mak' verses which
'Ud notably enrich
'Oor Scots tradition'—in the minds
O' ministers and hinds;
And fain I'd keep as faur frae that
As Proust frae Johnnie Gibb—that's flat!

—Can I get faurer frae't than here
Whaur a' life's fictions disappear
And I'm left face to face wi' nocht
But sicna drab splash as brocht
My like to be, to mak' wi't what I can,
Back at the stert whaur a' began?

Seed in my womb, I ken nae mair
Than ony wife what bairn I'll bear
—Christ or a village idiot there
A throned king, or corpse i' the air? . . .

Nature to Art is still a witch
Confinin't by waefu' metamorphosis
To Life, a memory mindin' which
It bairnlies itsel' again like this . . .

---

wudden dream, nightmare   gar, make   dwine, dwindle
a haunfu' haar, a handful of mist   joukin', dodging   feck, majority
waefu', woeful   bairnlies itsel', makes a child of itself

For if it's no' by thocht that Poetry's wrocht
It's no' by want o' thocht
The verse that flatters ignorance maun seem
To ignorant folk supreme
Sin' nane can read the verse that disna
The damned thing bides as if it isna!

Maun I tae sing a useless sang
  'La chanson grise
Où l'Indécis au Précis se joint.'
Naebody else can listen to
—Like shades o' music missin' to
A' but ane in a listenin' thrang,

And perfect it forever mair
Like Proust wha thocht he couldna sleep
Sae lang that, sleepin', he'd still a deep
Unsleepin' sense o' sleeplessness there,
And borrowed frae that in turn the thocht
That he'd been soond asleep frae the stert;
And syne—but och! the sang in my hert
Coonts like shadow frae nicht to nocht!

—Like Proust, or the Glesca man wha deed
And said to Charon: 'It's unco queer;
I dreamt I was deid, and no' juist here
At hame on a Sawbath day insteed!' . . .

Enclosed in silence, Earth's sang, unhurried
Dwines through the endless stages it needs
As 'twere the kind o' life Daith leads
In the deid aince they are buriet . . .

That's the condition o't or near
Grey glumshin' o' the winda here,
—As fit a subject for immortal sang
As ocht wi' which men's minds are thrang . . .

Here in the hauf licht waitin' till the clock
Chops: while the winnock
Hauds me, as a serpent hauds a rabbit
Afore it's time to grab it

---

wrocht, wrought   disna, does not   thrang, throng
deed, died   unco, very   glumshin', sulky appearance

—A serpent faded to a shadow
In the stelled een its een hae haud o' . . .

Here in the hauf licht hoo I've grown!
Seconds but centuries hae flown
Sin I was a reporter here
Chroniclin' the toon's sma' beer
Tinin' the maist o' life to get
The means to hain the least wee bit.

I wha aince in Heaven's height
Gethered to me a' the licht
Can nae mair reply to fire,
'Neth deid leafs buriet in the mire.

Sib to dewdrop, rainbow, ocean,
No' for me their hues and motion.
This foul clay has filed me till
It's no' to ken I'm water still.

Pars aboot meetins, weddins, sermons, a'
The crude events o' life-in-the-raw
Vanish like snowflakes on this river . . .
Dans le flot sans honneur de quelque noir mélange . . .
On wha's black bank I stand and shiver;
Nakit!—What gin the boss, as weel he micht,
Comes in and switches on the licht?

The Twentieth Century at Eternity
Gapes—and the clock strikes: Tea!
And sombrous I arise
Under his silly eyes
And doon the stairs, the devil at my back.
I doot the morn I'll get the sack!

'What was I da'en sittin' in the dark?'
'Huntin' like Moses for the vital spark,
—A human mole
Wi' a hole for a soul?'
'I sud think o' my wife and faimly'
I listen to him tamely.

---

sib, related   filed, defiled   tinin', losing   hain, preserve

'Cut oot this poetry stuff, my lad. Get on
Wi' advts. and puffs, and eident con
The proofs; it's in you gin you care
To dae't and earn (your maister) mair.
    Furth Fortune fill the fetters!
Apply yersel' to what's worth while
And I'll reward ye: that's my style.'

'Yessir, I'm sorry. It'll no'
Heppen again. The clock was slow
And I was slower still, I'm sorry
In gettin' back again afore ye
To sicna state as fits the job
O ane wha's brains you lout to rob.'

Curse on the system that can gie
A coof like this control o' me
—No' that he's in the least bit waur
Or better, than ither bosses are—
And on the fate that gars a poet
Toady to find a way to show it!

Curse his new hoose, his business, his cigar,
His wireless set, and motor car
Alsatian, gauntlet gloves, plus fours and wife,
—A'thing included in his life;
And, abune a', his herty laughter,
And—if he has yin—his hereafter.

Owre savage? Deil the bit! That's nocht
To what men like the Boss deserve;
Maist men that is—anon I'll gie
Them a' their paiks, wi' muckle verve.

He has an angry birthmark on his cheek,
    . . . *Le roy Scotiste*
    Qui demy face ot, ce dit-on,
    Vermeille comme une amathiste
    Depuys le front jusqu'au menton . . .
A purple pig's fit—a' his skin
Sud lowe forever in black burnin' shame
To mak' his ootside like his in.

---

lout, stoop   coof, fool   waur, worse   paiks, deserved punishment
lowe, blaze

I'd send it owre him like a flypin knife
Till like a carcase in a butcher's shop
He fronts the world—affrontin' it;
A rinn in' wound that nocht'll stop.

For sae the will to ignorance o' his kind,
Their line o' least resistance ruins life
As wha maun tine through foul disease
The heich ideas wi' which he's rife . . .

Curse a'thing that gars me pretend or feel
That life as maist folk hae't is real
Or waste my time on their ideas
Or silly sociabilities,
Service, meanin' or ocht that'll tak'
My mind off ony verse it'll mak.

> *I'm no' the kind o' poet*
> *That opens sales o' work . . .*

Curse on my dooble life and dooble tongue,
—Guid Scots wi' English a' hamstrung—

Speakin' o' Scotland in English words
As it were Beethoven chirpt by birds;
Or as if a Board school teacher
Tried to teach Rimbaud and Neitzsche.

And on this curst infirmity o' will
That hauds me bletherin' this way still
On things that like a midge-swarm pass
Sub specie aeternatatis.

Gin but the oor 'ud chop and set me free
Frae this accursed drudgery
Aiblins—aince I had my tea—
I could address mysel' to poetry,
Sufferin' nae mair th'embarrassment o' riches
Wi' which desire brute circumstance bewitches
Till my brain reels and canna faddom which is,
'Mid endless cues, the ane for which it itches.

---

flypin knife, skinning knife   maun tine, must lose   hae't, have it
aiblins, perhaps

Thrang o' ideas that like fairy gowd
'll leave me the 'Review' reporter still
Waukenin' to my clung-kite faimly on a hill
O' useless croftin' whaur naething's growed
But Daith, sin Christ for an idea died
On a gey similar but less heich hillside.
Ech, weel for Christ: for he was never wed
And had nae weans clamourin' to be fed!

As 'tis I ken that ilka instant gies,
If I could haud it lang eneuch to seize
Them, coontless opportunities
For reams o' verse in as mony different keys,
—And that's damned nonsense for they canna a'
Lead t'owt worth while—gin owt's worth while ava'.

> *Hell tak this improvisin'*
> *That leads a' airts and nane;*
> *A kind o' anti-poetry*
> *That is true poetry's bane!*

I'm weary o' the shapes mere chance can thraw
In this technique and that; and seek that law
To pit the maitter on a proper basis
My faith in which a feature o' the case is
I canna deal wi' here but efter tea
Will—if the wife and bairns—we'll wait and see . . .
A' this is juist provisional and 'll hae
A tea-change into something rich and Scots
When I wha needs use English a' the day
Win back to the true language o' my thochts.

---

clung-kite faimly, shrunken-bellied family   weans, little ones   ava', at all
thraw, cast   pit the maitter, put the matter

Hokum

It isna fair to my wife and weans
It isna fair to mysel',
To persist in poverty-stricken courses
And never ring Fortune's bell.
Thoosands o' writers wi' nae mair brains
In their heids than I've in my pinkie
Are rowin' in wealth while I toil for a dole,
O hoo's that accoontit for, thinkee?

Oh, it's easy, easy accoontit for, fegs.
I canna gie the folk hokum.
I can poke 'em and shock 'em and mock 'em,
But the a'e thing needfu' is hokum!
It pits a'thing else on its legs.

Losh! They'd ha' put me a brass plate up
In Langholm Academy,
And asked me to tak' the chair
At mony a London Scots spree.
They'd a' gien me my portrait in oils
By Henry Kerr, and the LL.D.,

And my wife and weans 'ud been as weel aff
As gin I'd been a dominie,
    If I'd only had hokum, hokum,
    Juist a wee thing common hokum!

A seat on the Bank o' Scotland buird,
And a public for my poetry . . .
    If I'd only had hokum, hokum,
    A modicum o' hokum!

It maitters little what line ye tak'
If you hae hokum wi't;
Butter or snash, it's a' alike,
Gar them laugh or greet.
There's naething the public winna stand
And pay for through the nose,
Barrin' the medicine that's ser'd up neat,
Whether it's bitter or whether it's sweet,
Wi' nae hokum to the dose.

---

pinkie, little finger   dominie, schoolmaster
butter or snash, flattery or sneers   greet, weep

But what I canna accoont for's no'
Bein' able to gie folk hokum.
I can joke 'em and sock 'em and choke 'em
But the a'e thing needfu' is hokum.
—I wish I was Neil Munro.

It isna fair to my wife and weans,
It isna fair to mysel'.
The day's lang by when Gaels gaed oot
To battle and aye fell.
I wish I was Harry Lauder,
Will Fyffe or J. J. Bell,
—Or Lauchlan Maclean Watt
For the maitter o' that!
—Dae I Hell!

Oh, it's hokum, hokum, hokum,
And this is as near't as I'll get.
The nearest I've got yet,
Losh, but it's unco like *it*,
      —That sine-qua-non,
      A soupçon
      O precious hokum-pokum!

North of the Tweed

Cauld licht and tumblin' cloods. It's queer
There's never been a poet here . . .

Shades o' the Sun-King no' yet risen
Are sleepin' in a corner on the straw.
Despair seems to touch bottom time and again
But aye Earth opens and reveals fresh depths.
The pale-wa'd warld is fu' o' licht and life
Like a glass in which water faintly stirs.
Gie owre a' this tomfoolery, and sing
The movin' spirit that nae metaphor drawn
Frae water or frae licht can dim suggest.

113

Leid in nae mere Longinian hypsos come
But in inhuman splendours, triumphin' wi'
'A dazzlin' disregard o' the soul.'
      Nocht else'll dae.

Water nor licht nor yet the barley field
That shak's in silken sheets at ilka braith,
Its lang nap thrawin' the quick licht aboot
In sic a maze that tak's and gies at aince
As fair oot-tops the coontless ripplin' sea.
There's nae chameleon like the July fields;
Their different colours change frae day to day
While they shift instantly neath the shiftin' licht
Yet they're owre dull for this, stagnant and dull;
And even your een, beloved, and your hair
Are like the barley and the sea and Heaven
That flaw and fail and are defeated by
      The blind turns o' chance.

Thinkna' that I'm ungratefu', wi' nae mind
O' Deirdre and the fauld o' sunbeams* yet,
Or canna find on bracken slopes abune the bog
The orchis smellin' like cherry-pie;
Or that the sun's blade cuttin' straightly through
A cloudy sea fails wi' my cloudy hert,
Releasin' it frae self-disgust until I tine
A' sense o' livin' under set conditions
And live in an unconditioned space o' time
Perfect in ilka pulse and impulse, and aince mair
A seven-whistler in Kintyre, or yon broon hill
That's barren save for fower pale violets on
      A South-leanin' bank.

I've sat amang the crimson buds o' thrift
Abune the sea whaur Buachaille herds the waves;
And seen the primrose nightglow to the North
Owre Moray and the flat sea while the West
Still held a twinkle o' the morning-star,
(For in the Cairngorms simmer nicht and dawn
Come close, but canna thraw the larks' hours oot);

---

leid, language

* 'Fold of sunbeams'—Glendaruel.

And hoo should I forget the Langfall
On mornings when the hines were ripe but een
Ahint the glintin' leafs were brichter still
Than sunned dew on them, lips reider than the fruit,
And I filled baith my basket and my hert
        Mony and mony a time?

And yet you mind, dear, on the bridal hill
Hoo yon laich loch ootshone my een in yours,
Nor wi' the heather could oor bluid compete,
Nor could the ring I gi'ed you when your hand
Lay on the crucifers compare wi' them
Save for a second when the sun seized on't.
Hair of the purple of Strathendrick Hill,
Slant e'en wi' pupils like blue-stane washed wi' rain
And the whites owre white and the hunted look.
Here tak' your bairn; I've cairried it lang eneuch,
Langer than maist men wad, as weel you ken.
Noo I'll pipe instead—what tune'll you hae?
        On Rudha nam Marbh.*

Unconscious Goal of History

Unconscious goal of history, dimly seen
In Genius whiles that kens the problem o' its age,
And works at it; the mass o' men pursue
Their puir blind purposes unaware o' you,
And yet frae them emerges tae your keen
Clear consequences nae man can gauge
Save in relation to some ancient stage;
Sae History mak's the ambitions o' great men
Means to ends greater than themsels could ken,
—Greater and ither—and mass ignorance yields,
Like corruption o' vegetation in fallow fields,
The conditions o' richer increase;—at last
The confusion's owre, the time comes fast

* 'The Point of the Dead'.

When men wauk to the possibility
O' workin' oot and makin, their destiny
In fu' consciousness and cease to muddle through
Wi' nae idea o' their goal—and nae mair grue!

Let nane cry that the right men arena here
—That urgent tasks await that nane can dae.
Times oft mistak' their problems in that way.
At the richt time the richt men aye appear.
If Scotland fills us wi' despair we may
Be proposin' a goal that disna lie
Onywhaur in history's plan the noo; we sigh
In vain—because we canna think in vain
And oor desire'll hae its due effect
In the lang run altho' oor age rejects.
But a'e thing's certain—nae genius'll come,
Nae maitter hoo he's shouted for, to recreate
The life and fabric o' a decadent State
That's dune its work, gien its Idea to the world,
The problem is to find in Scotland some
Bricht coil o' you that hasna yet uncurled,
And, hoosoever petty I may be, the fact
That I think Scotland isna dune yet proves
There's something in it that fulfilment's lacked
And my vague hope through a' creation moves.

The Unconscious Ideas that impel a race
Spring frae an ineffable sense o' hoo to be
A certain kind o' human being—Let's face
This fact in Scotland and we'll see
The fantasy o' an unconquerable soul
Neath nations' rivalries, persecutions, wars,
The golden casket o' their Covenant, their goal,
Shrined in a dwelling that ootshines the stars,
A dwelling o' delight no' made wi' hands,
For wha's sake till the gaen oot o' the Sun
They'll hew the Sassenach, the Amalekite, the Hun
Nor sacrifice the least fraction o' their will
To independence while they've a tittle still
O' their Unconscious Idea unrealised.

nae mair grue, no more revulsion

Is Scotland roupit that I su'd gie owre
My quest for onything, hooso'er disguised,
That wi' a new vitality may endower
My thieveless country: and mak' it mair
Intelligently allied to your hidden purpose there
Sae that my people frae their living graves
May loup and play a pairt in History yet
Wi' sufferin's mair like a Genius's than a slave's,
Vieve strands in your endless glories knit?
By thocht a man mak's his idea a force
Or fact in History's drama: He canna foresee
The transformations and uses o' the course
The dialectics o' human action and interaction'll gie
The contribution he mak's—it'll a' depend
On his sincerity and clearness in the end
And his integrity—his unity with you;
Strivin' to gie birth to that idea through
Him wha o' makin' his meanin' clear
May weel despair when you disappear—or appear.
Stir me, Cencrastus. If the faintest gleam
O' you kyths in my work fu' weel I ken
That your neist movement may lowse a supreme
Glory—tho' I'm extinguished then!

If there is ocht in Scotland that's worth ha'en
There is nae distance to which it's unattached
—Nae height, nae depth, nae breadth, and I am fain
To see it frae the hamely and the earthly snatched
And precipitated to what it will be in the end
A' that's ephemeral shorn awa' and rhyme nae mair
Mere politics, personalities, and mundane things,
Nor mistak' ony philosophy's elaborate and subtle form
That canna fit the changed conditions, for your trend
Drawin' a' life's threids thegither there
Nor losin' on the roonaboots, nor gainin' on the swings
But like the hairst that needs baith sun and storm,
Simmer and winter, Life and Daith . . . A' roads are closed;
North, South, East, West nae mair opposed.

roupit, auctioned   thieveless, purposeless   vieve, vivid
Cencrastus, the curly snake (ancient Celtic symbol of wisdom)
kyths, appears   lowse, set loose

Withoot a leg to stand on, like a snake
Wi' impossible lustres I shake.
Earth contracts to a single point of licht
As men, deceived by their een, see stars at nicht,
And the religious attitude has found
In Scotland yet a balancin' ground . . .

An image o' the sea lies underneath
A' men's imaginations—the sea in which
A' life was born and that cradled us until
We cam' to birth's maturity. Its waves bewitch
Us still or wi' their lure o' peacefu' gleamin'
Or hungrily in storm and darkness streamin'.

The imagination has anither poo'er—the snake
He who beats up the waters into storm
Wha's touch electrifies us into action;
In th' abyss o' their origin, their basic form,
A' oor imaginations partake
O' ane or th'ither—the sea or the snake.

The twasome control a' the drama o' life.
Gin we talk o' love and freedom, and tell
Oor dreams o' order and peace, equality and joy
We are under the blissfu' waters' spell
And oor een and oor voices betray
Oor inspiration in the bricht sea's sway.

Gin we speak o' Imperial Poo'er, Aristocracy,
Authority, Privilege, Control o' the world
The music changes—on a rattle o' Drums
We rise to heights o' glory and death; we've unfurled
An oriflamme; in the glitter o' the latest ideas
The auld serpent is a' yin sees.

The words and ideas change; but under them still
The serpent stirs or the sea allures.
We're deceived nae mair; 'neath a' certain plane
Science, art, a's but the ravings
O' th' poo'ers o' th' abyss; men the instrument
O' the water or the serpent.

twasome, double

They strive forever to master the minds o' men
And rule them wi' strange rhythms. Few ken them.
Maist folk gang through life and never see
The marionettes they are—what forces pen them
Subservient to the serpent's magic or
The charmin' o' the sea that has nae shore.

But there are aye a wheen minds in whom
The surgings and writhings cease.
They dismay anger wi' their smile
And o' diverse notions mak' harmonies
Wi' freendly understandin's flashin' speech
Or unexpected tranquilisin' wit.

My love is to the light of lights
As a gold fawn to the sun
And men, wha love ocht else, to her
Their ways ha' scarce begun.

For God their God's a jealous God
And keeps her frae their sight.
He hasna had her lang eneuch
Himsel' to share his delight

And kens gin he'd been worth his saut
He'd ha' made her first, no' last,
Since but a'e glimpse, a'e thocht, o' her
Discredits a' the Past.

(A'e glimpse, a'e thocht, and men might cease
To honour his tardy pooers;
And he's no' shair she winna prove
To be no' his—but oors!)

Yet praise the Past sin' but for it
We never might ha' seen her
—And still to oor een maun temper wi't
The glory that's been gi'en her.

My love she is the hardest thocht
That ony brain can ha'e,
And there is nocht worth ha'en in life
That doesna lead her way.

My love is to a' else that is
As meaning's meaning, or the sun
Men see ahint the sunlight whiles
Like lint-white water run . . .

For them there's nae mair sea; the snake
Is chained in the depths o' a bottomless pit.
The serene fury o' ha'en seen th' ineffable's theirs
They are absolved frae a' worship and gang
In the strength o' their ain souls—it is they
Wha recreate man's thocht and change his state;
By what are they ken't—for whom nocht prepares?
Only their like'll no' guess wrang
But twa features they hae—whatever they say
Is something that few can believe; and yet
Never the opposite to general belief.
They never come except in due season
And croon a' controversies wi' a reason
Never heard o' before—yont ilka faction
—AND AYE A REASON FOR ACTION!

> *Is cam's is direach an lagh.*

Si l'orvet voyait,
Si le sourd entendait,
Pas un homme ne vivrait.

From *First Hymn to Lenin*
(1931)

At My Father's Grave

The sunlicht still on me, you row'd in clood,
We look upon each ither noo like hills
Across a valley. I'm nae mair your son.
It is my mind, nae son o' yours, that looks,
And the great darkness o' your death comes up
And equals it across the way.
A livin' man upon a deid man thinks
And ony sma'er thocht's impossible.

Charisma and My Relatives

(To William McElroy)

No' here the beloved group; I've gane sae faur
(Like Christ) yont faither, mither, brither, kin
I micht as weel try dogs or cats as seek
In sic relationships again to fin'
The epopteia I maun ha'e—and feel
        (Frae elsewhere) owre me steal.

But naewhere has the love-religion had
A harder struggle than in Scotland here
Which means we've been untrue as fechters even
To oor essential genius—Scots, yet sweer
To fecht in, or owre blin' to see where lay
        The hert o' the fray.

We've focht in a' the sham fechts o' the world.
But I'm a Borderer and at last in me
The spirit o' my people's no' content
Wi' ony but the greatest enemy,
And nae mair plays at sodgers but has won
        To a live battle-grun'.

---

row'd, wrapped   sweer, reluctant

A fiercer struggle than joukin it's involved.
Oorsels oor greatest foes. Yet, even yet,
I haud to 'I' and 'Scot' and 'Borderer'
And fence the wondrous fire that in me's lit
Wi' sicna barriers roond as hide frae'ts licht
  Near a'body's sicht.

And cry as weel try dogs or cats as seek
In sic relationships again to fin'
The epopteia that, yet f'und, like rain
'Ud quickly to the roots o' a'thing rin
Even as the circles frae a stane that's hurled
  In water ring the world.

Sae to my bosom yet a' beasts maun come,
Or I to theirs,—baudrons, wi' sides like harps,
Lookin' like the feel o' olives in the mooth,
Yon scabby cur at whom the gutter carps,
Nose-double o' the taste o' beer-and-gin,
  And a' my kin.

And yet—there's some folk lice'll no' live on,
I'm ane o' them I doot. But what a thocht!
What speculations maun a man sae shunned
No' ha'e until at last the reason's brocht
To view acceptable, as the fact may be
  On different grun's to them and me.

The Seamless Garment

*Whene'er the mist which stands 'twixt God and thee
Defecates to a pure transparency*
     Coleridge

You are a cousin of mine
 Here in the mill.
It's queer that born in the Langholm
 It's no' until
Juist noo I see what it means
To work in the mill like my freen's.

---

joukin, dodging sicna, such baudrons, cats

I was tryin' to say something
   In a recent poem
Aboot Lenin. You've read a guid lot
   In the news—but ken the less o'm?
Look, Wullie, here is his secret noo
In a way I can share it wi' you.

His secret and the secret o' a'
That's worth ocht.
The shuttles fleein' owre quick for my een
   Prompt the thocht,
And the coordination atween
   Weaver and machine.

The haill shop's dumfoonderin'
   To a stranger like me.
Second nature to you; you're perfectly able
   To think, speak and see
Apairt frae the looms, tho' to some
That doesna sae easily come.

Lenin was like that wi' workin' class life,
   At hame wi't a'.
His fause movements couldna been fewer,
   The best weaver Earth ever saw.
A' *he'd* to dae wi' moved intact
   Clean, clear, and exact.

A poet like Rilke did the same
   In a different sphere,
Made a single reality—a' a'e' oo'—
   O' his love and pity and fear;
A seamless garment o' music and thought
But you're owre thrang wi' puirer to tak' tent o't.

What's life or God or what you may ca'
   But something at ane like this?
Can you divide yoursel' frae your breath
   Or—if you say yes—
Frae your mind that as in the case
O' the loom keeps that in its place?

---

fause, false   a' a'e oo', all one   thrang, busy   tak' tent o't, take notice of it
ca't, call it

Empty vessels mak' the maist noise
   As weel you ken.
Still waters rin deep, owre fu' for soond.
   It's the same wi' men.
Belts fleein', wheels birlin'—a river in flood,
Fu' flow and tension o' poo'er and blood.

Are you equal to life as to the loom?
   Turnin' oot shoddy or what?
Claith better than man? D'ye live to the full,
   Your Poo'er's a' deliverly taught?
Or scamp a'thing else? Border claith's famous.
Shall things o' mair consequence shame us?

Lenin and Rilke baith gied still mair skill,
   Coopers o' Stobo, to a greater concern
Than you devote to claith in the mill.
   Wad it be ill to learn
To keep a bit eye on *their* looms as weel
And no' be hailly ta'en up wi' your 'tweel'?

The womenfolk ken what I mean.
   Things maun fit like a glove,
Come clean off the spoon—and syne
   There's time for life and love.
The mair we mak' natural as breathin' the mair
Energy for ither things we'll can spare,
   But as lang as we bide like this
Neist to naething we ha'e, or miss.

Want to gang back to the handloom days?
   Nae fear!
Or paintin' oor hides? Hoo d'ye think we've got
   Frae there to here?
We'd get a million times faurer still
If maist folk change profits didna leav't till
A wheen here and there to bring it aboot
—Aye, and hindered no' helped to boot.

Are you helpin'? Machinery's improved, but folk?
   Is't no' high time

---

birlin', whirling   claith, cloth   deliverly, continually   wheen, little

We were tryin' to come into line a' roon?
  (I canna think o' a rhyme.)
Machinery in a week mak's greater advances
Than Man's nature twixt Adam and this.

Hundreds to the inch the threids lie in,
  Like the men in a communist cell.
There's a play o' licht frae the factory windas.
  Could you no' mak' mair yoursel'?
Mony a loom mair alive than the weaver seems
For the sun's still nearer than Rilke's dreams.

Ailie Bally's tongue's keepin' time
  To the vibration a' richt.
Clear through the maze your een signal to Jean
  What's for naebody else's sicht
Short skirts, silk stockin's—fegs, hoo the auld
  Emmle-deugs o' the past are curjute and devauld!

And as for me in my fricative work
  I ken fu' weel
Sic an integrity's what I maun ha'e,
Indivisible, real,
Woven owre close for the point o' a pin
  Onywhere to win in.

Water of Life

Wha looks on water and's no' affected yet
By memories o' the Flood, and, faurer back,
O' that first flux in which a' life began,
And won sae slowly oot that ony lack
O' poo'er's a shrewd reminder o' the time
  We ploutered in the slime?

It's seldom in my active senses tho'
That water brings sic auld sensations as that

emmle-deugs, tatters of clothes   curjute, overthrown   devauld, relinquished
ploutered, floundered

(Gin it's no' mixed wi' something even yet
A wee taet stronger); but in lookin' at
A woman at ony time I mind oor source
 And possible return of course.

Happy wha feels there's solid ground beneath
His feet at ony time—if ony does.
Happy? That's aiblins ga'en a bit owre faur.
I only mean he differs frae me thus
Tho' I'm whiles glad when a less shoogly sea
 Than ithers cradles me.

And if I'm no' aye glad o't it's because
I was sae used to waters as a loon
That I'm amphibious still. A perfect maze
O' waters is aboot the Muckle Toon,
Apairt frae't often seemin' through the weather
 That sea and sky swap places a'thegither.

Ah, vivid recollection o' trudgin' that
Crab-like again upon the ocean-flair!—
Juist as in lyin' wi' a woman still
I feel a sudden cant and sweesh aince mair
Frae Sodom or Gomorrah wi' yon Eastern whore
 T'oor watery grave o' yore.

She clung to me mair tightly at the end
Than ane expects or wants in sic a case,
Whether frae love or no' I needna say,
A waste o' guid material—her face
Fastened on mine as on a flag a sooker
 And naething shook her.

Although my passion was sair diluted then
I mind the cratur' still frae tip to tae
Better than ony that I've troked si' syne
—The gowden pendants frae her lugs, her skin
Sae clear that in her cheeks the glints 'ud play
As whiles wi' bits o' looking-glass as loons
 We'd gar the sun loup roon's.

taet, bit   aiblins, perhaps   shoogly, insecure   loon, boy
swap, exchange   flair, floor   sweesh, swish   sooker, sucker
cratur', creature   troked, had to do with   si' syne, since then
lugs, ears   loup roon's, jump around us

Nae doot the sudden predicament we shared
Has fixed her in my mind abune the lave,
A kind o' compensation for the way
She was sae tashed and lightlied by the wave
Oot o' my recognition and slarried by
   The infernal sly.

A man never faced wi' death kens nocht o' life.
But a' men are? But micht as weel no' be!
The ancient memory is alive to few
And fewer when it is ken what they see,
But them that dae fear neither life nor death,
   Mindin' them baith.

Nae man can jouk and let the jaw gang by.
To seem to's often to dodge a silly squirt
While bein' whummled in an unseen spate
Lodgin' us securely in faur deeper dirt
Or carryin' us to heichts we canna see
   For th' earth in oor e'e.

Nae gulfs that open 'neath oor feet'll find
Us hailly at a loss if we juist keep
The perspective the deluge should ha' gien's
And if we dinna, or if they're mair deep
Than even that is muckle guidance in,
   It's there altho' we're blin'.

Whatever is to be, what's been has been;
Even if it's hailly undune that deed'll bear
A sense o' sequence forever in itsel',
Implyin', and dependent on, what erst was there,
Tho' it's no' conscious o't—less conscious o't
   Than men o' their historic lot.

Hoo I got oot o' yon I dinna ken,
But I am ready noo at ony time
To be hurled back or forrit to ony stage
O' ocht we've ever been twixt sun and slime
Or can become, trustin' what's brocht aboot
   A' th' ither sequels to the water-shute.

---

lave, remainder   tashed, ruined   lightlied, slighted   slarried, bedogged
sly, green slime on water   jaw, wave   whummled, overturned
gien's, given us   hailly, wholly   forrit, forward   ocht, ought

Shall wellspring and shower, ebb-tide and neap,
Refuse their separate pairts cryin' let's be ane,
In function as natur', appearance as fact?
Foul here, fair there, to sea and sky again
The river keeps its course and ranges
    Unchanged through a' its changes.

Wha speak o' vice and innocence, peace and war,
Culture and ignorance, humility and pride,
Describe the Fairy Loup, the thunder-plump,
The moss-boil on the moor, the white-topped tide;
And the ane as sune as the tither 'll be
    Brocht doon to uniformity.

Ah, weel I ken that ony ane o' them,
Nae maitter hoo vividly I ca't to mind,
Kennin' the world to men's as light to water,
Has endless beauties to which my een are blind,
My ears deaf—aye, and ilka drap a world
    Bigger than a' Mankind has yet unfurled.

Excelsior

Sae worked the instinct in the seas
And jungles we were born in
But sicna cares are useless noo
Tho' aiblins no' for scornin'.

Sae worked the kindnesses we got
Frae shadows gane ayont recall.
Sae work whatever relationships
May haud us still in thrall.

Still on we fare and tine oor need
O' modern mither's as monkey's care,
Syne wives, bairns, freens, and in the end
Oorsels we weel can spare.

---

thunder-plump, thunder-shower   moss-boil, a spring in a mossy place
tither, other
sicna, such   aiblins, perhaps   tine, lose

And aye the force that's brocht life up
Frae chaos to the present stage
Creates new states as ill for us
As oors for eels to gauge.

The promise that there'll be nae second Flood
I tak' wi' a' the salt I've saved since then.
Extinction? What's that but to return
To juist anither Muckle Toon again?
—A salutary process bringin' values oot
    Ocht less 'ud leave in doot.

It teach't me mony lessons I've ne'er forgot—
That it's no' easy to thraw cauld water on life;
The changes a man can safely undergang
And bide essentially unchanged; the strife
To tak' new forms and in it no' forget
    We've never managed yet.

The Factory Gullets and the Skipper's Pool
Are different as Dr. Jekyll and Mr. Hyde
But the quick changes o' the Esk that joins
These twa afore it meets the Solway Tide
'Ud faur ootrin the divers thochts o' Man
    Sin' Time began.

And yet, tho' hospitable to them a',
The Esk is drawn on like a knotless threid
Juist owre lang for's to see the end o't yet,
Tho' noo and then I tak' it in my heid
That the pirn in the hills it's birlin' frae
    Maun near ha' ser'd its day.

Or else I feel like payin' oot line
Forever to an unimaginable take,
And ken that in the Buck and Croon Hotels
They'd lauch my tale to scorn, altho' gudesake,
They credit mony hardly less faur-fetched.
    Heaven kens if mine is stretched!

The Buck and Croon Hotels—guid judges baith
O' credibility I've cause to ken;

ocht, ought   teach't, taught   pirn, reel   birlin', whirling

A wee hauf wi' the emphasis on the wee,
And day and daily d'they no' see again
A miracle clean-flypit, in the maitter
   O' wine turn't back to water?

Weel the Waterside folk kent what I mean;
They were like figures seen on fountains whiles.
The river made sae free wi' them—poored in and oot
O' their een and ears (no' mooths) in a' its styles,
Till it clean scooped the insides o' their skulls
   O' a' but a wheen thochts like gulls.

Their queer stane faces and hoo green they got!
Juist like Rebecca in her shawl o' sly.
I'd never faur to gang to see doon there
A wreathed Triton blaw his horn or try,
While at his feet a clump o' mimulus shone
   Like a god's een wi' a' the world a bone.

flypit, turned inside out   wheen, few   sly, green slime on water

From *The Modern Scot*
(1931)

Kinsfolk

Gin scenic beauty had been a' I sook
I never need ha' left the Muckle Toon.
I saw it there as weel as ony man
(As I'll sune prove); and sin syne I've gane roon'
Hauf o' the warld wi' faculties undulled
      And no' seen't equalled.

But scenic beauty's never maittered much
To me afore, sin poetry isna made
O' anything that's seen, toucht, smelt, or heard,
And no' till lately ha'e the hame scenes played
A pairt in my creative thocht I've yet
      To faddom, and permit.

Gin there's an efter life hoo can I guess
What kind o' man I'll be wha canna tell
What's pairted me here frae my kith and kin
In a' airts mair than Heaven is frae Hell
(To bate the question which is which a wee)
      As't seems to them and me.

Nor tell what brings me unexpectedly back
Whaur't seems nae common thocht or interest's left.
Guid kens it wasna snobbery or hate,
Selfishness, ingratitude, or chance that reft
Sae early, sae completely, ties that last
      Maist folk for life—or was't?

I bein' a man made ither human ties
But they—my choice—are broken (in this case
No' a' my choice) as utterly as those
That bound me to my kin and native place.
My wife and bairns, is't tinin' them that thraws
      Me back on my first cause?

Foreseein' in Christine's or in Walter's mind
A picture o' mysel' as in my ain
My mither rises or I rise in hers
Incredible as to a Martian brain
A cratur' o' this star o' oors micht be
      It had nae point o' contact wi'.

---

sook, sought   sin syne, since then   a' airts, all ways   tinin', losing
cratur', creature

Daith in my faither's case. I ha'e his build,
His energy, but no' his raven hair,
Rude cheeks, clear een. I am whey-faced. My een
Ha'e dark rings roon' them and my pow is fair.
A laddie when he dee'd, I kent little o'm and he
        Kent less o' me.

Gin he had lived my life and wark micht weel
Ha' been entirely different, better or waur,
Or neither, comparison impossible.
It wadna ha' been the same. That's hoo things are.
He had his differences frae some folks aroon'
        But never left the Muckle Toon.

He had his differences but a host o' freen's
At ane wi' him on maist things and at serious odds
In nane, a kindly, gin conscientious, man,
Fearless but peacefu', and to man's and God's
Service gi'en owre accordin' to his lichts
        But fondest o' his ain fireside o' nichts.

Afore he dee'd he turned and gied a lang
Last look at pictures o' my brither and me
Hung on the wa' aside the bed, I've heard
My mither say. I wonder then what he
Foresaw or hoped and hoo—or gin—it squares
        Wi' subsequent affairs.

I've led a vera different life frae ocht
He could conceive or share I ken fu' weel
Yet gin he understood—or understands
(His faith, no' mine)—I like to feel, and feel,
He wadna wish his faitherhood undone
        O' sic an unforeseen unlikely son.

I like to feel, and yet I ken that a'
I mind or think aboot him is nae mair
To what he was, or aiblins is, than yon
Picture o' me at fourteen can compare
Wi' what I look the day (or looked even then).
        He looked in vain, and I again.

---

pow, head   waur, worse   aiblins, perhaps

Gin he had lived at warst we'd ha' been freen's
Juist as my mither (puir auld soul) and I
—As maist folk are, no' ga'en vera deep,
A maitter o' easy-ozie habit maistly, shy
O' fundamentals, as it seems to me,
          —A minority o' ane, may be!

Maist bonds 'twixt man and man are weel ca'd bonds.
But I'll come back to this, since come I maun,
Fellow-feelin', common humanity, claptrap (or has
In anither sense my comin'-back begun)
I've had as little use for to be terse
          As maist folk ha'e for verse.

My wife and weans in London never saw
The Muckle Toon that I'm concerned wi' noo
(Sittin' in Liverpool) and never may.
What maitters't then, gin a' life's gantin' through,
Biggit on sicna kittle sands as these,
          Wi' like haphazardries?

My clan is darkness 'yont a wee ring
O' memory showin' catsiller here or there
But nocht complete or lookin' twice the same.
Graham, Murray, Carruthers, Frater, and faur mair
Auld Border breeds than I can tell ha' been
          Woven in its skein.

Great hooses keep their centuried lines complete.
Better than I can mind my faither they
Preserve their forbears painted on their wa's
And can trace ilka tendency and trait
O' bluid and spirit in their divers stages
          Doon the ages.

---

maun, must   weans, children   gantin', gaping   biggit, built
sicna kittle, such difficult   catsiller, mica

To mind and body I ha' nae sic clue,
A water flowin' frae an unkent source
Wellin' up in me to catch the licht at last
At this late break in its hidden course,
Yet my blin' instincts nurtured in the dark
  Sing sunwards like the lark.

I canna signal to a single soul
In a' the centuries that led up to me
In happy correspondence, yet to a'
These nameless thanks for strength and cleanness gi'e,
And mair, auld Border breeds, ken I inherit,
  And croun, your frontier spirit.

Reivers to weavers and to me. Weird way!
Yet in the last analysis I've sprung
Frae battles, mair than ballads, and it seems
The thrawn auld water has at last upswung
Through me, and's mountin' like the vera devil
  To its richt level!

---

reivers, freebooters thrawn, obstinate

From *Scots Unbound* (1932)

Milk-Wort and Bog-Cotton

(To Seumas O'Sullivan)

Cwa' een like milk-wort and bog-cotton hair!
I love you, earth, in this mood best o' a'
When the shy spirit like a laich wind moves
And frae the lift nae shadow can fa'
Since there's nocht left to thraw a shadow there
Owre een like milk-wort and milk-white cotton hair.

Wad that nae leaf upon anither wheeled
A shadow either and nae root need dern
In sacrifice to let sic beauty be!
But deep surroondin' darkness I discern
Is aye the price o' licht. Wad licht revealed
Naething but you, and nicht nocht else concealed.

Water Music

(To William and Flora Johnstone)

Wheesht, wheesht, Joyce, and let me hear
Nae Anna Livvy's lilt,
But Wauchope, Esk, and Ewes again,
Each wi' its ain rhythms till't.

I

Archin' here and arrachin there,
Allevolie or allemand,
Whiles appliable, whiles areird,
The polysemous poem's planned.

---

cwa', come away   een, eyes   laich, low   lift, sky   dern, hide

wheesht, hush   till't, to it   arrachin, tumultuous   allevolie, at random
allemand, to conduct in a formal and courtly style   appliable, compliant
areird, stubborn

Lively, louch, atweesh, atween,
    Auchimuty or aspate,
Threidin' through the averins
    Or bightsom in the aftergait.

Or barmybrained or barritchfu',
    Or rinnin' like an attercap,
Or shinin' like an Atchison,
    Wi' a blare or wi' a blawp.

They ken a' that opens and steeks,
    Frae Fiddleton Bar to Callister Ha',
And roon aboot for twenty miles,
    They bead and bell and swaw.

Brent on or boutgate or beschact,
    Bellwaverin' or borne-heid,
They mimp and primp, or bick and birr,
    Dilly-dally or show speed.

Brade-up or sclafferin', rouchled, sleek,
    Abstraklous or austerne,
In belths below the brae-hags
    And bebbles in the fern.

Bracken, blaeberries, and heather
    Ken their amplefeysts and toves,
Here gangs ane wi' aiglets jinglin',
    Through a gowl anither goves.

Lint in the bell whiles hardly vies
    Wi' ane the wind amows,

---

louch, downcast   atweesh, between   atween, between
auchimuty, paltry   averins, heather stems   bightsom, ample
aftergait, outcome   barmybrained, wanton, giddy   barritchfu', troublesome
attercap, spider   Atchison, a copper coin washed with silver   blawp, belch
steeks, shuts   bead, gather   bell, bubble up   swaw, ripple
brent on, straight ahead   boutgate, roundabout   beschact, crooked
bellwaverin', undecided   borne-heid, headlong   mimp, act affectedly
bick and birr, make a cry like a grouse
brade-up, with address   sclafferin', slovenly   rouchled, ruffled
abstraklous, outrageous   austerne, austere   belths, sudden swirls
brae-hags, overhanging banks   bebbles, droplets   amplefeysts, fits of sulks
toves, moods   aiglets, tipped boot-laces   gowl, glen   goves, comes angrily
lint in the bell, flax in flower   whiles, sometimes   amows, vexes

While blithely doon abradit linns
   Wi' gowd begane anither jows.

Cougher, blocher, boich and croichle,
   Fraise in ane anither's witters,
Wi' backthraws, births, by-rinnin's,
   Beggar's broon or blae—the critters!

Or burnet, holine, watchet, chauve,
   Or wi' a' the colours dyed
O' the lift abune and plants and trees
   That grow on either side.

Or coinyelled wi' the midges,
   Or swallows a' aboot,
The shadow o' an eagle,
   The aiker o' a troot.

Toukin' ootrageous face
   The turn-gree o' your mood,
I've climmed until I'm lost
   Like the sun ahint a clood.

But a tow-gun frae the boon-tree,
A whistle frae the elm,
A spout-gun frae the hemlock,
And, back in this auld realm,
Dry leafs o' dishielogie
To smoke in a 'partan's tae!'

And you've me in your creel again,
   Brim or shallow, bauch or bricht,
Singin' in the mornin',
   Corrieneuchin' a' the nicht.

---

abradit linns, worn rocky stairways   gowd, gold   begane, decorated
jows, rocks along   cougher, onomatopoetic sound
blocher, to cough noisily because of phlegm   boich, to cough
croichle, onomatopoetic sound
fraise in ane anither's witters, to run through each other
backthraws, recoilings   by-rinnin's, side-runs   beggar's broon, snuff
blae, blue   critters, creatures   burnet, brown   holine, holly green
watchet, dark green   chauve, black and white   coinyelled, pitted
aiker, motion   toukin', distorted   turn-gree, winding stair
climmed, climbed
tow-gun, pop gun   boon-tree, elder tree   spout-gun, hollow stem (blow-pipe)
dishielogie, colt's foot   partan's tae, clay pipe   bauch, dull
corrieneuchin', murmuring

II

Lappin' on the shirrel,
    Or breengin' doon the cleuch,
Slide-thrift for stars and shadows,
    Or sun-couped owre the heuch.

Wi' the slughorn o' a folk,
    Sightsmen for a thoosand years,
In fluther or at shire
    O' the Border burns' careers,

Let them popple, let them pirl,
    Plish-plash and plunk and plop and ploot,
In quakin' quaw or fish-currie
    I ken a' they're aboot.

And 'twixt the pavvy o' the Wauchope,
    And the paspey o' the Ewes,
And the pavane o' Esk itsel',
    It's no' for me to choose.

Be they querty, be they quiet,
    Flow like railya or lamoo,
Only turn a rashmill or
    Gar a' the country tew,

As it's froggin' in the hills,
    Or poors pipestapples and auld wives,
Sae Waich Water glents and scrows,
    Reels and ratches and rives.

---

shirrel, turf   breengin', hurtling   cleuch, ravine
slide-thrift, a game of chequers   couped owre, tumbled over   heuch, cliff
slughorn, characteristic   sightsmen, observers of the movement of salmon
fluther, in flood   shire, at high water   popple, bubble   pirl, to purl
quaw, quagmire   fish-currie, hiding place for fish   pavvy, bustle
paspey, dance   querty, lively   railya, striped cloth   lamoo, lamb's wool
rashmill, toy mill made of rushes   tew, toil   froggin', sleeting intermittently
poors, pours   pipestapples, broken pipe stems   auld wives, old women
glents, sparkles   scrows, swarms   ratches, wrenches   rives, rends

Some day they say the Bigly Burn
　　'Ll loup oot frae its scrabs and thistles,
And ding the bonnie birken shaw
　　A' to pigs and whistles.

And there's yon beck—I winna name't—
　　That hauds the fish that aince was hookit
A century syne—the fisher saw't,
　　And flew, and a' his graith forsookit.

And as for Unthank Water,
　　That seeps through miles o' reeds and seggs,
It's aye at pilliewinkie syne
　　Wi' the gowdnie's eggs.

Nae mair than you could stroan yoursel'
　　The biggest o' them you may say,
Yet lood and still I see them stoan
　　To oceans and the heaven's sway.

Fleetin' owre the meadows,
　　Or cleitchin' in the glaur,
The haill world answers to them,
　　And they rein the faurest star.

Humboldt, Howard, Maury,
　　Hildebrandsson, Hann, and Symons,
A digest o' a' their work's
　　In these dour draps or diamonds.

And weel I ken the air's wild rush
　　As it comes owre the seas,
Clims up and whistles 'twixt the hills,
　　Wi' a' the weather gie's

O' snaw and rain and thunder,
　　Is a single circle spun
By the sun's bricht heat and guided by
　　Earth's spin and the shapes o' the grun'.

loup, leap　　scrabs, heather stumps　　ding, knock
bonnie birken shaw, the beautiful beech wood　　graith, gear
forsookit, forsook　　seggs, broad leaved rushes　　pilliewinkie, a barbarous
children's sport against birds　gowdnie, sea bird　　stroan, urinate
stoan, swell　　cleitchin', chattering　　glaur, mud, ooze　　grun', ground

145

Lappin' on the shirrel,
 Or breengin' doon the cleuch,
I can listen to the waters
 Lang—and no' lang—eneuch.

Wheesht, wheesht, Joyce, and let me hear
No' Anna Livvy's lilt,
But Wauchope, Esk, and Ewes again,
 Each wi' its ain rhythms till't.

Tarras

This Bolshevik bog! Suits me doon to the grun'!
For by fike and finnick the world's no' run.
Let fools set store by a simperin' face,
Ithers seek to keep the purale in place
Or grue at vermin—but by heck
The purpose o' life needs them—if us.
Little the bog and the masses reck
O' some dainty-davie or fike-ma-fuss.
Ho for the mother of usk and adder
Spelderin' here in her coal and madder
Faur frae Society's bells and bladder.

The fog-wa' splits and a gair is set
O' corbie oats and corcolet
And drulie water like sheepeik seeps
Through the duffie peats, and cranglin' creeps,
Crowdles like a crab, syne cowds awa',
Couthless eneuch, yet cuttedly tae,
Tho' here and there in a sudden swaw
Corky-heidit as if in a playsome way,

fike, fuss purale, the poor grue, be revolted
dainty-davie, stately person fike-ma-fuss, fussy person spelderin', sprawling
fog-wa', moss wall gair, patch of green hillside corbie oats, black oats
corcolet, a lichen drulie, muddy sheepeik, sheep-grease duffie, spongy
cranglin', winding crowdles, crawls cowds, floats slowly couthless, cold
cuttedly, tartly swaw, ripple corky-heidit, giddy

But its lichtest kinks are a cowzie sport,
That nocht can cuddum—nocht can sort
For't, endless torsion, riddlin' port.

Ah, woman-fondlin'! What is that to this?
Saft hair to birssy heather, warm kiss
     To cauld black waters' suction.
     Nae ardent breists' erection
But the stark hills'! In what dry-gair-flow
Can I pillow my lowin' cheek here
Wi' nae paps' howe below?

    What laithsome parodies appear
    O' my body's secrets in this oorie growth
    Wi' its peerieweeries a' radgie for scouth
    And the haill ratch and rive o' a world uncouth?

Her cautelles! On cods o' crammasy sundew
Or wi' antrin sprigs o' butterwort blue,
Here in a punk-hole, there in a burn,
She gecks to storm and shine in turn,
Trysts wi' this wind and neist wi' that,
Now wi' thunder and syne wi' snaw,
Bare to the banes or wi' birds in her hat,
    —And has bairns by them a',
      ——Bairns!

Bycomes o' bogs and gets o' cairns,
Ultimate flow of her flosh and ferns . . .
The doup of the world is under you here

---

kinks, twists   cowzie, boisterous   cuddum, tame   birssy, bristly
dry-gair-flow, place where two hills join   lowin', blazing   howe, valley
laithsome, loathesome   oorie, weird   peerieweeries, very small things
radgie, ready   scouth, freedom   ratch, wrench   rive, rend
cautelles, stratagems   cods, pillows   crammasy, crimson
antrin, occasional   punk-hole, hole in the moss
gecks, tosses the head affectedly   neist, next   bycomes, illegitimate offspring
gets, bastards   flosh, swamp   doup, hindquarters

And, fast in her shochles, she'll find ye,
When you're drawn to where wind and water shear,
Shuttles o' glaur, and shot-heuch, to wind ye,
Till you peugle and hoast in the shug-bog there,
While she lies jirblin' wide to the air
And now and then lets a scannachin flare.

Come pledge her in a horse-punckin then!
Loons to a byssim, pock-shakin's o' men,
Needna come vauntin' their poustures to her.
Their paramuddle is whey to her heather.
To gang through her mill they maun pay
Ootsucken multure to the auld vulture,
Nor wi' their flauchter-spades ettle to play,
Withoot thick paikies to gaird their cul-ture!

What's ony schaftmon to this shud moss?
Or pooky-hair to her matted boss?
—Pledge her wha's mou' can relish her floss!

Of John Davidson

I remember one death in my boyhood
That next to my father's, and darker, endures;
Not Queen Victoria's, but Davidson, yours,
And something in me has always stood
Since then looking down the sandslope
On your small black shape by the edge of the sea,
—A bullet-hole through a great scene's beauty,
God through the wrong end of a telescope.

shochles, legs
shot-heuch, fallen surface caused by undermining by water
peugle and hoast, cough in a stifled manner   shug-bog, quaking bog
jirblin', spilling   scannachin, glancing
horse-punckin, hole in the mud made by a horse's hoof   loons, boys
byssim, bawd   pock-shakin', the youngest, smallest and weakest of a family
poustures, bodily abilities   paramuddle, blood supply
ootsucken multure, mill duties   flauchter-spades, turf-cutting spades
ettle, try   paikies, protective aprons for turf cutters
cul-ture, pun on 'cull', testicle   ony, any   schaftmon, a measure of six inches
shud, coagulated   moss, bog   pooky-hair, scraggly hair
boss, front of body from chest to loins   floss, pubic hair

From *The Modern Scot*
(1933)

Whuchulls*

Il ne peut y avoir du progres (vrai, c'est-à-dire moral), que dans l'individu et par l'individu et par l'individu lui-même.

Charles Baudelaire

Gie owre your coontin', for nae man can tell
The population o' a wud like this
In plants and beasts, and needna pride himsel'
On ocht he marks by a' he's boond to miss.
What is oor life that we should prize't abune
Lichen's or slug's o' which we ken scarce mair
Than they o' oors when a'thing's said and dune,
Or fancy it ser's 'heicher purposes'?
The wice man kens that a fool's brain and his
Differ at maist as little 'gainst a' that is
As different continents and centuries,
Time, station, caste, culture, or character—
Triflin' distinctions that dinna cairry faur—
And if at ony point he stops and says:
'My lot has fa'n in mair enlightened days,
I'm glad to be a European, no' a black
—Human, no' hotchin' glaur,' ahint his back
Let him forehear as foolish a future set
Him in a class as seemin' laicher yet,
Or ten pasts damn him for a graceless get.
Original forest, Whuchulls, public park,
Mysel', or ony man, beast, mineral, weed,
I clearly see are a' aside the mark.
The poet hauds nae brief for ony kind,
Age, place, or range o' sense, and no' confined
To ony nature can share Creation's insteed.
First speir this bowzie bourach if't prefers
The simmer or the winter, day or night,
New or forhooied nests, rain's pelts or smirrs,

Gie owre, leave off   wud, wood   heicher, higher   hotchin', seething
glaur, slime   laicher, lower   get, illegitimate offspring   speir, ask
bowzie, branchy   bourach, cluster   forhooied, forsaken   smirrs, drizzles

* Local pronunciation of Whitshiels, a wood near Langholm.

Bare sticks or gorded fullyery; and syne invite
My choice twixt good and evil, life and death.
What hoar trunk girds at ivy or at fug
Or what sleek bole complains it lacks them baith?
Nae foliage hustle-farrant in windy light
Is to the Muse a mair inspirin' sight
Than fungus poxy as the mune; nae blight
A meaner state than flourish at its height.
Leaf's music weel accords wi' gloghole's glug.
Then cite nae mair this, that, or onything.
To nae belief or preference I cling,
Earth—let alane the mucklest mountain in't—
Is faur owre kittle a thing to hide ahint.
I'll no' toy wi' the fragments o't I ken
—Nor seek to beshield it, least o' a' men! . . .
Yet here's a poem takin' shape again,
Inevitable shape, faur mair inevitable
Than birks and no' bamboos or banyans here,
Impredictable, relentless, thriddin' the rabble
O' themes and aspects in this thrawart scene.
O freedom constrainin' me as nae man's been
Mair constrained wha wasna, as I'll yet be, freer! . . .

'Clearlier it comes. I winna ha'e it. Quick
And gi'e me tutors in arboriculture then.
Let me plunge where the undergrowth's mair thick.
Experts in forestry, botany—a' that ken
Mair than I dae o' onything that's here.
I ken sae little it easily works its will.
Fence me frae its design wi' endless lear.

Pile up the facts and let me faurer ben.
Multiply my vocabulary ten times ten.
Let me range owre a' prosody again.
Mak' yon a lammergeir, no' juist a wren.
Is that owre muckle for a Scotsman yet,
Needin' a soupler leid, great skills, he lacks?
Is he in silence safer frae attacks?

gorded, fullblown   fullyery, foliage   fug, moss
hustle-farrant, tattered   gloghole, deep hole   mucklest, highest
kittle, ticklish   birks, birches   thriddin', threading   thrawart, perverse
lear, learning   faurer ben, further in   yon, that   muckle, much
soupler, suppler   leid, language

Yet wha can thole to see it cavalierly choose
In God's green wud—tak' this and that refuse?
Yon knoul-taed trees, this knurl, at least 't'll use!
Gar memory gie the place fower seasons at aince.'
The world's no' mine. I'll tak' nae hen's care o't.
'Is that Creation's nature you evince,
Sma-bookin' Whuchulls to a rice or twa
Sae arbitrarily picked, and voidin' a'
The lave as gin it wasna worth a jot?'

There is nae reason but on unreason's based
And needs to mind that often to hain its sense,
Dodo and Mammoth had the same misplaced
Trust in their *données*—and hae lang gane hence.
Why fash sae muckle owre Nature's present stock
In view o' a' past changes and to come?
Its wipin' oot 'ud be nae greater shock
Than mony afore; and Poetry isna some
Society for Preservin' Threatened Types,
But strokes a cat or fiddles on its tripes,
And for inclusions or exclusions, fegs,
Needna apologize while a'e bird's eggs
Are plain, anither's speckled, beasts ha'e legs,
Birds wings, Earth here brairds trees, here nocht but seggs.
'Troth it's an insult for a man to seek
A'e woman owre anither. A' women hae
Their differences and resemblances, but whatna freak
Thinks, frae the latter, ony ane'll dae
Or, frae the former, fain 'ud sair them a'?

The world o' a' the senses is the same.
Creation disna live frae hand to mooth
Juist improvisin' as it gangs, forsooth,
And there's nae meanin' in life that bode to da'
Until we came—or bides a wicer day—
'Yont brute creation, fools, bairns, unborn, deid.
I'd sing bird-mooth'd wi' ony ither creed,

---

thole, bear   knoul-taed, swollen-toed   fower, four
sma'-bookin', shrinking   rice, branch   lave, rest
hain, keep   fash, bother   brairds, sprouts   seggs, marsh plants
fain 'ud sair, gladly would serve   bode to da', waited to dawn   wicer, wiser

No' wi' Creation's nature and its aim;
Or sing like Miffy—wheesht, world, while he speaks.
In English—hence, the Universal Speech.
He has nae wings; let birds pit on the breeks
Nae fins. Fish, copy him! And sae let each
O' Nature's sorts be modelled upon him
Frae animalculae to Seraphim.
He is nae poet, but likes the Laureate best.
What, write like that?—Ah! here's the crucial test!
I ha'e the courage to be a Scotsman then
(Nae Scot'll e'er be Laureate we ken!)★
Divided frae ither folk to Eternity's en',
And, if I hadna, ken it wadna maitter.
I'd be it still. Exclusive forms are nature.

It means to be and comes in Nature's way.
—In its ain nature's, as a' in Nature does.
Supersessions, innovations, variations, display
Nature, no' hide; and Scotland, Whuchulls, us
Interest me less for what they are than as
Facts o' the creative poo'er that, tho' they pass,
'll aye be qualified by their ha'en been.
It is nae treason then to stell my een
No' on their fleetin' shapes but on their deep
Constituent principles destined to keep
A mystery greater than the sight o' eels
Kelterin' through a' the seven seas reveals.
These to a'e spot converge, but we gang oot
Aye faurer frae oor source—ne'er back, I doot.
'I like to see the ramel gowd-bestreik,
And sclaffer cuit-deep through the birsled leafs.
Here I dung doon the squirrels wi' my sling
And made the lassies brooches o' their paws,
Set girns for rabbits and for arnuts socht,
Herried my nests and blew the eggs, and lit
Fires o' fir-burrs and hag in tinker style.

---

breeks, trousers   stell, fix   kelterin', snaking   ramel, branches
gowd-bestreik, gold-veined   sclaffer, shuffle   cuit-deep, ankle deep
birsled, crackled   dung, knocked   girns, snares   arnuts, earth-nuts
herried, plundered   -burrs, -cones   hag, peat

★ 'There are poets little enough to envy even a poet-laureate'—Gray.

Hoo faur the interests o' progress warrant
Meddlin' wi' Whuchulls' auld amenities,
And their dependent livelihoods and ploys,
I'm no' to say; I'm glad to see it still
Temporarily triumphant against control.
It's pleasant nae doot for a woman to dream
O' yieldin' hersel' to some buirdly man
Wha kens what he wants and willy-nilly'll ha'e't
But when the time comes she'll aye find, I think,
Guid reasons for no' yieldin'—bless her hert!
Sae wi' the Whuchulls. May the Lord be praised.'
Nae doot primeval beasts felt juist the same
Aboot the place—tho' different frae this
As ony change that's still in store for it.
Hauf saurian-emeritus, hauf prentice spook,
You'll never see the plantin' for the trees,
This Eden where Adam comes fu' circle yet.

There is nae ither way. For weel or woe
It is attained. Tho' idle side-winds blow
In on me still and inferior questions thraw
Their crockets up, a' doots and torments cease.
The road is clear. I gang in perfect peace,
And my idea spreids and shines and lures me on,
O lyric licht auld chaos canna dam!
Celestial, soothin', sanctifyin' course, wi' a'
The high sane forces o' the sacred time
Fechtin' on my side through it till I con
This blainy blanderin' and ken that I'm
Delivered frae the need o' trauchlin' wi't,
Accommodated to't, but in my benmaist hert
Acknowledgementless, free, condition or reform,
Or sunny lown or devastatin' storm,
Indifferent to me; where the Arts stert
Wi' a' else *corpore vili*—'God's mercy-seat!'

---

ploys, business   buirdly, well-built   plantin', plantation   crockets, ornaments
blainy blanderin', patchy sowing   trauchlin', struggling   benmaist, inmost
lown, calm

From *Poems to Paintings by William Johnstone 1933* (1963)

A Point in Time

Now you understand how stars and hearts are one with another
And how there can nowhere be an end, nowhere a hindrance;
How the boundless dwells perfect and undivided in the spirit,
How each part can be infinitely great, and infinitely small,
How the utmost extension is but a point, and how
Light, harmony, movement, power
All identical, all separate, and all united are life.

Conception

I have reached the stage when questioning myself
Concerning the love of Scotland and turning inward
Upon my own spirit, there comes to me
The suggestion of something utterly unlike
All that is commonly meant by loving
One's country, one's brother man, not altruism,
Not kindly feeling, not outward-looking sympathy,
But something different from all these,
Something almost awful in its range,
Its rage and fire, its scope and height and depth,
Something growing up, within my own
Separate and isolated lonely being,
Within the deep dark of my own consciousness,
Flowering in my own heart, my own self
(Not the Will to Power, but the Will to Flower!)
So that indeed I could not be myself
Without this strange, mysterious, awful finding
Of my people's very life within my own
—This terrible blinding discovery
Of Scotland in me, and I in Scotland,
Even as a man, loyal to a man's code and outlook,
Discovers within himself woman alive and eloquent,
Pulsing with her own emotion,
Looking out on the world with her own vision.

From *Stony Limits* (1934)

The Point of Honour

(On watching the Esk again)

I would that once more I could blend her
With my own self as I did then
Vivid and impulsive in crystalline splendour
Cold and seething champagne.

(Cut water. Perfection of craft concealed
In effects of pure improvisation,
Delights of dazzle and dare revealed
In instant inscapes of fresh variation.

Exhilarating, effortless, divinely light,
In apparent freedom yet reined by unseen
And ubiquitous disciplines; darting, lint-white,
Fertile in impulse, in control—keen.

Pride of play in a flourish of eddies,
Bravura of blowballs, and silver digressions,
Ringing and glittering she swirls and steadies,
And moulds each ripple with secret suppressions.)

Once, with my boy's body little I knew
But her furious thresh on my flesh;
But now I can know her through and through
And, light like, her tide enmesh.

Then come, come, come, let her spend her
Quivering momentum where I lie here,
Wedding words to her waves, and able to tend her
Every swirl and sound with eye and ear.

No more of mere sound, the least part!
I know how it acts, connecting words, implying
A rate of movement, onomatopoeic art,
Or making a reader start trying
To interpret the mouth's actual movement
As a gesture; or acting directly
Like a tune—a mode that is different
From the rest as darkness from light to me.
These intelligible, this a mystery.

Is not consciousness of a sound an act
Of belief in it; are not movements of muscles
Transferred, apprehended, as rhythms, or fact
Of nature some other sense claims, like the tussles
You arouse of thought, hearing, touch and sight
Variety of experience, a baffling medley
Till one wins, and I cease to know you aright
Yet dare not embezzle the dramatic insights,
The generative questionableness, knowing well
The greater risk of taking no risks,
Creating no ecstasies, changing the mights
Of old safe ecstasies to counters, discs,
Transports reduced to play-level,
The problematic, the murderous, element
Of all art eschewed; no mad leap taken
Into the symbol, driving like your stream
Through all mere images, all that may seem
Its very character; the engagement
Twixt man and being forsaken.
All stale, unprofitable, flat and thin,
No restless eager poem that speaking in
A thousand moods achieves a unity,
No wracking indispensable energy,
Only emotions forgotten in tranquillity.
Seductive solutions, genteel clarities,
What have I or you to do with these?
Am I too old to spring like a salmon
And confined to Goethean gammon?
—And yet in the summer-time you
Sometimes come down to that too.

Nay, the boy's spirit its lessoning got;
Dissympathy with nature, sheer sensual force,
Lust of light and colour, the frequent note
Of free enthusiasm in its course.

What troubling flavour in this heady wine?
It hides not Dionysos' but Astarte's sting?
Mid the elemental enemies—cold, ravening brine—
The intellectual flame's survival I sing.

Malicious and unaccountable twinkle, free
Beyond human freedom from the laws of causation?
Nay, gaily, daily, over abysses more ghastly
Men cast spider-webs of creation.

(Nay, the last issue I have all but joined
But my muse still lacks—and so has missed all—
The right temper, like yours, which goes to the point
Of the terrible; the terrible crystal.

Some day I cry—and may cry my life through—
Serene and modest in self-confidence like you
I will capture the world-free illusion two
Of naught, and they one, like me and the sun's rays.

For in you and in me moves a thought
So passionate and live like a plant or beast
It has its own architecture and has brought
A new thing to Nature—mine vague, yours exprest.

If I find yours I will find my own.
What lack of integrity prevents me?
Where is the reach-point (it exists I've known long
Waiting for me) of this integrity?

Found I shall know it like a turned lock's click
But I fumble and juggle again and again.
Your every least move does the trick
But I watch your quick tumblers in vain.)

But one sweep of motion in the world to-day,
The unwearying flood of the river,
Inexplicable, alien! Water, whither away
In a flight that passes and stays forever?

Full from the rains, but the flood sediment gone;
Under the brace of the glancing current
Each pebble shines as with a life of its own,
Electric, autonymous, world-shaking-divergent.

Or comes the disturbing influence with which I tingle
Only from the shoals of fishes that seem
As though they'd be stranded there on the shingle
From the swaying waters they teem?

A wagtail flits but noiseless—by knowledge awed
Of some great unseen presence? Or food its gob in?—
Then suddenly, with expanding sweetness, a glad
Clear note rings out: Revelation!; Robin?

Stranded. I with them! Would I wish to bend her
    To me as she veers on her way again
Vivid and impulsive in crystalline splendour
    Cold and seething champagne?

No. So life leaves us. Already gleam
In the eyes of the young the flicker, the change,
The free enthusiasm that carries the stream
Suddenly out of my range.

On a Raised Beach

(To James H. Whyte)

All is lithogenesis—or lochia,
Carpolite fruit of the forbidden tree,
Stones blacker than any in the Caaba,
Cream-coloured caen-stone, chatoyant pieces,
Celadon and corbeau, bistre and beige,
Glaucous, hoar, enfouldered, cyathiform,
Making mere faculae of the sun and moon,
I study you glout and gloss, but have
No cadrans to adjust you with, and turn again
From optik to haptik and like a blind man run
My fingers over you, arris by arris, burr by burr,
Slickensides, truité, rugas, foveoles,
Bringing my aesthesia in vain to bear,
An angle-titch to all your corrugations and coigns,
Hatched foraminous cavo-rilieva of the world,
Diectic, fiducial stones, Chiliad by chiliad
What bricole piled you here, stupendous cairn?
What artist poses the Earth écorché thus,

Pillar of creation engouled me?
What eburnation augments you with men's bones,
Every energumen an Endymion yet?
All the other stones are in this haecceity it seems,
But where is the Christophanic rock that moved?
What Cabirian song from this catasta comes?

Deep conviction or preference can seldom
Find direct terms in which to express itself.
To-day on this shingle shelf
I understand this pensive reluctance so well,
This not discommendable obstinacy,
These contrivances of an inexpressive critical feeling,
These stones with their resolve that Creation shall not be
Injured by iconoclasts and quacks. Nothing has stirred
Since I lay down this morning an eternity ago
But one bird. The widest open door is the least liable to intrusion,
Ubiquitous as the sunlight, unfrequented as the sun.
The inward gates of a bird are always open.
It does not know how to shut them.
That is the secret of its song,
But whether any man's are ajar is doubtful.
I look at these stones and know little about them,
But I know their gates are open too,
Always open, far longer open, than any bird's can be,
That every one of them has had its gates wide open far longer
Than all birds put together, let alone humanity,
Though through them no man can see,
No man nor anything more recently born than themselves
And that is everything else on the Earth.
I too lying here have dismissed all else.
Bread from stones is my sole and desperate dearth,
From stones, which are to the Earth as to the sunlight
Is the naked sun which is for no man's sight.
I would scorn to cry to any easier audience
Or, having cried, to lack patience to await the response.
I am no more indifferent or ill-disposed to life than death is;
I would fain accept it all completely as the soil does;
Already I feel all that can perish perishing in me
As so much has perished and all will yet perish in these stones.
I must begin with these stones as the world began.

Shall I come to a bird quicker than the world's course ran?
      To a bird, and to myself, a man?
      And what if I do, and further?
I shall only have gone a little way to go back again
And be like a fleeting deceit of development,
Iconoclasts, quacks. So these stones have dismissed
All but all of evolution, unmoved by it,
(Is there anything to come they will not likewise dismiss?)
As the essential life of mankind in the mass
Is the same as their earliest ancestors yet.

Actual physical conflict or psychological warfare
      Incidental to love or food
Brings out animal life's bolder and more brilliant patterns
      Concealed as a rule in habitude.
      There is a sudden revelation of colour,
      The protrusion of a crest,
      The expansion of an ornament,
—But no general principle can be guessed
From these flashing fragments we are seeing,
These foam-bells on the hidden currents of being.
The bodies of animals are visible substances
And must therefore have colour and shape, in the first place
Depending on chemical composition, physical structure, mode of
   growth,
Psychological rhythms and other factors in the case,
But their purposive function is another question.
Brilliant-hued animals hide away in the ocean deeps;
The mole has a rich sexual colouring in due season
Under the ground; nearly every beast keeps
Brighter colours inside it than outside.
What the seen shows is never anything to what it's designed to hide,
The red blood which makes the beauty of a maiden's cheek
Is as red under a gorilla's pigmented and hairy face.
Varied forms and functions though life may seem to have shown
They all come back to the likeness of stone,
So to the intervening stages we can best find a clue
In what we all came from and return to.
There are no twirly bits in this ground bass.

We must be humble. We are so easily baffled by appearances
And do not realise that these stones are one with the stars.

It makes no difference to them whether they are high or low,
Mountain peak or ocean floor, palace, or pigsty.
There are plenty of ruined buildings in the world but no ruined
  stones.
No visitor comes from the stars
But is the same as they are.
—Nay, it is easy to find a spontaneity here,
An adjustment to life, an ability
To ride it easily, akin to 'the buoyant
Prelapsarian naturalness of a country girl
Laughing in the sun, not passion-rent,
But sensing in the bound of her breasts vigours to come
Powered to make her one with the stream of earth-life round her,'
But not yet as my Muse is, with this ampler scope,
This more divine rhythm, wholly at one
With the earth, riding the Heavens with it, as the stones do
And all soon must.
But it is wrong to indulge in these illustrations
Instead of just accepting the stones.
It is a paltry business to try to drag down
The arduus furor of the stones to the futile imaginings of men,
To all that fears to grow roots into the common earth,
As it soon must, lest it be chilled to the core,
As it will be—and none the worse for that.
Impatience is a poor qualification for immortality.
Hot blood is of no use in dealing with eternity,
It is seldom that promises or even realisations
Can sustain a clear and searching gaze.
But an emotion chilled is an emotion controlled;
This is the road leading to certainty,
Reasoned planning for the time when reason can no longer avail.
It is essential to know the chill of all the objections
That come creeping into the mind, the battle between opposing
  ideas
Which gives the victory to the strongest and most universal
Over all others, and to wage it to the end
With increasing freedom, precision, and detachment
A detachment that shocks our instincts and ridicules our desires.
All else in the world cancels out, equal, capable
Of being replaced by other things (even as all the ideas
That madden men now must lose their potency in a few years

And be replaced by others—even as all the religions,
All the material sacrifices and moral restraints,
That in twenty thousand years have brought us no nearer God
Are irrelevant to the ordered adjustments
Out of the reach of perceptive understanding
Forever taking place on the Earth and in the unthinkable regions
    around it;
This cats' cradle of life; this reality volatile yet determined;
This intense vibration in the stones
That makes them seem immobile to us)
But the world cannot dispense with the stones.
They alone are not redundant. Nothing can replace them
Except a new creation of God.

I must get into this stone world now.
Ratchel, striae, relationships of tesserae,
      Innumerable shades of grey,
      Innumerable shapes,
And beneath them all a stupendous unity,
Infinite movement visibly defending itself
Against all the assaults of weather and water,
Simultaneously mobilised at full strength
At every point of the universal front,
      Always at the pitch of its powers,
      The foundation and end of all life.
I try them with the old Norse words—hraun
Duss, rønis, queedaruns, kollyarum;
They hvarf from me in all directions
Over the hurdifell—klett, millya, hellya, hellyina bretta,
Hellyina wheeda, hellyina grø, bakka, ayre,—
      And lay my world in kolgref.

This is no heap of broken images.
Let men find the faith that builds mountains
Before they seek the faith that moves them. Men cannot hope
To survive the fall of the mountains
Which they will no more see than they saw their rise
Unless they are more concentrated and determined,
Truer to themselves and with more to be true to,
Than these stones, and as inerrable as they are.
Their sole concern is that what can be shaken
Shall be shaken and disappear

And only the unshakable be left.
What hardhihood in any man has part or parcel in this latter?
It is necessary to make a stand and maintain it forever.
These stones go through Man, straight to God, if there is one.
What have they not gone through already?
Empires, civilisations, aeons. Only in them
If in anything, can His creation confront Him.
They came so far out of the water and halted forever.
That larking dallier, the sun, has only been able to play
With superficial by-products since;
The moon moves the waters backwards and forwards.
But the stones cannot be lured an inch further
Either on this side of eternity or the other.
Who thinks God is easier to know than they are?
Trying to reach men any more, any otherwise, than they are?
These stones will reach us long before we reach them.
Cold, undistracted, eternal and sublime.
They will stem all the torrents of vicissitude forever
With a more than Roman peace.
Death is a physical horror to me no more.
I am prepared with everything else to share
Sunshine and darkness and wind and rain
And life and death bare as these rocks though it be
In whatever order nature may decree,
But, not indifferent to the struggle yet
Nor to the ataraxia I might get
By fatalism, a deeper issue see
Than these, or suicide, here confronting me.
It is reality that is at stake.
Being and non-being with equal weapons here
Confront each other for it, non-being unseen
But always on the point, it seems, of showing clear,
Though its reserved contagion may breed
This fancy too in my still susceptible head
And then by its own hidden movement lead
Me as by aesthetic vision to the supposed
Point where by death's logic everything is recomposed,
Object and image one, from their severance freed,
As I sometimes, still wrongly, feel 'twixt this storm beach and me.
What happens to us
Is irrelevant to the world's geology

But what happens to the world's geology
Is not irrelevant to us.
We must reconcile ourselves to the stones,
Not the stones to us.
Here a man must shed the encumbrances that muffle
Contact with elemental things, the subtleties
That seem inseparable from a humane life, and go apart
Into a simple and sterner, more beautiful and more oppressive
    world,
Austerely intoxicating; the first draught is over-powering;
Few survive it. It fills me with a sense of perfect form,
The end seen from the beginning, as in a song.
It is no song that conveys the feeling
That there is no reason why it should ever stop,
But the kindred form I am conscious of here
Is the beginning and end of the world,
The unsearchable masterpiece, the music of the spheres,
Alpha and Omega, the Omnific Word.
These stones have the silence of supreme creative power.
The direct and undisturbed way of working
Which alone leads to greatness.
What experience has any man crystallised,
What weight of convictions accumulated,
What depth of life suddenly seen entire
In some nigh supernatural moment
And made a symbol and lived up to
With such resolution, such Spartan impassivity?
It is a frenzied and chaotic age,
Like a growth of weeds on the site of a demolished building.
How shall we set ourselves against it,
Imperturbable, inscrutable, in the world and yet not in it,
Silent under the torments it inflicts upon us,
      With a constant centre,
With a single inspiration, foundations firm and invariable;
      By what immense exercise of will,
Inconceivable discipline, courage, and endurance,
      Self-purification and anti-humanity,
        Be ourselves without interruption,
          Adamantine and inexorable?
It will be ever increasingly necessary to find
In the interests of all mankind

Men capable of rejecting all that all other men
　　Think, as a stone remains
Essential to the world, inseparable from it,
　　And rejects all other life yet.
Great work cannot be combined with surrender to the crowd,
　　—Nay, the truth we seek is as free
From all yet thought as a stone from humanity.
Here where there is neither haze nor hesitation
Something at least of the necessary power has entered into me.
I have still to see any manifestation of the human spirit
That is worthy of a moment's longer exemption than it gets
From petrifaction again—to get out if it can.
All is lithogenesis—or lochia;
And I can desire nothing better,
An immense familiarity with other men's imaginings
Convinces me they cannot either
(If they could, it would instantly be granted
—The present order must continue till then)
Though, of course, I still keep an open mind,
A mind as open as the grave.
You may say that the truth cannot be crushed out,
That the weight of the whole world may be tumbled on it,
And yet, in puny, distorted, phantasmal shapes, albeit,
It will braird again; it will force its way up
Through unexpectable fissures? Look over this beach.
What ruderal and rupestrine growth is here?
What crop confirming any credulties?
Conjure a fescue to teach me with from this
And I will listen to you, but until then
Listen to me—Truth is not crushed;
It crushes, gorgonises all else into itself.
The trouble is to know it when you see it?
You will have no trouble with it when you do.
Do not argue with me. Argue with these stones.
Truth has no trouble in knowing itself.
This is it. The hard fact. The inoppugnable reality,
Here is something for you to digest.
Eat this and we'll see what appetite you have left
For a world hereafter.
I pledge you in the first and last crusta,
The rocks rattling in the bead-proof seas.

O we of little faith,
As romanticists viewed the philistinism of their days
As final and were prone to set over against it
Infinite longing rather than manly will—
Nay, as all thinkers and writers find
The indifference of the masses of mankind,—
So are most men with any stone yet,
Even those who juggle with lapidary's, mason's, geologist's words
      And all their knowledge of stones in vain,
Tho' these stones have far more differences in colour, shape and
   size
         Than most men to my eyes—
Even those who develop precise conceptions to immense distances
         Out of these bleak surfaces.
All human culture is a Goliath to fall
To the least of these pebbles withal.
A certain weight will be added yet
To the arguments of even the most foolish
And all who speak glibly may rest assured
That to better their oratory they will have the whole earth
For a Demosthenean pebble to roll in their mouths.

I am enamoured of the desert at last,
The abode of supreme serenity is necessarily a desert.
My disposition is towards spiritual issues
Made inhumanly clear; I will have nothing interposed
Between my sensitiveness and the barren but beautiful reality;
The deadly clarity of this 'seeing of a hungry man'
Only traces of a fever passing over my vision
Will vary, troubling it indeed, but troubling it only
In such a way that it becomes for a moment
Superhumanly, menacingly clear—the reflection
Of a brightness through a burning crystal.
A culture demands leisure and leisure presupposes
A self-determined rhythm of life; the capacity for solitude
Is its test; by that the desert knows us.
It is not a question of escaping from life
But the reverse—a question of acquiring the power
To exercise the loneliness, the independence, of stones,
And that only comes from knowing that our function remains
However isolated we seem fundamental to life as theirs.

We have lost the grounds of our being,
We have not built on rock.
Thinking of all the higher zones
Confronting the spirit of man I know they are bare
Of all so-called culture as any stone here;
Not so much of all literature survives
As any wisp of scriota that thrives
On a rock—(interesting though it may seem to be
As de Bary's and Schwendener's discovery
Of the dual nature of lichens, the partnership,
Symbiosis, of a particular fungus and particular alga).
These bare stones bring me straight back to reality.
I grasp one of them and I have in my grip
The beginning and the end of the world,
My own self, and as before I never saw
The empty hand of my brother man,
The humanity no culture has reached, the mob.
Intelligentsia, our impossible and imperative job!

'Ah!' you say, 'if only one of these stones would move
—Were it only an inch—of its own accord
This is the resurrection we await,
—The stone rolled away from the tomb of the Lord.
I know there is no weight in infinite space
No impermeability in infinite time,
But it is as difficult to understand and have patience here
As to know that the sublime
Is theirs no less than ours, no less confined
To men than men's to a few men, the stars of their kind.'
(The masses too have begged bread from stones,
From human stones, including themselves,
And only got it, not from their fellow-men,
But from stones such as these here—if then.)
Detached intellectuals, not one stone will move,
Not the least of them, not a fraction of an inch. It is not
The reality of life that is hard to know.
It is nearest of all and easiest to grasp,
But you must participate in it to proclaim it.
—I lift a stone; it is the meaning of life I clasp
Which is death, for that is the meaning of death;
How else does any man yet participate

In the life of a stone,
How else can any man yet become
Sufficiently at one with creation, sufficiently alone,
Till as the stone that covers him he lies dumb
And the stone at the mouth of his grave is not overthrown?
—Each of these stones on this raised beach,
Every stone in the world,
Covers infinite death, beyond the reach
Of the dead it hides; and cannot be hurled
Aside yet to let any of them come forth, as love
Once made a stone move
(Though I do not depend on that
My case to prove).
So let us beware of death; the stones will have
Their revenge; we have lost all approach to them,
But soon we shall become as those we have betrayed,
And they will seal us as fast in our graves
As our indifference and ignorance seals them;
But let us not be afraid to die.
No heavier and colder and quieter then,
No more motionless, do stones lie
In death than in life to all men.
It is no more difficult in death than here
—Though slow as the stones the powers develop
To rise from the grave—to get a life worth having;
And in death—unlike life—we lose nothing that is truly ours.

Diallage of the world's debate, end of the long auxesis,
Although no ébrillade of Pegasus can here avail,
I prefer your enchorial characters—the futhore of the future—
To the hieroglyphics of all the other forms of Nature.
Song, your apprentice encrinite, seems to sweep
The Heavens with a last entrochal movement;
And, with the same word that began it, closes
Earth's vast epanadiplosis.

With the Herring Fishers

'I see herrin'.'—I hear the glad cry
And 'gainst the moon see ilka blue jowl
In turn as the fishermen haul on the nets
And sing: 'Come, shove in your heids and growl.

'Soom on, bonnie herrin', soom on,' they shout,
Or 'Come in, O come in, and see me,'
'Come gie the auld man something to dae.
It'll be a braw change frae the sea.'

O it's ane o' the bonniest sichts in the warld
To watch the herrin' come walkin' on board
In the wee sma' 'oors o' a simmer's mornin'
As if o' their ain accord.

For this is the way that God sees life,
The haill jing-bang o's appearin'
Up owre frae the edge o' naethingness
—It's his happy cries I'm hearin'.

'Left, right—O come in and see me',
Reid and yellow and black and white
Toddlin' up into Heaven thegither
At peep o' day frae the endless night.

'I see herrin',' I hear his glad cry,
And 'gainst the moon see his muckle blue jowl,
As he handles buoy-tow and bush-raip
Singin': 'Come, shove in your heids and growl!'

---

ilka, every   soom, swim   dae, do   braw, fine
wee sma' 'oors, the early hours   simmer, summer
haill jing-bang o's, the whole collection of us   thegither, together
buoy-tow, buoy rope   bush-raip, rope attached to net

Mirror Fugue

Whiles I've seen a wheen gulls
Seem to equal the croods
O' the white waves by joinin'
Hands wi' the cloods,
Till atween them they've made
   A complete and clear
Heavenly facsimile
O' the hydrosphere
   —Till the shapes in the lift
   And the seas' wild smother
   Seemed baith to mak'
   And to mirror each other.

But my thochts that gang questin'
   Abune the haill earth
Whiles fly where there's naething
   To eke oot their dearth.
   They are to the laigh then
Like the stars or the sun
Where ony reflection's
Confined to the one
   —They are to the Earth
   Like licht, or its lack,
   Earth maun tak' as it gets
   And no' answer back.

And they are to the heich
   —Wha can tell what they are?
Or chart the diplomacy
   O' star upon star?
For the Earth is a star
As weel as the neist
Tho' few are alive
To the fact in the least
   —And for a' I can ken
   My fremt notions may be
   Hand in glove wi' a' else
   In ways kittle to see.

---

wheen, few   laigh, low   heich, high   neist, next   fremt, isolated
kittle, difficult

Ostentatiously tho' the gulls
Wi' the cloods dado up
I'm content to establish
A mair gingerly grup.
As wi' flash upon flash
O' sheet-lichtnin' in space
The relation atween them
Is whiles ill to trace.
  Sae wi' thocht upon thocht
  There's a structure nae doot,
  But I'm blithe in the meantime
  Juist to hae them glint oot.

Aye, wi' thocht upon thocht,
Like the wild-fire playin'
My richt hand needna ken
What my left hand's da'en.
Tho' the seas' wud marble
In a mackerel lift's glassed
Through the hollow globe flaughts
Frae ootside it are cast
  Flames fickler to partner
  Than the gulls and the cirrus.
  But the cutchack can wait
  While the gleids still bewhirr us.

For the queerest sensation
Intriguin' the air
A' agog for the former
Is there—and no' there.
The queerest sensation
Intriguin' the air
Kyths kir as a rabbit.
And whuds through a gair.

Glory on the water and grace in the welkin
But how sall I follow this flicker away,
Why follow, how fail, this fey flicker there,

---

grup, grip   da'en, doing   wud, mad   lift, sky   flaughts, flames
cutchack, clearest part of a fire   gleids, sparks   bewhirr, whirl about
kyths, appears   kir, wanton   whuds, dashes   gair, green patch

This faint flicker where,
Wi' my wingbeats biddin' good-bye to the gulls,
To the sea, and the sun, and a' the laigh?

Harry Semen

I ken these islands each inhabited
Forever by a single man
Livin' in his separate world as only
In dreams yet maist folk can.

Mine's like the moonwhite belly o' a hoo
Seen in the water as a fisher draws in his line.
I canna land it nor can it ever brak awa'.
It never moves, yet seems a' movement in the brine;
A movin' picture o' the spasm frae which I was born,
It writhes again, and back to it I'm willy-nilly torn.
A' men are similarly fixt; and the difference 'twixt
    The sae-ca'd sane and insane
Is that the latter whiles ha'e glimpses o't
    And the former nane.

Particle frae particle'll brak asunder,
Ilk ane o' them mair livid than the neist.
A separate life?—incredible war o' equal lichts,
Nane o' them wi' ocht in common in the least.
Nae threid o' a' the fabric o' my thocht
Is left alangside anither; a pack
O' leprous scuts o' weasels riddlin' a plaid
    Sic thrums could never mak.'
Hoo mony shades o' white gaed curvin' owre
To yon blae centre o' her belly's flower?
Milk-white, and dove-grey, wi' harebell veins.
Ae scar in fair hair like the sun in sunlicht lay,
And pelvic experience in a thin shadow line;
Thocht canna mairry thocht as sic saft shadows dae.

---

hoo, dogfish   sae-ca'd, so-called   ilk ane, each one   ocht, anything
sic thrums, ravelled loose threads   blae, ghastly

Grey ghastly commentaries on my puir life,
A' the sperm that's gane for naething rises up to dam
In sick-white onanism the single seed
Frae which in sheer irrelevance I cam.
What were the odds against me? Let me coont.
What worth am I to a' that micht ha'e been?
To a' the wasted slime I'm capable o'
Appeals this lurid emission, whirlin' lint-white and green.
Am I alane richt, solidified to life,
Disjoined frae a' this searin' like a white-het knife,
And vauntin' my alien accretions here,
Boastin' sanctions, purpose, sense the endless tide
I cam frae lacks—the tide I still sae often feed?
O bitter glitter; wet sheet and flowin' sea—and what
     beside?

Sae the bealin' continents lie upon the seas,
     Sprawlin' in shapeless shapes a' airts,
Like ony splash that ony man can mak'
     Frae his nose or throat or ither pairts,
Fantastic as ink through blottin'-paper rins.
But this is white, white like a flooerin' gean
Passin' frae white to purer shades o' white,
Ivory, crystal, diamond, till nae difference is seen
Between its fairest blossoms and the stars
Or the clear sun they melt into,
And the wind mixes them amang each ither
Forever, hue upon still mair dazzlin' hue.

Sae Joseph may ha'e pondered; sae a snawstorm
Comes whirlin' in grey sheets frae the shadowy sky
And only in a sma' circle are the separate flakes seen.
White, whiter, they cross and recross as capricious they fly,
Mak' patterns on the grund and weave into wreaths,
Load the bare boughs, and find lodgements in corners frae
The scourin' wind that sends a snawstorm up frae the earth
To meet that frae the sky, till which is which nae man can
     say.

---

bealin', festering   a' airts, all directions
flooerin' gean, flowering cherry tree

They melt in the waters. They fill the valleys. They scale
    the peaks.
There's a tinkle o' icicles. The topmaist summit shines oot.
Sae Joseph may ha'e pondered on the coiled fire in his seed,
The transformation in Mary, and seen Jesus tak' root.

From Ode to All Rebels

The angelic state to which I've attained
Disna lust for bluid and a bowler hat again
Or for onything else that men can ha'e.
I ken I canna be seen by men.
Maist things in the warld are like that they ken,
And maist folk fancy that they'll win tae
       To a similar state to mine noo
—Tho' they're no' in ony great hurry to,
And hing on for a' they are worth
To the empty things o' the earth.
They believe in ither things they canna see,
Then why should they no' believe in me
But presume to pick and choose atween
The things they themsel's ca' the unseen?
Nonsense? But dae they get as muckle fun
Frae my antics as frae theirs I've whiles won,
—Tho' angels lack humour and it's no' sae easy
To divert me noo as it used to be.
The haill warld's vanished like Kate and Jean
       As it had never been.
     I tell you it never existed
       And even if it had
I could never ha'e filed mysel' as I did
Wi' filthy life, and will again—no' me
But yon imbecile facsimile.
I want naething—naething.
Oot o' the mirror wi' that chowlin' face
Or I'll smash 't wi' my invisible wing!

---

bluid, blood   win tae, attain also   filed, filthied   chowlin', mournful

Come test my een. I tell you there's nocht,
There's naebody alive or can be, on this plane.
Measure my een. They're as guid as yours.
Average een and fell like your ain.
No' sea-green een, but a common colour
Yet they can see naething you say you see.
I dinna believe it exists ava',
And I'm shair you canna prove it to me.
The self-same een, but a different world
And you canna imagine what my een see.
If I tried to tell, it would seem to you
—I'm content that it should—sheer idiocy,
While, if I believed a' you believe in was,
And you tried to describe it I'd feel still mair
Something I was time oot o' mind mowed
As 'twere my ain foetus hauntin' me there,
Blether nae mair aboot justice and crime,
Guid and ill, life and daith, man and wumman, God and man.
My een are as guid as yours and see nocht
O' ony o' these—fegs, shairly you can
Credit your ain een withoot needin' me
To see the same things in order to see.
Besides, you've the rest o' humanity.
Needin' me to a' that's puir testimony.
I tell you my een are the marrows o' yours
But mine canna see the truth and yours can
—Or is't the ither way roond?—and that's juist
The essence o' a' that can be ca'd God's plan.
Wi' nae fairness or reason as you will agree.
Wha sae wanton as that but God can be?
There's only a'e thing that you maun see
And that's—that there's nae necessity,
   And that the essence o' a' law
    Is that there is nae law ava'.
Twirp, think what you like, but let me be.

---

fell, greatly ava', at all mowed, violated blether, talk nonsense
puir, poor marrows, equals a'e, one single

I'd be better deid? Nae doot! Wha wadna?
      A' the Christians think they will
      Or think or say they dae
      But, in a sort o' way,
Maist o' them keep on livin' still.
But I've deed a wheen times noo and ken
It'll no help maitters to dae't again.
Besides there's nae ither way
O' deein' than the ways they ha'e.
If I could think o' a completely new kind
O' daith, to try't aince I michtna mind.
Puir Judas—wrangly—thocht it worth a hang.
Frae a *nouveau riche* what mair could you hope?

But, in this alien form, to keep livin' amang
Self-styled life gie's my funny gifts mair scope.
Why d'ye no' kill me? You canna. That's why,
Aye roond the neist corner in wait I lie.
For my quarrel is endless and winna dee.
      My quarrel is endless and no' wi' you
      Or wi' onybody or ocht else noo,
      Or that ever can be, in view,
And nocht can dae ocht wi' a man like me.
My interests are foreign to history,
      And still mair foreign to hope.

For oot o' naething what beauty arises
We poets ken—if we dinna ken hoo—
Wha only the impossible pursue
(A' else comes to us owre easily
Needin' nae pursuit—oor job's to keep free)
Till naething suddenly surprises
—Seize the vision, my spirit, seize it, mak' haste!—
Wi' $\tau\iota\ \tau\iota\mu\iota\omega\tau\alpha\tau\upsilon$, wi' 'what maitters maist,'
What else unmisnamed can you stand for, rebels?
      (Leave a' that to MacDonald; he'll manage the lot.
      I'm certain o' that—I was aince a Scot.)
And why, oh why, on onything else waste
A quiver o' the precious strength that alane

---

dae, do   deed, died   wheen, number of   neist, next   ocht, anything
hoo, how

Can live in the void that by that's whiles graced?
The revolutionary spirit's ane wi' spirit itsel'!
    Let a'thing else gang to Hell.
        Responsibility's a fearsome load
          Nae man can bear.
          Rebels, try nae mair.
          Be as irresponsible as God.
(The Baccarat scandal was bad eneuch
But to see the King o' Kings cheatin'—wheuch!)
The advice I gi'e you is simply this:
Keep oot o' a' else except the abyss.
Rive Joy oot o' Terror's clenched neive,
Gie't a'e look, syne back again heave.
You'll no' see it twice. The Beauty that's won
Frae Terror's aye something new under the sun.

Blindin' licht is waur than the dark.
Cataclysm in the mirror. What's that I see?
I heard reason shriek and saw her flee
        Through the weiks o' my e'e
        And kent it was me.
(It was bound to be. The fact can be proved
For the simple reason that I hadna moved.)
She was richt! It is. But I ken vera weel
Nae man can believe that anither can don
Sic impossible lustres as yon.
I am poured oot like water and a' my banes are oot o' joint.
My hert is like wax; it's melted in the midst o' my bowels.
Yon boat, the sun, I aince burnt ahint me
Had never a lowe like this ava';
But as the lourd earth is the same alow
Tho' insubstantialised in the sunshine
I see the slack mooth and gogglin' een
Ahint this glory and ken them for mine
Nor if I could wad I tine for a meenut
Divine in human or human in divine.

---

whiles, sometimes   eneuch, enough
wheuch, expression of disgust   rive, tear   neive, fist
waur, worse   weiks, corners   lowe, flame   lourd, heavy   tine, lose

O dooble vision fechtin' in the glass!
Noo licht blots oot sic last distinctions o' class.
O magical change. O miracle.
I am suddenly beyond mysel'.
Reid, white, and square.
Tearin' the soul to rags.
Folk recognise—wi' regret it may be—
Man's kinship wi' the maist laithsome brute
Jogglin' his protrudin' sternum there
And lettin' his animal noises oot.
A' they can ha'e patience wi',
A' they can pity,
A' they can hide in their madhouses,
In their gaols and hospital wards,
Fat herts, lourd lugs, shut een,
A' that's badly, malformed, obscene,
Mankind accepts and guards;
But when an angel kyths, a man
Infinitely superior to man, as here,
Frae a man nae better than ither men,
An idiot like them, they howl wi' fear,
Or perjure their sicht, and gibe and jeer
And deny that the like can ever appear,
Let alane be ane wi' the ither.

It's against a' sense and what's the use
O' decency, worship, a shepherded soul,
If a cratur like this can suddenly emerge?
—Regairdless o' a' that maist men can thole,
Yet visibly dowered wi' the licht o' lichts,
The glory o' God he shows yet denies,
When even if they tried like vices themsel's
Instead o' the wisdom and virtues they prize
Nane o' them, no' even the maist reverend and upright,
'Ud ever be transfigured in similar wise.
God s'ud consult wi' the King or the Kirk
Or get the medical profession to advise,

---

maist laithsome, most loathsome   jogglin', lurching
lourd lugs, heavy ears   kyths, appears   cratur, creature   thole, endure

No' act in sic an irrational way
In decidin' on wha he glorifies
And no'—as owre often—let scallywags,
Topers and lechers, win sic a prize.
Wi' a' due respect we'll no' follow his lead.
Mankind at least maun aye keep its heid.
The wise are confounded; calculations upset,
Law set at naught, and order contemned.
—O the Angel o' Daith is covered wi' een
But I stand in a guise still mair terribly gemmed.
—I think you are richt.
Culture's leadin' to the extinction o' Man.
   What? Stop the culture?
    That's no' my plan.
   I am Ishmael, the only man,
    Wha's the freend o' a' men.
  (And wha has ever been certain o' ocht
   Here recognises certainty's voice again.)
   I tell you a' else is vain.
  Eden's wide-open, unchanged; and nocht shuts us
    frae 't
   But impious delusions o' oor ain.

Skald's Death

 I have known all the storms that roll.
 I have been a singer after the fashion
 Of my people—a poet of passion.
   All that is past.
 Quiet has come into my soul.
 Life's tempest is done.
   I lie at last
 A bird cliff under a midnight sun.

From *Second Hymn to Lenin*
(1935)

Second Hymn to Lenin

Ah, Lenin, you were richt. But I'm a poet
(And you c'ud mak allowances for that!)
Aimin' at mair than you aimed at
Tho' yours comes first, I know it.

An unexamined life is no' worth ha'in'.
Yet Burke was richt; owre muckle concern
Wi' Life's foundations is a sure
Sign o' decay; tho' Joyce in turn

Is richt, and the principal question
Aboot a work o' art is frae hoo deep
A life it springs—and syne hoo faur
Up frae't it has the poo'er to leap.

And hoo muckle it lifts up wi' it
Into the sunlicht like a saumon there,
Universal Spring! For Morand's richt—
It s'ud be like licht in the air—

Are my poems spoken in the factories and fields,
    In the streets o' the toon?
Gin they're no, then I'm failin' to dae
    What I ocht to ha' dune.

Gin I canna win through to the man in the street,
    The wife by the hearth,
A' the cleverness on earth 'll no' mak' up
    For the damnable dearth.

Haud on, haud on; what poet's dune that?
    Is Shakespeare read,
Or Dante or Milton or Goethe or Burns?
    —You heard what I said.

—A means o' world locomotion,
The maist perfected and aerial o' a'.
Lenin's name's gane owre the haill earth,
But the names o' the ithers?—Ha!

---

ha'in', having

What hidie-hole o' the vineyard d'they scart
Wi' minds like the look on a hen's face,
Morand, Joyce, Burke, and the rest
That e'er wrote; me noo in like case?

Great poets hardly onybody kens o'?
Geniuses like a man talkin' t'm sel'?
Nonsense! They're nocht o' the sort
Their character's easy to tell.

They're nocht but romantic rebels
Strikin' dilettante poses;
Trotsky—Christ, no' wi' a croon o' thorns
But a wreath o' paper roses.

A' that's great is free and expansive.
What ha' they expanded tae?
They've affected nocht but a fringe
O' mankind in ony way.

Barbarian saviour o' civilization
Hoo weel ye kent (we're owre dull witted)
Naething is dune save as we ha'e
Means to en's transparently fitted.

Poetry like politics maun cut
The cackle and pursue real ends,
Unerringly as Lenin, and to that
Its nature better tends.

Wi' Lenin's vision equal poet's gift
And what unparalleled force was there!
Nocht in a' literature wi' that
Begins to compare.

Nae simple rhymes for silly folk
But the haill art, as Lenin gied
Nae Marx-without tears to workin' men
But the fu' course insteed.

Organic constructional work,
Practicality, and work by degrees;

---

scart, scratch at   t'm sel', to himself

First things first; and poetry in turn
'Ll be built by these.

You saw it faur off when you thocht
O' mass-education yet.
Hoo lang till they rise to Pushkin?
And that's but a fit!

Oh, it's nonsense, nonsense, nonsense,
Nonsense at this time o' day
That breid-and-butter problems
S'ud be in ony man's way.

They s'ud be like the tails we tint
On leavin' the monkey stage;
A' maist folk fash aboot's alike
Primaeval to oor age.

We're grown ups that haena yet
Put bairnly things aside
—A' that's material and moral—
And oor new state descried.

Sport, love, and parentage,
Trade, politics, and law
S'ud be nae mair to us than braith
We hardly ken we draw.

Freein' oor poo'ers for greater things,
And fegs there's plenty o' them,
Tho' wha's still trammelt in alow
Canna be tenty o' them—

In the meantime Montéhus' sangs—
But as you were ready to tine
The Russian Revolution to the German
Gin that ser'd better syne,

---

fit, foot   tint, lost   fash, bother   bairnly, childish   fegs, faith   alow, below
tenty, mindful   tine, lose

Or foresaw that Russia maun lead
The workers' cause, and then
Pass the lead elsewhere, and aiblins
Fa' faur backward again,

Sae here, twixt poetry and politics,
There's nae doot in the en'.
Poetry includes that and s'ud be
The greatest poo'er amang men.

—It's the greatest, *in posse* at least,
That men ha'e discovered yet
Tho' nae doot they're unconscious still
O' ithers faur greater than it.

You confined yoursel' to your work
—A step at a time;
But, as the loon is in the man,
That'll be ta'en up i' the rhyme,

Ta'en up like a pool in the sands
Aince the tide rows in,
When life opens its hert and sings
Withoot scruple or sin.

Your knowledge in your ain sphere
Was exact and complete
But your sphere's elementary and sune by
As a poet maun see't.

For a poet maun see in a'thing,
Ev'n what looks trumpery or horrid,
A subject equal to ony
—A star for the forehead!

A poet has nae choice left
Betwixt Beaverbrook, say, and God.
Jimmy Thomas or you,
A cat, carnation, or clod.

He daurna turn awa' frae ocht
For a single act o' neglect

---

aiblins, perhaps   loon, boy   rows, rolls   sune by, soon past
daurna, dare not

And straucht he may fa' frae grace
And be void o' effect.

Disinterestedness,
Oor profoundest word yet,
But how far yont even that
The sense o' onything's set!

The inward necessity yont
Ony laws o' cause
The intellect conceives
That a'thing has!

Freend, foe; past, present, future;
Success, failure; joy, fear;
Life, Death; and a'thing else,
For us, are equal here.

Male, female; quick or deid,
Let us fike nae mair;
The deep line o' cleavage
Disna lie there.

Black in the pit the miner is,
The shepherd reid on the hill,
And I'm wi' them baith until
The end of mankind, I wis.

Whatever their jobs a' men are ane
In life, and syne in daith
(Tho' it's sma' patience I can ha'e
Wi' life's ideas o' that by the way)
And he's nae poet but kens it, faith,
And ony job but the hardest's ta'en.

The sailor gangs owre the curve o' the sea,
The housewife's thrang in the wash-tub,
And whatna rhyme can I find but hub
And what else can poetry be?

The core o' a' activity,
Changin't in accordance wi'
Its inward necessity
And mede o' integrity.

---

straucht, immediately   fike, trouble   wis, know

Unremittin', relentless,
Organized to the last degree,
Ah Lenin, politics is bairns' play
To what this maun be!

On the Ocean Floor

Now more and more on my concern with the lifted
        waves of genius gaining
I am aware of the lightless depths that beneath them lie;
And as one who hears their tiny shells incessantly raining
On the ocean floor as the foraminifera die.

O Ease My Spirit

*And as for their appearances they had one likeness as if a
wheel had been in the midst of a wheel.*
                            Ezekiel

O ease my spirit increasingly of the load
Of my personal limitations and the riddling differences
Between man and man with a more constant insight
Into the fundamental similarity of all activities.

And quicken me to the gloriously and terribly illuminating
Integration of the physical and the spiritual till I feel how easily
I could put my hand gently on the whole round world
As on my sweetheart's head and draw it to me.

bairns', children's

Light and Shadow

Like memories of what cannot be
Within the reign of memory . . .
That shake our mortal frames to dust.
            Shelley

On every thought I have the countless shadows fall
Of other thoughts as valid that I cannot have;
Cross-lights of errors, too, impossible to me,
Yet somehow truer than all these thoughts, being with
    more power aglow.

May I never lose these shadowy glimpses of unknown thoughts
That modify and minify my own, and never fail
To keep some shining sense of the way all thoughts at last
Before life's dawning meaning like the stars at sunrise pale.

Lo! A Child is Born

I thought of a house where the stones seemed suddenly changed
And became instinct with hope, hope as solid as themselves,
And the atmosphere warm with that lovely heat,
The warmth of tenderness and longing souls, the smiling anxiety
That rules a home where a child is about to be born.
The walls were full of ears. All voices were lowered.
Only the mother had the right to groan or complain.
Then I thought of the whole world. Who cares for its travail
And seeks to encompass it in like lovingkindness and peace?
There is a monstrous din of the sterile who contribute nothing
To the great end in view, and the future fumbles,
A bad birth, not like the child in that gracious home
Heard in the quietness turning in its mother's womb
A strategic mind already, seeking the best way
To present himself to life, and at last, resolved,
Springing into history quivering like a fish,
Dropping into the world like a ripe fruit in due time—
But where is the Past to which Time, smiling through her tears
At her new-born son, can turn crying: 'I love you'?

In the Slums of Glasgow

I have caught a glimpse of the seamless garment
And am blind to all else for evermore.
The immaculate vesture, the innermost shift,
   Of high and low, of rich and poor,
The glorious raiment of bridegroom and bride,
   Whoremonger and whore,
I have caught a glimpse of the seamless garment
And have eyes for aught else no more.

Deep under the γνῶθι σεαυτον of Thales I've seen
The Hindu Atmānam ātmanā pāsya, and far deeper still
In every man, woman, and child in Scotland even
The inseparable inherent cause, the inalienable thrill
The subtle movement, the gleam, the hidden well-water,
All the lin-gāni of their souls, God's holy will.
As a shining light needs no other light to be seen
The soul is only known by the soul or knows anything still.

It was easier to do this in the slums, as who prefers
A white-faced lass—because the eyes show better, so.
Life is more naked there, more distinct from mind,
Material goods and all the other extraneous things that grow
Hardening over and hiding the sheer life. Behind speech, mind and
   will
Behind sensation, reflection, knowledge, and power —lo!
Life, to which all these are attached as the spokes of a wheel to the
   nave;
The immensity abiding in its own glory of which I have caught the
   glow.

The same earth produces diamonds, rock-crystal, and vermilion,
The same sun produces all sorts of plants, the same food
Is converted into hair, nails and many other forms.
These dogmas are not as I once thought true nor as afterwards false
But each the empty shadow of an intimate personal mood.
I am indifferent to shadows, possessing the substance now.
I too look on the world and behold it is good.

I am deluded by appearances no more—I have seen
The goodness, passion, and darkness from which all things spring,
Identical and abundant in the slums as everywhere else

Taking other forms—to which changing and meaningless names
    cling,—
But cancelling out at last, dissolving, vanishing,
  Like the stars before the rising sun.
Foam, waves, billows and bubbles are not different from the sea,
But riding the bright heavens or to the dark roots of earth sinking
Water is multiform, indivisible and one,
Not to be confused with any of the shapes it is taking.

I have not gained a single definite belief that can be put
In a scientific formula or hardened into a religious creed.
A conversion is not, as mostly thought, a turning towards a belief.
It is rather a turning round, a revolution indeed.
It has no primary reference to any external object.
It took place in me at last with lightning speed.

I suddenly walk in light, my feet are barely touching the ground,
I am free of a million words and forms I no longer need.
In becoming one with itself my spirit is one with the world.
The dull, aching tension is gone, all hostility and dread.
All opposing psychic tendencies are resolved in sweet song
My eyes discard all idle shows and dwell instead
In my intercourse with every man and woman I know
On the openings and shuttings of eyes, the motions of mind, and,
    especially, life, and are led
Beyond colour, savour, odour, tangibility, numbers, extensions,
Individuality, conjunction, disjunction, priority, posteriority—like
    an arrow sped,
And sheer through intellection, volition, desire, aversion,
Pleasure, pain, merit and demerit—to the fountain-head,
To the unproduced, unproducing, solitary, motionless soul
By which alone they can be known, by which alone we are not
    misled.

I have seen this abhyasa most clearly in the folk of these slums,
Even as I have known the selfless indefatigable love of a mother
Concerned only for the highest possible vitality of her children,
Leaving their lives free to them, not seeking to smother
Any jet of their spirits in her own preconceptions or wishes.—
Would such were the love of every one of us for each other!
I have seen this abhyasa most clearly in the folk of these slums
Even as I know how every one of the women there,

Irrespective of all questions of intelligence, good looks, fortune's
    favour,
Can give some buck-navvy or sneak-thief the joy beyond compare—
Naked, open as to destitution and death, to the unprudential
Guideless life-in-death of the ecstasy they share—
Eternity, as Boethius defined it,—though few lovers give it his
    terms—
'To hold and possess the whole fulness of life anywhere
In a moment; here and now, past, present and to come.'—
The bliss of God glorifying every squalid lair.

The sin against the Holy Ghost is to fetter or clog
The free impulse of life—to weaken or cloud
The glad wells of being—to apply the other tests,
To say that there pure founts must be hampered, controlled,
Denied, adulterated, diluted, cowed,
The wave of omnipotence made recede, and all these lives, these
    lovers,
Lapse into cannon-fodder, sub-humanity, the despised slum-crowd.

I am filled forever with a glorious awareness
Of the inner radiance, the mystery of the hidden light in these dens,
I see it glimmering like a great white-sailed ship
Bearing into Scotland from Eternity's immense,
Or like a wild swan resting a moment in mid-flood.
It has the air of a winged victory, in suspense
By its own volition in its imperious way.
As if the heavens opened I gather its stupendous sense.

For here too, Philosophy has a royal and ancient seat,
And, holding an eternal citadel of light and immortality,
With Study her only comrade, sets her victorious foot
On the withering flower of the fast ageing world.—Let all men see.
Now the babel of Glasgow dies away in our ears,
The great heart of Glasgow is sinking to rest,
Na nonanunno nunnono nana nananana nanu,
Nunno nunnonanunneno nanena nunnanunnanut.
We lie cheek to cheek in a quiet trance, the moon itself no more
    still.
There is no movement but your eyelashes fluttering against me,
And the fading sound of the work-a-day world.
Dadadoduddadaddadi dadadodudadidadoh,
Duddadam dadade dudde dadadadadadodadah.

The Storm-Cock's Song

My song today is the storm-cock's song.
When the cold winds blow and the driving snow
Hides the tree-tops, only his song rings out
In the lulls in the storm. So let mine go!

On the topmost twig of a leafless ash
He sits bolt upright against the sky
Surveying the white fields and the leafless woods
And distant red in the East with his buoyant eye.

Surely he has little enough cause to sing
When even the hedgerow berries are already pulped by
    the frost
Or eaten by other birds—yet alone and aloft
To another hungry day his greeting is tossed.

Blessed are those who have songs to sing
When others are silent; poor song though it be,
Just a message to the silence that someone is still
Alive and glad, though on a naked tree.

What if it is only a few churning notes
Flung out in a loud and artless way?
His 'Will I do it? Do it I will!' is worth a lot
When the rest have nothing at all to say.

From *The Islands of Scotland*
(1939)

Island Funeral

The procession winds like a little snake
Between the walls of irregular grey stones
Piled carelessly on one another.
Sometimes, on this winding track,
The leaders are doubled back
Quite near to us.

It is a grey world, sea and sky
Are colourless as the grey stones,
And the small fields are hidden by the walls
That fence them on every side.

Seen in perspective, the walls
Overlap each other
As far as the skyline on the hill,
Hiding every blade of grass between them,
So that all the island appears
One jumble of grey boulders.
The last grey wall outlined on the sky
Has the traceried effect
Of a hedge of thorns in winter.

The men in the stiff material
Of their homespun clothes
Look like figures cut from cardboard,
But shod in their rawhide rivelins
They walk with the springing step of mountaineers.
The women wear black shawls,
And black or crimson shirts.

A line of tawny seaweed fringes the bay
Between high-water mark and low.
It is luminous between the grey of rocky shore
And the grey of sullen water.

We can now and then look over a wall
Into some tiny field. Many of these
Are nothing but grey slabs of limestone,
Smooth as any pavement,
With a few blades of grass
Struggling up through the fissures,

And the grey surface of that rock
Catches and holds the light
As if it was water lying there.

At last the long line halts and breaks up,
And, like a stream flowing into a loch,
The crowd pours from the narrow lane
Into the cemetery where on an unfenced sandhill
The grey memorial stones of the island
Have no distinction from the country.
The coffin lies tilted a little sideways
On the dark grey sand flung up from the grave.

A little priest arrives; he has a long body and short legs
And wears bicycle clips on his trousers.
He stands at the head of the grave
And casts a narrow purple ribbon round his neck
And begins without delay to read the Latin prayers
As if they were a string of beads.
Twice the dead woman's son hands him a bottle
And twice he sprinkles the coffin and the grave
With holy water. In all the faces gathered round
There is a strange remoteness.
They are weather-beaten people with eyes grown clear,
Like the eyes of travellers and seamen,
From always watching far horizons.
But there is another legend written on these faces,
A shadow—or a light—of spiritual vision
That will seldom find full play
On the features of country folk
Or men of strenuous action.
Among these mourners are believers and unbelievers,
And many of them steer a middle course,
Being now priest-ridden by convention
And pagan by conviction,
But not one of them betrays a sign
Of facile and self-lulling piety,
Nor can one see on any face
'A sure and certain hope
Of the Resurrection to eternal life.'
This burial is just an act of nature,
A reassertion of the islanders' inborn certainty

That 'in the midst of life we are in death.'
It is unlike the appointed funerals of the mainland
With their bitter pageantry
And the ramp of undertakers and insurance companies
That makes death seem incredible and cruel.
There are no loafing onlookers.
Everyone is immediately concerned
In what is taking place.
All through their lives death has been very close to them,
And this funeral of one who had been 'a grand woman'
Seems to be but a reminder
Of the close comradeship between living and dying.

Down in the bay there is a row of curraghs
Drawn up on the sand. They lie keel upwards,
Each one shining black and smooth
Like some great monster of the sea,
Symbols to the island folk of their age-long
Battle with the waves, a battle where in daily life
The men face death and the women widowhood.

Four men fill in the grave with dark grey sand,
Then they cover the sand
With green sods and rough-hewn boulders,
And finally an old man with a yellow beard
Helps the four young gravediggers
In levering a great slab of stone
Until it lies flat upon the grave,
And the people watch all this in silence.
Then the crowd scatters east and west
And, last, the four gravediggers,
All of them laughing now
With the merriment of clowns.

There are few and fewer people
On the island nowadays,
And there are more ruins of old cottages
Than occupied homes.
I love to go into these little houses
And see and touch the pieces of furniture.
I know all there is to know
About their traditional plenishing

And native arts and crafts,
And can speak with authority
About tongue-and-groove cleats,
The lipped drawer, and the diameters of finials.
But I know them also in their origin
Which is the Gaelic way of life
And can speak with equal authority
About a people one of whose proverbs
Is the remarkable sentence:
'Every force evolves a form.'
While this thing lasted
It was pure and very strong.
In an old island room the sense is still strong
Of being above and beyond the familiar,
The world as we know it,
In an atmosphere purified,
As it were, from the non-essentials of living
—An intangible feeling,
Difficult to describe,
But easy to recall to anyone
Who has stood in such a room
And been disturbed by the certainty
That those who once inhabited it
Were sure of every thought they had.

To enter almost any of the island rooms even today
Is to be profoundly conscious of this emanation,
At once so soothing and so strangely agitating.
Fifty years ago a visitor wrote: 'They are there to stay,
And that fact accounts for a great deal.
It is partial explanation of the contentment
On the faces of the island women.
It is a reason for the repose and settledness
Which pervade an island village
—That indefinable something,
So altogether unlike the life of ordinary villages,
And which you feel in the air,
And are conscious of by some instinct, as men claim
To be aware of the presence of spirits.
There is no restlessness,
Or fret of business,

Or anxiety about anything.
It is as if the work was done,
And it was one eternal afternoon.'
But they have not, in fact, stayed,
Foully forced out by their inferiors—
Red-faced, merely physical people
Whose only thought looking over
These incomparable landscapes
Is what sport they will yield
—How many deer and grouse.
The old stock are few and ever fewer now.
But they expected to stay,
And they deserved to stay,
Just as they expected there would always be
Thousands of them to work incessantly and serenely
At the making of objects which said:
'There is great beauty in harmony.'
They lived as much like one another as possible,
And they kept as free as they could of the world at large.
It is not their creed as such, however,
That explains them and the beauty of their work.

It is rather the happiness with which they held it,
The light-heartedness with which they enslaved themselves
To the various rituals it demanded,
And also the circumstance that they were all
Poor people—whose notions of form
Were both ancient and basic.
They began with the barest patterns, the purest beginnings
Of design, in their minds, and then
Something converted them into artists
With an exalted lyric gift.
What that something was
No one can claim perfectly to know.
Some of them were reported as believing
In assistance from the angels.
Whatever the source, the result was some
Of the most beautiful work the world has ever seen.

And even now, in Edinburgh or Glasgow or London,
I often move my ear up close
The better to distinguish in the raucous mixture

The sound of the cornet I want to hear,
And you may see my face light up
With recognition and appreciation at various points,
And hear me comment, 'The greatest of them all.'
The term is justified—this island note,
This clear old Gaelic sound,
In the chaos of the modern world,
Is like a phrase from Beiderbecke's cornet,
As beautiful as any phrase can be.
It is, in its loveliness and perfection,
Unique, as a phrase should be;
And it is ultimately indescribable.

Panassié speaks of it as 'full and powerful,'
But also as 'so fine
As to be almost transparent,'
And there is in fact
This extraordinary delicacy in strength.
He speaks of phrases that soar;
And this, too, is in fact
A remarkable and distinguishing quality.
Otis Ferguson speaks of 'the clear line
Of that music,' of 'every phrase
As fresh and glistening as creation itself,'
And there is in fact
This radiance, and simple joyousness.
These terms tell a great deal, but there remains
Much that eludes words completely
And can only be heard.
And though one can account for the music
Up to a certain point by the quality of the person
—The 'candour, force, personal soundness, good humour'—
There have been other people—and still are, no doubt—
With candour, force, personal soundness and good humour
And one has still to explain, as always,
How these qualities translated themselves
In this instance into such musical phrases.
In the din of our modern world
The Gaelic spirit plays merely
As an unfeatured member of well-known bands
—Which means that one hears it sometimes—very rarely!—

For a full chorus, sometimes merely for a phrase,
Sometimes only in the background with the rest of the brass.
But even the phrase detaches itself from its surroundings
As something exquisite and perfect; and even playing
Along with the others in the background
It stands out from them,
Not through any aggressiveness but solely
Through the distinctive quality of its style.
'The greatest of them all'—but
There is little life left on the island now,
And soon the last funeral
Will take place there,
And in the rowdy chaos of the world
The sound of this cornet will be heard no more
—One will listen and one's face will never
Light up with recognition and appreciation again.

Yet if the nature of the mind is determined
By that of the body, as I believe,
It follows that every type of human mind
Has existed an infinite number of times
And will do so. Materialism promises something
Hardly to be distinguished from eternal life.
Minds or souls with the properties I love
—The minds or souls of these old islanders—
Have existed during an eternal time in the past
And will exist for an eternal time in the future.
A time broken up of course
By enormous intervals of non-existence,
But an infinite time.
If one regards these personalities
As possessing some value
There is a certain satisfaction
In the thought that in eternity
They will be able to develop
In all possible environments
And to express themselves
In all the ways possible to them
—A logical deduction from thoroughgoing Materialism
And independent of the precise type

Of materialism developed.
It is quite unimportant whether we call
Our ultimate reality matter, electric charge,
Ψ-waves, mind-stuff, neural stuff, or what not,
Provided it obeys laws which can, in principle,
Be formulated mathematically.

The cornet solo of our Gaelic islands
Will sound out every now and again
Through all eternity.

I have heard it and am content for ever.

From *The Battle Continues*
(1957)

Major Road Ahead*

The workers of Spain have themselves become the Cid
    Campeador.
A name whose original meaning is 'to be in the field,
The pasture.'
It has the further meanings of
'To frisk in the field,'
And so 'to be in the field of battle,'
And, especially, 'to be prominent in the field of battle,'
And so it came to mean 'surpassing in bravery'
And, in the mouths of their detractors,
'Men of the field, yokels.'
The word went from mouth to mouth among the timorous
Who had no better defence than their irony;
It slipped glibly from lips unctuous with envy.
'We are men of the field,' they cried,
Catching the jesting word like a ball hard driven,
Accepting the nickname with pride,
And launching it into the firmament,
And on their lips
The jesting word assumed a dignity
And sparkled and shone and flashed
And became a blazon and a star.

Who was the first to say it?
No man can tell. None of them knew.
It found itself suddenly upon all lips.
Was it born from the earth?
Did it fall from the sky,
From stones and trees,
From the dust and the air,
It was born from everywhere
At the same time,
It filled all space like light.

The heart of Spain expanded at the name
And embraced the world.
The name rose up,

---

*Written soon after the end of the Spanish Civil War.

Rose up into space,
Was charged and condensed
And fell again in a heroic rain.
A flight of swallows flying overhead
Caught up the name on the wing
And carried it to all the corners of the world.
The swallows sang it as they flew
And Spain grew by leagues
As it heard the name.

So their name issued suddenly
From all the pores of the earth,
And found itself upon all tongues,
Singing like a tree in the sun.
It was born and grew and ascended into Heaven,
Multiplied and was one with the forests,
Invaded the plains, crossed the mountains,
Covered Spain, leapt the frontiers and seas,
Filled all Europe,
Burst the boundaries of the world,
And grew and ascended,
And stayed only at Hope's zenith.

History and geography
Were obsessed with the name.
To the north, to the south,
To the east, to the west,
It was borne by the wind like a rose.
It passed above all banners and all birds
With a noise like a thousand banners,
A thousand birds,
While, beneath, a multitude
Weeping for joy,
Followed its passage on their knees
—Millions of heads
Raised in a branch of offering.
That heroic name is an eagle's nest
On the highest peak of History,
Sending through History a surge of song.
And there it remains through all eternity
Nestling on the strings of a lute.

You come to me shining from beyond the bourne of death,
You come to me across life,
Over a wide sea beneath a sky of doves.
The tide of the battle surges upon the gleaming shore of
    your eyes.

Your eyes are two bas-reliefs of your glory.
Your hands are folded to offer up your heart.
Clothed in a comet,
You soar above Spain,
Above human history,
Into the infinite.

Your fury of love and faith
Planted four crosses to the wind
The garland of the four corners of the compass.
The hurricanes of God conjured you above your battles.
I saw you dedicate yourself
And arise out of your flesh
In a divine frenzy
Drawn up towards the infinite
In a mystic ecstasy,
A celestial drunkenness.

You are a tree which climbs and climbs
To bear up once more the Christ
Who came down to visit souls.
Bent over a flight of thunderbolts,
With your eyes fixed upon a journey,
Whither are you going?
In an immense sweep you soar resplendent
Up to the kingdom that is within yourself.
He who would now seek to follow the march of your
    thoughts
Would lose his reason in dismay,
Would go astray in abysses of vertigo.
There are no limits to your soul.
Whither are you going?
How can I follow you?

The courses of the seven planets
Are reflected in the mirror of your shield.

Go your ways, go your ways,
Leave your flesh behind and go your ways
Clad in Epic.
I will watch beside you
As you roam the spaces of the stars
Without form and void,
As you circle the ellipse of God
I will keep vigil at the foot of your memory.
Your heart leaves a wake of spreading deeds
And perhaps I can follow you with my eyes.

They are gone.
Before my eyes
Their sword gleams and twists in a sudden blaze
And sprouts wings—two great wings of fire and
    flaming feather.

The sword moves, it is lifted up,
It soars, soars above my head, above the world.
I hear a hecatomb of planets falling into chaos.
I hear windows opening in space.
I hear eternity rushing in my ears.
Where am I? What is happening to me?
A whirlpool of light sucks me into its centre
And I fall down, down, down . . .

I have returned to earth,
To Spain.
I have come back to myself.

They were the people of destiny.
Of destiny, not fate.
Destiny went tied to their saddle-bow,
Linked with them in some mysterious fashion.
I do not know why.
In the presence of the fact
There is nothing to do
But bow the head.
As in a pack of cards
There is one ace of trumps,
So it is the habit of life;
Suddenly there emerges a man, a people,
Who is life's ace of trumps.

They were people of more than genius or than talent.
They were people of electricity.
Genius may fail of inspiration,
Talent may fail in calculation,
But the electric man
Does not fail in current.
Higher than the inspiration of genius
And a nicety of calculation
Is the discharge of a high potency,
The current of irresisitible voltage,
Which a people can make pass
From one pole of the world to the other.

They were faith,
Ardour transfigured by faith,
The unconsciousness of faith,
The madness of faith which multiplies strength
And knows no possible barrier.
Wherever they passed there sprang behind their footprints
Mystic signs—I put it to the wisest
To reveal the mystery, to solve the problem.

The truth is that the problem has no solution.
They regarded themselves, they contemplated their work,
And they saw themselves escape from all laws
And enter into that region of the imponderable
Where things cannot be reduced to logic
So they were—and that was all about it.

Their bodies were a stupendous factory
Which manufactured the imponderable.
It was a factory
Which created the supernatural out of the natural,
Which created excess out of proportion,
Because all this factory worked
In the service of an exaltation
And this exaltation made them sublime
And made them illogical.

It was not logical that the Spanish workers should
    fight one against ten
Against World Fascism.—But so it was.
It was not logical that they should contend

Against superior numbers, superior armaments,
   superior civilisation.
But it was so. And in the end
It will be seen that they have won,
And are consubstantial with all that has ever really lived
And lives forever as part and parcel
Of the very meaning and purpose of life.
An imperishable honour to Man;
One of the great glories of human life,
At the greatest turning point in human history
When mankind was faced at last with the sign:
   MAJOR ROAD AHEAD.

The Battle continues.

For the spirit knows no compromise.

From *Lucky Poet* (1943)

From The Kind of Poetry I Want

A poetry full of erudition, expertise, and ecstasy
—The acrobatics and the faceted fly-like vision,
The transparency choke-full of hair-pin bends,
'Jacinth work of subtlest jewellery', poetry *à quatre épingles*—
(Till above every line we might imagine
A tensely flexible and complex curve
Representing the modulation,
Emphasis, and changing tone and tempo
Of the voice in reading;
The curve varying from line to line
And the lines playing subtly against one another
—A fineness and profundity of organization
Which is the condition of a variety great enough
To express all the world's,
As subtle and complete and tight
As the integration of the thousands of brush strokes
In a Cézanne canvas),
Alive as a bout of all-in wrestling,
With countless illustrations like my photograph of a Mourning
  Dove
Taken at a speed of 1/75,000 of a second.
A poetry that speaks 'of trees,
From the cedar tree that is in Lebanon
Even unto the hyssop that springeth out of the wall',
And speaks also 'of bests and of fowl,
And of creeping things and of fishes',
And needs, like Marya Sklodowska on her laboratory table,
For its open-eyed wonderment at the varied marvels of life,
Its insatiable curiosity about the mainspring,
Its appetite for the solution of problems,
Black fragments of pitch-blende from Saxony and Bohemia,
Greenish-blue chalcolite from Portugal and Tonkin,
Siskin-green uranium mica from France,
Canary-yellow veined carnotite from Utah,
Greenish-grey tjujamunite from Turkestan,
Pinkish-grey fergusonite from Norway,
Gold-tinted Australian monazite sand,
Greenish-black betafite from Madagascar,
And emerald-green tobernite from Indo-China.
And like my knowledge of, say, interlocking directorships,

Which goes far beyond such earlier landmarks
As the Pujo Committee's report
Or Louis Stanley's 'Spider Chart';
And everywhere without fear of Chestov's 'suddenly',
Never afraid to leap, and with the unanticipatedly
Limber florescence of fireworks as they expand
Into trees or bouquets with the abandon of 'unbroke horses'.
Or like a Beethovian semitonal modulation to a wildly remote
    key,
As in the Allegretto where that happens with a sudden jump of
    seven sharps,
And feels like the sunrise gilding the peak of the Dent Blanche
While the Arolla valley is still in cloud.
And constantly with the sort of grey-eyed gaiety
So many people feel exalted by being allowed to hear
But are unable to laugh at—as in the case of the don
Who, lecturing on the first Epistle to the Corinthians,
In a note on the uses of αλλα mentioned αλλα *precantis*,
Which an undergraduate took down as Allah *precantis*.
In photographic language, 'wide-angle' poems
Taking in the whole which explains the part,
Scientifically accurate, fully realized in all their details,
As Prudentius's picture of the gradually deputrifying Lazarus,
Or Baudelaire's of the naked mulatto woman,
Or Pope's most accurate particularities
In the Epistle to Lord Bathurst,
Or like a magic of grammar, a syntactical magic,
Of the relations of thought with thought whereby
By means of the syntax a whole world of ideas
Is miraculously concentrated into what is almost a point.
No mere passive hyperaesthesia to external impressions
Or exclusive absorption in a single sense,
But a many-sided active delight in the wholeness of things
And, therefore, paradoxically perhaps,
A poetry like an operating theatre,
Sparkling with a swift, deft energy,
Energy quiet and contained and fearfully alert,
In which the poet exists only as a nurse during an operation,
Who only exists to have a sponge ready when called for,
Wads of sterilized cotton wool—nothing else
Having the smallest meaning for her.

A poetry not for those who do not love a gaping pig,
Or those made mad if they behold a cat,
And least, those who, when the bagpipe sings i' the nose,
Cannot contain their urine.

The Glen of Silence

By this cold shuddering fit of fear
My heart divines a presence here,
Goddess or ghost yclept;
Wrecker of homes . . .

Where have I heard a silence before
Like this that only a lone bird's cries
And the sound of a brawling burn to-day
Serve in this wide empty glen but to emphasize?

Every doctor knows it—the stillness of foetal death,
The indescribable silence over the abdomen then!
A silence literally 'heard' because of the way
It stands out in the auscultation of the abdomen.

Here is an identical silence, picked out
By a bickering burn and a lone bird's wheeple
—The foetal death in this great 'cleared' glen
Where the *fear-tholladh nan tighem* has done his foul work
—The tragedy of an unevolved people.

---

fear-tholladh nan tighem, destroyer of homes

Direadh III

So, in the sudden sight of the sun, has man stopped, blinded,
paralysed and afraid?

I am reft to the innermost heart
Of my country now,
History's final verdict upon it,
The changeless element in all its change,
Reified like the woman I love.

Here in this simple place of clean rock and crystal water,
With something of the cold purity of ice in its appearance,
Inhuman and yet friendly,
Undecorated by nature or by man
And yet with a subtle and unchanging beauty
Which seems the antithesis of every form of art,

Here near the summit of Sgurr Alasdair
The air is very still and warm.

The Outer Isles look as though
They were cut out of black paper
And stuck on a brilliant silver background,
(Even as I have seen the snow-capped ridges of Hayes
    Peninsula
Stand out stark and clear in the pellucid Arctic atmosphere
Or, after a wild and foggy night, in the dawn
Seen the jagged line of the Tierra del Fuego cliffs
Looking for all the world as if they were cut out of tin,
Extending gaunt and desolate),
The western sea and sky undivided by horizon,
So dazzling is the sun
And its glass image in the sea.
The Cuillin peaks seem miniature
And nearer than is natural
And they move like liquid ripples
In the molten breath
Of the corries which divide them.
I light my pipe and the match burns steadily
Without the shielding of my hands,
The flame hardly visible in the intensity of light
Which drenches the mountain top.

I lie here like the cool and gracious greenery
Of the water-crowfoot leafage, streaming
In the roping crystalline currents,
And set all about on its upper surface
With flecks of snow blossom that, on closer looking,
Shows a dust of gold.
The blossoms are fragile to the touch
And yet possess such strength and elasticity
That they issue from the submergence of a long spate
Without appreciable hurt—indeed, the whole plant
Displays marvellous endurance in maintaining
A rooting during the raging winter torrents.
Our rivers would lose much if the snowy blossom
And green waving leafage of the water-crowfoot
Were absent—aye, and be barer of trout too!
And so it is with the treasures of the Gaelic genius
So little regarded in Scotland to-day.
Yet emerging unscathed from their long submergence,
Impregnably rooted in the most monstrous torrents★
—The cataracting centuries cannot rive them away—
And productive of endless practical good,
Even to people unaware of their existence,
In the most seemingly-unlikely connections.
I am possessed by this purity here
As in a welling of stainless water
Trembling and pure like a body of light
Are the webs of feathery weeds all waving,
Which it traverses with its deep threads of clearness
Like the chalcedony in moss agate
Starred here and there with grenouillette.

It is easy here to accept the fact
That that which the 'wisdom' of the past
And the standards of the complacent elderly rulers
Of most of the world to-day regard
As the most fixed and eternal verities—
The class state, the church,
The old-fashioned family and home,
Private property, rich and poor,

★ See John Ruskin's description of the spring at Carshalton.

'Human nature' (to-day meaning mainly
The private-profit motive), their own race,
Their Heaven and their 'immortal soul',
Is all patently evanescent,
Even as we know our fossil chemical accumulations
Of energy in coal, peat, oil, lignite and the rest
Are but ephemeral, a transitory blaze
Even on the small time-scale of civilized man,
And that running water, though eminently convenient and
    practicable
For the present, will give us a mere trickle
Of the energy we shall demand in the future.

And suddenly the flight of a bird reminds me
Of how I once went out towards sunset in a boat
Off the rocky coast of Wigtownshire
And of my glimpse of the first rock-pigeon I saw,
It darted across one of the steep gullies
At the bottom of which our boat lay rocking
On the dark green water—and vanished into safety
In a coign of the opposite wall
Before a shot could be fired.
It swerved in the air,
As though doubtful of its way,
Then with a glad swoop of certainty
It sped forward, turned upward,
And disappeared into some invisible cranny
Below the overhanging brow of the cliff.

There was such speed, such grace, such happy confidence
    of refuge in that swoop
That it struck me with the vividness of a personal experience.
For an instant I seemed to see into the bird's mind
And to thrill with its own exhilaration of assured safety.
Why should this be? It was as though
I had seen the same occurrence,
Or some part of it, before.

Then I knew. Into the back of my mind had come
The first line of the loveliest chorus in *Hippolytus*,
That in which the Troezenian women,
Sympathizing with the unhappy Phaedra,

Who is soon to die by her own hand,
Sing of their yearning to fly away from the palace
Whose sunny terraces are haunted by misery and
    impending doom.
They long to escape with the flight of the sea-birds
To the distant Adriatic and the cypress-fringed waters of
    Eridanus
Or to the fabulous Hesperides,
Where beside the dark-blue ocean
Grow the celestial apple-trees.
It is the same emotion as filled the Hebrew poet
Who cried: 'O for the wings of a dove,
That I might flee away and be at rest.'
'ἠλιβάτοις ὑπὸ χενθμῶσὶ γενοίμαν'.
The untranslatable word in that line
Is the ὑπὸ. It includes more
Than a single word of English can contain.
Up-in-under: so had the pigeon
Flown to its refuge in 'steep hiding places',
So must Euripides have seen a sea-bird
Dart to its nest in the cliffs of Attica.
For an instant, sitting in that swaying boat
Under the red rocks, while the sunset ebbed down the sky
And the water lapped quietly at my side,
I again felt the mind of the poet reaching out
Across the centuries to touch mine.
Scotland and China and Greece!
Here where the colours—
Red standing for heat,
Solar, sensual, spiritual;
Blue for cold—polar, bodily, intellectual;
Yellow luminous and embodied
In the most enduring and the brightest form in gold—
Remind me how about this
Pindar and Confucius agreed.
Confucius who was Pindar's contemporary
For nearly half a century!
And it was Pindar's 'golden snow'
My love and I climbed in that day!
I in Scotland as Pindar in Greece
Have stood and marvelled at the trees

And been seized with honey-sweet yearning for them;
And seen too mist condensing on an eagle,
His wings 'streamlined' for a swoop on a leveret,
As he ruffled up the brown feathers on his neck
In a quiver of excitement;
Pindar, greatest master of metaphor the world has seen,
His spirit so deeply in tune
With the many-sidedness of both Man and Nature
That he could see automatically all the basal resemblances
His metaphors imply and suggest.
Scotland and China and Greece!

So every loveliness Scotland has ever known,
Or will know, flies into me now,
Out of the perilous night of English stupidity,
As I lie brooding on the fact
That 'perchance the best chance
Of reproducing the ancient Greek temperament
Would be to "cross" the Scots with the Chinese.'*
The glory of Greece is imminent again to me here
With the complete justification his sense of it
In Germany—his participation in that great awakening
Taking the form of an imaginative reliving,
On behalf of his people, of the glory of Athens—
Lacked in Hölderlin. I see all things
In a cosmic or historical perspective too.
Love of country, in me, is love of a new order.
In Greece I also find the clue
To the mission of the poet
Who reveals to the people
The nature of their gods,
The instrument whereby his countrymen
Become conscious of the powers on whom they depend
And of whom they are the children,
Knowing, in himself, the urgency of the divine creativeness
    of Nature
And most responsive to its workings in the general world.
'Wer das Tiefste gedacht, liebt das Lebendigste.'
And remembering my earlier poems in Scots

---

* Sir Richard Livingstone.

Full of my awareness 'that language is one
Of the most cohesive or insulating of world forces
And that dialect is always a bond of union,'*
I covet the mystery of our Gaelic speech
In which *rughadh* was at once a blush,
A promontory, a headland, a cape,
Leadan, musical notes, litany, hair of the head,
And *fonn*, land, earth, delight, and a tune in music,†
And think of the Oriental provenance of the Scottish Gael,
The Eastern affiliations of his poetry and his music,
'... the subtler music, the clear light
Where time burns back about th' eternal embers',
And the fact that he initiated the idea of civilization
That to-day needs renewal at its native source
Where, indeed, it is finding it, since Georgia,
Stalin's native country, was also the first home of the Scots.

The Gaelic genius that is in this modern world
As sprays of quake grass are in a meadow,
Or light in the world, which notwithstanding
The *Fiat Lux* scores of thousands of years ago,
Is always scanty and dubious enough
And at best never shares the empery of the skies
On more than equal terms with the dark,
Or like sensitive spirits among the hordes of men,
Or seldom and shining as poetry itself.
Quake grass, the 'silver shakers', with their plumes
    shaped and corded
Like miniature cowrie shells, and wrapped
In bands of soft green and purple, and strung
(Now glittering like diamonds,
Now chocolate brown like partridge plumage)
On slender stems and branchlets, quick
To the slightest touch of air!

So Scotland darts into the towering wall of my heart
And finds refuge now. I give
My beloved peace, and her swoop has recalled
That first day when my human love and I,

---

* Sir James Crichton-Browne.
† Macfarlane's *English and Gaelic Vocabulary* (Constable, Edinburgh, 1815).

Warmed and exhilarated by the sunny air,
Put on our skis and began
A zigzag track up the steep ascent.
There was no sound but the faint hiss and crush
Of the close-packed snow, shifting under our weight.
The cloudless bowl of the sky
Burned a deep gentian. In the hushed, empty world,
Where nothing moved but ourselves,
Our bodies grew more consciously alive.
I felt each steady beat of my heart.
The drawing and holding of my breath
Took on a strange significance.
Nor was I merely conscious of myself.
I began to be equally aware of my love;
Her little physical habits
Sinking into my mind
Held the same importance as my own.

How fragrant, how infinitely refreshing and recreating
Is the mere thought of Deirdre!
How much more exhilarating to see her, as now!

'She said that she at eve for me would wait;
Yet here I see bright sunrise in the sky.'*

Farewell all else! I may not look upon the dead,
Nor with the breath of dying be defiled,
And thou, I see, art close upon that end.

I am with Alba—with Deirdre—now
As a lover is with his sweetheart when they know
That personal love has never been a willing and efficient
    slave
To the needs of reproduction, that to make
Considerations of reproduction dictate the expression of
    personal love
Not infrequently destroys the individual at his spiritual core,
Thus 'eugenic marriages' cannot as a whole
Be successful so far as the parents are concerned,
While to make personal love master over reproduction

---

* From a Chinese eight-line lyric, twenty-seven centuries old.

Under conditions of civilization is to degrade
The germ plasm of the future generations,
And to compromise between these two policies
Is to cripple both spirit and germ,
And accept the only solution—unyoke the two,
Sunder the fetters that from time immemorial
Have made them so nearly inseparable,
And let each go its own best way,
Fulfilling its already distinct function,
An emancipation the physical means for which
Are now known for the first time in history!

Let what can be shaken, be shaken,
And the unshakeable remain.
The Inaccessible Pinnacle★ is not inaccessible.
So does Alba surpass the warriors
As a graceful ash surpasses a thorn,
Or the deer who moves sprinkled with the dewfall
Is far above all other beasts
—Its horns glittering to Heaven itself.†

Edinburgh

Most of the denizens wheeze, sniffle, and
exude a sort of snozzling whnoff whnoff,
apparently through a hydrophile sponge.
                                    Ezra Pound

The capital of Scotland is called Auld Reekie,
Signifying a monstrous acquiescence
In the domination of the ends
By the evidences of effort.
—Not the mastery of matter
By the spirit of man
But, at best, a damnable draw,
A division of the honours

★ Of Sgurr Dearg, in Skye.
† See *Volsungakvida en forna*, 41 (Saemundar Edda, Jonsson).

And, far more, the dishonours!
—Dark symbol of a society
Of 'dog eat dog'.
Under which the people reveal themselves to the world
Completely naked in their own skin,
Like toads!
Yes, see, the dead snatch at the living here.
So the social corpse, the dead class,
The dead mode of life, the dead religion,
Have an after life as vampires.
They are not still in their graves
But return among us.
They rise with the fumes
From the chimney of the crematorium
And again settle down on the earth
And cover it with black filth.

To repossess ourselves of the primal power
'Let there be light' and apply it
In our new, how ever more complex, setting
Is all. And let us not cry
'Too difficult! Impossible!' forgetting
That the stupendous problems that obsess us to-day
Are as nothing to the problems overcome
By the miraculous achievements of men in the past
—Yes, the first problems in the very dawn of human history
Were infinitely greater, and our troubles are due
To the fact that we have largely lost
The earliest, the most essential,
The *distinctively human* power
Our early ancestors had in abundant measure
Whatever else they lacked that we possess.
Possess thanks to them!—and thanks to the primal
    indispensable power
They had and we have lost progressively
And affect to despise—
Fools who have lost the substance
And cling to the shadow.
Auld Reekie indeed!
Preferring darkness rather than light
Because our deeds are evil!

I see the dark face of an early mother of men
By a primitive campfire of history.
Her appearance is rendered all the more remarkable
Because of the peculiar performance of the smoke.
By some process, natural no doubt but mysterious to us,
She exercises a strange control over the smoke
As she shuffles round—with vast protruding lips
And with wide rings hanging from her ears,
Weaving her hands. And it is
As if the billows of thick white vapour
Are forced to follow her will
And make a magical dancing cloud
Behind her as she moves.
Learn again to consume your own smoke like this,
Edinburgh, to free your life from the monstrous pall,
To subdue it and be no longer subdued by it,
Like the hand of the dyer in his vat.
So all the darkness of industrialism yet
Must be relegated like a moth that pursues
The onward dance of humanity.

So the mighty impetus of creative force
That seeks liberation, that shows even through
The scum of swinish filth of bourgeois society,
The healthy creative force will break through
—Even in Edinburgh—and good, human things grow,
Protecting and justifying faith
In regeneration to a free and noble life
When labour shall be a thing
Of honour, valour, and heroism
And 'civilization' no longer like Edinburgh
On a Sabbath morning,
Stagnant and foul with the rigid peace
Of an all-tolerating frigid soul!

This is the great skill that mankind has lost,
The distinctively human power.
Lo! A poor negress teaches this rich university city
Something more important than all it knows,
More valuable than all it has!
But Edinburgh—Edinburgh—is too stupid yet
To learn how not to stand in her own light.

Scotland Small?

Scotland small? Our multiform, our infinite Scotland *small*?
Only as a patch of hillside may be a cliché corner
To a fool who cries 'Nothing but heather!' where in
    September another
Sitting there and resting and gazing round
Sees not only heather but blaeberries
With bright green leaves and leaves already turned scarlet,
Hiding ripe blue berries; and amongst the sage-green leaves
Of the bog-myrtle the golden flowers of the tormentil shining;
And on the small bare places, where the little Blackface sheep
Found grazing, milkworts blue as summer skies;
And down in neglected peat-hags, not worked
In living memory, sphagnum moss in pastel shades
Of yellow, green, and pink; sundew and butterwort
And nodding harebells vying in their colour
With the blue butterflies that poise themselves delicately
    upon them,
And stunted rowans with harsh dry leaves of glorious colour.
'Nothing but heather!'—How marvellously descriptive!
    And incomplete!

Bagpipe Music

Let me play to you tunes without measure or end,
Tunes that are born to die without a herald,
As a flight of storks rises from a marsh, circles,
And alights on the spot from which it rose.

Flowers. A flower-bed like hearing the bagpipes.
The fine black earth has clotted into sharp masses
As if the frost and not the sun had come.
It holds many lines of flowers.
First faint rose peonies, then peonies blushing,
The again red peonies, and, behind them,
Massive, apoplectic peonies, some of which are so red
And so violent as to seem almost black; behind these
Stands a low hedge of larkspur, whose tender apologetic
    blossoms

Appear by contrast pale, though some, vivid as the sky
above them,
Stand out from their fellows, iridescent and slaty as a
pigeon's breast,
The bagpipes—they are screaming and they are sorrowful.
There is a wail in their merriment, and cruelty in their
triumph.
They rise and they fall like a weight swung in the air at the
end of a string.
They are like the red blood of those peonies.
And like the melancholy of those blue flowers.
They are like a human voice—no! for the human voice lies!
They are like human life that flows under the words.
That flower-bed is like the true life that wants to express itself
And does . . . while we human beings lie cramped and fearful.

From *Poetry Scotland No. 1*
(1943)

The Glass of Pure Water

Hold a glass of pure water to the eye of the sun!
It is difficult to tell the one from the other
Save by the tiny hardly visible trembling of the water.
This is the nearest analogy to the essence of human life
Which is even more difficult to see.
Dismiss anything you can see more easily;
It is not alive—it is not worth seeing.
There is a minute indescribable difference
Between one glass of pure water and another
With slightly different chemical constituents.
The difference between one human life and another
Is no greater; colour does not colour the water:
You cannot tell a white man's life from a black man's.
But the lives of these particular slum people
I am chiefly concerned with, like the lives of all
The world's poorest, remind me less
Of a glass of water held between my eyes and the sun
—They remind me of the feeling they had
Who saw Sacco and Vanzetti in the death cell
On the eve of their execution.
—One is talking to God.

I dreamt last night that I saw one of His angels
Making his centennial report to the Recording Angel
On the condition of human life.

Look at the ridge of skin between your thumb and
    forefinger.
Look at the delicate lines on it and how they change
—How many different things they can express—
As you move out or close in your forefinger and thumb.
And look at the changing shapes—the countless
Little gestures, little miracles of line—
Of your forefinger and thumb as you move them.
And remember how much a hand can express,
How a single slight movement of it can say more
Than millions of words—dropped hand, clenched fist,
Snapping fingers, thumb up, thumb down,
Raised in blessing, clutched in passion, begging,
Welcome, dismissal, prayer, applause,
And a million other signs, too slight, too subtle,
Too packed with meaning for words to describe,
A universal language understood by all.
And the Angel's report on human life
Was the subtlest movement—just like that—and no more;
A hundred years of life on the Earth
Summed up, not a detail missed or wrongly assessed,
In that little inconceivably intricate movement.

The only communication between man and man
That says anything worth hearing
—The hidden well-water; the finger of destiny—
Moves as that water, that angel, moved.
Truth is the rarest thing and life
The gentlest, most unobtrusive movement in the world.
I cannot speak to you of the poor people of all the world
But among the people in these nearest slums I know
This infinitesimal twinkling, this delicate play
Of tiny signs that not only say more
Than all speech, but all there is to say,
All there is to say and to know and to be.
There alone I seldom find anything else,
Each in himself or herself a dramatic whole,
An 'agon' whose validity is timeless.

Our duty is to free that water, to make these gestures,
To help humanity to shed all else,
All that stands between any life and the sun,
The quintessence of any life and the sun;
To still all sound save that talking to God;
To end all movements save movements like these.
India had that great opportunity centuries ago
And India lost it—and became a vast morass,
Where no water wins free; a monstrous jungle
Of useless movement; a babel
Of stupid voices, drowning the still small voice.
It is our turn now; the call is to the Celt.

This little country can overcome the whole world of
    wrong
As the Lacedaemonians the armies of Persia.
Cornwall—Gaeldom—must stand for the ending
Of the essential immorality of any man controlling
Any other—for the ending of all Government
Since all Government is a monopoly of violence;
For the striking of this water out of the rock of Capitalism;
For the complete emergence from the pollution and fog
With which the hellish interests of private property
In land, machinery, and credit
Have corrupted and concealed from the sun,
From the gestures of truth, from the voice of God,
Hundreds upon hundreds of millions of men,
Denied the life and liberty to which they were born
And fobbed off with a horrible travesty instead
—Self-righteous, sunk in the belief that they are human,
When not a tenth of one per cent show a single gleam
Of the life that is in them under their accretions of filth.

And until that day comes every true man's place
Is to reject all else and be with the lowest,
The poorest—in the bottom of that deepest of wells
In which alone is truth; in which
Is truth only—truth that should shine like the sun,
With a monopoly of movement, and a sound like
    talking to God . . .

From *Poetry Scotland No. 2*
(1945)

Talking with Five Thousand People in Edinburgh

God forbid that I should justify you: till I die I will not remove
mine integrity from me.
Job 27:5.

Talking with five thousand people in Edinburgh yesterday
I was appalled at their lack of love for each other,
At their lack of ecstasy at the astounding miracle
Of being alive in the flesh and together with one another,
And amazed that men and women each superficially so different
Should be so obviously the product of the same temperament,
Dyed in the same vat to a uniform hue.
In each the mood, the atmosphere, the peculiar nature
Of the tension produced, all the intangibles in fact,
Were almost identical—the same unresolved discords,
The same sultry hates, the same murderous impulses
Below the surface of decorous lives, the same
Hopeless struggle against an evil no one dares name
—The same growing understanding that the substitute names
They use for it are wide of the mark, that the name must be
    spoken,
That it will be impossible soon not to speak it out plump and
    plain,
The whole five thousand of them, as with a single voice.

But yesterday I listened to the mutual criticisms,
The sneers, the belittlings, the cynical acceptances,
Misunderstandings, indifferences, looking down their noses,
Pursing their mouths, giving meaning looks, till I saw all these
    people
As specialists in hates and frustrations, students of helpless rages,
Articulators of inarticulate loathings, and suddenly understood
That the trouble was no one knew where the centre lay
Of the system of discontent in which they were pent,
All emotionally suspended and dubious
(Saying all sorts of things with the single exception
Of what they ought to be saying—what they needed to say;
Their powers of speech all hopelessly misapplied)
Because their talk evaded, deserted, their real theme.

They expressed themselves in despairs, doubts, grumblings and
   fears.
None of them had yet made clear contact with the sources of
   his or her power.
They were all fascinated by their hatred of something—but of
   what?
The passion of that nameless hatred got itself partially expressed
By seizing on this or that—on anything—in lieu of its true object.
These were occasions for the rages but not the causes.
Edinburgh produces and sustains agonising tensions of life
—Edinburgh, a blinded giant who has yet to learn
What the motive spirit behind his abilities really is.

So that as I spoke with these five thousand people
Each of us was more or less lost
In the midst of the events so powerfully presented.
All who should help to open the way for true expression
—The teachers, the ministers, the writers—are living like maggots
On dead words in an advanced state of decomposition,
Big words that died over twenty years ago
—For most of the important words were killed in the
   First World War—
And Edinburgh has not given birth to new words yet
In which it can say anything worth saying, make anything
   but animal noises.

Edinburgh—But Edinburgh is no worse than anywhere else;
All the big centres of mankind are like thunder-clouds to-day
Forming part of the horrific structure of a storm
That fills the whole sky—but ere long
Will disappear like the fabric of a dream.

Perhaps Edinburgh's terrible inability to speak out,
Edinburgh's silence with regard to all it should be saying,
Is but the hush that precedes the thunder,
The liberating detonation so oppressively imminent now?
For what are its people standing in their own light,
Denying life infinitely more abundant,
Preferring darkness to light, and death to life?
Edinburgh is capable here and now of a human life
As illimitably greater than any it has yet known,
As any human being's is to the lowest order of animal existence.

All they need to do is to lift up their hearts
And conceive nobler conditions of life, acquire
The feelings which will give forms to such a life, and at once
The necessary organs of these will appear,
Just as life at first put out arms and legs.
All they need to do is to be true to themselves
And not like some foolish woman who cries
There's thunder in the air and stuffs her ears with cotton wool
And goes to bed and hides herself under the blankets
Afraid of the thunder and lightning—the bridegroom who
    enters in.

There is no one really alive in Edinburgh yet:
They are all living on the tiniest fraction
Of the life they could easily have,
Like people in great houses who prefer
To live in their cellars and keep all the rest sealed up.

There is nothing to prevent them except themselves
Having all that the mind of man can know
Or the heart of man conceive.

Total strangers to all the events
Taking place around and in and through them.

No one with either the scientific training
Or the courage and desire to learn
What is going on beneath the surface of life.

Few, if any, of life's collisions here
Are on the purely individual plane.
There is no general scheme behind it,
No real general purpose,
No genuine fighting spirit.
Is there no one to fight this decline of honour,
This hypocrisy, meanness, and boredom?

Let the demagogues denounce me,★ and betray me too
As Burns was betrayed and Bakunin and Maclean;
Serve me as Utin served Marx, with vile slanders to expel
Bakunin and James Guillaume, *Veritas odium parit.*

★ 'Au milieu de douces imbéciles, c'est l'homme d'esprit qui est une bête'—
Maria Star.

Friends, you know. I am guilty of it. Let it rest.
At the worst, *in magnis et voluisse sat est.*
I stand to my position, do what I can,
And will never be turned into a 'strong, silenced man,'
For I am corn and not chaff, and will neither
Be blown away by the wind, nor burst with the flail,
     But will abide them both
     And in the end prevail.

For I am like Zamyatin. I must be a Bolshevik
Before the Revolution, but I'll cease to be one quick
When Communism comes to rule the roost,
For real literature can exist only where it's produced
By madmen, hermits, heretics,
Dreamers, rebels, sceptics,
—And such a door of utterance has been given to me
As none may close whosoever they be.

Let a look at Edinburgh be called
Just an educational film then
Such as we see any day on the screen,
'The Abortion,' say, or 'Why Does It Rain?'
Or 'How Silk Stockings Are Made,' or, finally,
'What Is the Difference Between A Man and A Beaver?'

It's far too late in the day
     For a fellow like this
Trying to organise a conspiracy of feelings
     In Edinburgh of all places.

Let us fall in with the wishes of Authority,
Hush to treasonable rubbish like 'The Red Flag';
Let us study—and in the end be content to be
Each of us no better than a carted stag.

From *A Kist of Whistles*
(1947)

On Reading Professor Ifor Williams's 'Canu Aneurin'* in Difficult Days

*Only barbarism, villainy, and ignorance do not respect the past,
cringing before the present alone.*

Pushkin

Stay me with mosses, comfort me with lichens.

Opening the Gododdin again and renewing
My conscious connection with the gwyr y gogledd†
I who never fail to detect every now and again,
In the Hebridean and Shetland and Cornish waters I
    most frequent,
By subtile signs Myrddin's ship of glass‡
Which has floated invisibly around the seas
Ever since Arfderydd a millennium and a half ago,
(Since Arfderydd—a few miles from where I was born!)§
I am as one who sees again in a stark winter wood
(And the forest of Celyddon‖ is indeed in death's grip
    to-day)

The lichens and mosses, earth's first mercies, shine forth
—The dusk of Lincoln green warming the ragged tree-
    bole,
Dark flaked liverwort on dank cliff,
Rich velvet mosses making a base
For the old stone dykes—all glowing
In a lustrous jewel-like beauty for the enjoyment of which
One might well endure the rigours of winter!
Contrary to common belief, the lichens and mosses
Love the winter sunlight as wise human beings do!
(Thus, of two retaining walls of a sunk lane,

---

* Published by the University of South Wales Press Board, Cardiff, 1939.
† Men of the North.
‡ After the battle of Arfderydd, Myrddin, sometimes called Myrddin Wyllt or Merlinus Sylvestris, the Merlin of the Arthurian romance, fled to the Caledonian forest and finally escaped with his paramour, Chwimleian (Vivien) in a ship of glass.
§ Arthuret, near Carlisle (A.D. 575). The author was born twenty miles away, just over the Scottish border.
‖ The Caledonian forest.

The lichens and mosses are most abundant and vigorous
On the side that receives the largest volume of sunlight,
And a warm stretch of dykefoot facing the low-set
Southern winter sun is the most resplendent
In fair velvet of any exposure known to me.)

Even so, at the feet of the great grim vertical problems
Of contemporary life I am sustained and cheered
By the perennial shining of a few
Little personal relationships
Surely in these days of Massenmensch
A singularly blessed example
Of the transcendent function⋆ emerging
From an enantiodromic movement.

Even so in these sterile and melancholy days
The ghastly desolation of my spirit is relieved
As a winter wood by glowing moss or lichen,
And the sunk lane of my heart is vivified,
And the hidden springs of my life revealed
Still patiently potent and humbly creative
When I spy again the ancestral ties between Scotland
　　and Wales,
And, weary of the senseless cacophony of modern
　　literature,
Recur to Aneirin's Gododdin, one of the oldest poems
In any European vernacular—far older indeed
Than anything ever produced on the Continent
Outside Greek and Latin; and not only
Note how (great topical lesson for us to-day)
It is not the glory, but the pity and waste, of war
That inspires its highest passages, but realise
That the profoundest cause in these Islands to-day,
The Invisible War upon which Earth's greatest issues
　　depend,
Is still the same war the Britons fought in at Catraeth†
And Aneirin sings. The Britons were massacred then.
　　Only one
Escaped alive. His blood flows in my veins to-day

⋆ C. G. Jung's term.
† Catterick in Yorkshire.

Stronger than ever, inspires me with his unchanged purpose,
And moves me alike in Poetry and Politics.

Between two European journeys of Neville Chamberlain's
And two important speeches of Herr Hitler's
I return to the Taliesin and Llywarch Hen poems,
Full of hiraeth, of angry revolt
Against the tyranny of fact, even as Malesherbes
Spent the time lesser men would have devoted
To preparing their case against the forty-three accusations
Contained in the Acte enonciatif
Of December 11, 1792
In reading Hume's History of the House of Stuart.

So I am delivered from the microcosmic human chaos
And given the perspective of a writer who can draw
The wild disorder of a ship in a gale
Against the vaster natural order of sea and sky.
If man does not bulk too big in his rendering
He does not lose the larger half of dignity either.

Aneirin stays me with mosses
And comforts me with lichens
In the winter-bound wood of the world to-day
Where the gaunt branches rattle like gallows bones.

It is like one of the commonest and at the same time
One of the most indeterminate factors in the life of men
—An experience so intensely private
And so jealously guarded and protected
It scarcely reaches the level of articulation.
It is felt to be precious and indispensable.

It belongs to the very foundations
Of temperament and character,
Yet it seldom rises to the clear-cut stage
Of positive affirmation.
It lies somewhere between wistfulness and perception,
In the borderland between longing and knowing.
It is like music from some far-off shore
Or a light that never was on land or sea.

From Cornish Heroic Song for Valda Trevlyn

His attitude towards woman is the basic point
A man must have thought out to know
Where he honestly stands.
Since praise is well, and compliment is well,
But affection—that is the last and final
And most precious reward any man can win.
I remember when you were like that shrub
Which is smothered with carillons of little brick-red bells
Finely striped with yellow lines;
That, when the sun shines through them,
Glow like hot blown glass.
But ah! now, beloved, it is as when on the Carmine
    Cherry,
A hundred feet high and with a spread
Coinciding with the circumference of the earth,
The ruby-red flowerbuds open, and the whole tree
Bursts into carmine flame, a mass of blossom, stark
    crimson.
To see the sun through its branches
When the tree is in full bloom
Is a thing that can never be forgotten.
Nor the sight of your eyes now, Valda,
Through the toppling wave of love.
Love's scarlet banner is over us.
We conquer chaos, a new Creation.

A Golden Wine in the Gaidhealtachd

*(To W. D. MacColl and our hosts and hostesses in Arisaig,
Eigg, South Uist, Raasay, Skye, Barra, and Mull)*

In Scotland in the Gaidhealtachd there's a golden wine
Still to be found in a few houses here and there
Where the secret of its making has been kept for centuries
—Nor would it avail to steal the secret, since it cannot be
    made elsewhere.

In Scotland in the Gaidhealtachd there's a golden wine.
Carelessly and irreligiously quaffed it might be taken
For a very fine Champagne. But it is not an effervescing wine
Although its delicate piquancy produces a somewhat similar
  effect upon the palate.

In Scotland in the Gaidhealtachd there's a golden wine,
A wine that demands so deliberate a pause,
In order to detect its hidden peculiarities
And subtle exquisiteness of its flavour, that to drink it
Is really more a moral than a physical delight.
There is a deliciousness in it that eludes analysis
And like whatever else is superlatively good
Is better appreciated by the memory
Than by present consciousness.

In Scotland in the Gaidhealtachd there's a golden wine.
One of its most ethereal charms lies
In the transitory life of its richest qualities,
For while it requires a certain leisure and delay
Yet if you linger too long upon the draught it becomes
Disenchanted both of its fragrance and its flavour.

In Scotland in the Gaidhealtachd there's a golden wine.
The lustre should not be forgotten among the other
Admirable embodiments of this rare wine; for, as it stands in
  a glass
A little circle of light glows round about it,
The finest Orvieto or that famous wine,
The Est Est Est of Montefiascone,
Is vulgar in comparison. This is surely
The wine of the Golden Age such as Bacchus himself
First taught mankind to press from the choicest of his grapes.

In Scotland in the Gaidhealtachd there's a golden wine.
There is a tradition that if any of it were sent to market
This wine would lose all its wonderful qualities.
Not a drop of it therefore has ever been sold,
Or ever will be. Indeed the wine is so fond
Of its native home that a transportation
Of even a few miles turns it quite sour.
Yet the custom of those who have it has always been and still is
To let it flow freely whenever those

Whom they love and honour sit at the board.
But it cannot be drunk in all the world
Save under these particular roofs in Arisaig and Eigg,

In Tobermory, South Uist, Barra, Raasay and Skye,
Nor can they see or smell or taste it who are not
Competent receivers—nor could they bestow
Who lack the sense of operative form—this consecrated juice
Symbolising the holy virtues of hospitality and social kindness.

Through what else can Scotland recover its poise
Save, as Very Hope believes, this golden wine yet?

Off the Coast of Fiedeland

Shetland (West side) herring fishing, June 1936

Written during a week aboard the sailing ship *Valkyrie*

(To Skipper John Irvine, of Saltness, Whalsay)

Twenty miles out to the main deep
Due west o' the Ramna Stacks
And sou-west o' the Flugga Light
I ha'e a' that my pleasure lacks.

Gannet, havd wide. Seek the bush-raip alang
Till aiblins at last you may sight
A single white cork amang a' the broon
On which you may like to alight.

But awa' doon here on the inshore grunds
Twenty-miles sou-west o' the Flugga Light
I row at ease on a broon mysel'
And ha'e nae need to seek for a white.

---

bush-raip, rope attached to net   aiblins, perhaps

For shootin' oor nets parallel to the Ramna Stacks
I think o' the sixareens o' the auld Fiedeland fleet
And their hardy fishermen a' langsyne in the mools,
And life ony auld gait is fell sweet.

Rinnin' oor nets oot in line wi' the Stacks
Wi' oor ain broon sails clashed doon at oor feet
There's nae white to be seen save yon toom face o' a
    mune
Till we haul up syne, when oor shot may compete.

Gannet, haud wide. Swing awa' roon' the buoys.
It's my watch tonight while we lie to the nets,
And I'm blithe to be whaur the hert o' darkness
Wins back sae muckle day aye needs forgets.

My een compete wi' the Aeschiness Light,
There's little else to be seen wi' the ootward eye,
But it's no' the ootward eye that contents my mind,
Nor yet that difference, gannet, 'twixt you and me.

And I ken the morn we'll pit in at North Roe
And I'll see wi' the lassies in the guttin' ranks there
The wee Whalsay lassie I lo' best o' a'
Wi' a wreath o' white gulls roond her bonnie broon hair
—Aye, when her skinklan' tresses she combs
She's bonnier than ocht on the Floo'ery Holms.

Fillin' oor cran-baskets and swingin' them up
And alang on the trollies, a look and a smile,
A word in the bygaein', and, if I'm lucky, a touch,
'll haud me gaein' again for anither while.

Praise be, it's only a plain Shetland lad
At whom ony sweet Shetland lass e'er keeks.
God or the King o' Heaven kens wha
If they tried to butt in 'ud be deemed juist freaks.
Ony fisher lad 'ud hae them beat to the wide
If they cam' here ettlin' to find a bride.

---

sixareens, the old square sail boats   langsyne in the mools, all long dead
ony auld gait, any old way   toom, empty   shot, haul of herring
Roe, pronounced Rew   skinklan', shining   bygaein', passing
keeks, peeps   ettlin', trying

Syne we'll bear awa' yont the Stacks aince mair
Till I'll feel like a 'reincandescent' again,
But whaur the white light that glows in me's frae
Only mysel', and the lassie at North Roe, ken.

Oh, awa' yont the Ramna Stacks again
For anither night on the edge o' the Main Deep there!
—Lassie, I doot I never saw afore
Hoo bright the gowd glints in your bonnie broon hair.

Furth frae your breists and oot through the ocean
Pearl-white stream ne'er confused in the maelstrom o'
    waters.
As the needle to the Pole my hert to you,
Fairest 'mang the haill o' Hialtland's daughters!

Seaward again yont the Erne's Crag
And the horns o' the neeps o' Greevlan',
And I praise the Lord that your love for me
In the weavin' waters needs nae unreevlin'!

Look, there's a tystie fleein' wi' his boat full!
But I've dipped a raip owre and sprinkled oor deck
Wi' the sparklin' saut draps for luck's sake again
Or the tystie's gobbled the fish doon his neck.

Ho, there Jimmy! Jimmy Williamson, ho!
Sing to the herrin' as you used to do.
I'll go in wi' the chorus, but there's twa bright herrin'
Loupin' in my chest'll no answer to you!

Sing: 'Come on, peerie fish. Fill the hungry hold.
I see a straggle. I see white in the lum.
I see faither awa' there at the back o' the bed.
Here's a better bit strollie. Let her come. Let her come.
The seals are snuffin' a' alang the tow-heid,
Hannah abune is squealin' wi' greed.
Come on in. You're safer wi' us indeed,
Bonxie and maulie are seekin' their feed.

---

neeps, promontories   unreevlin', unravelling   tystie, Black Guillemot
wi' his boat full, with a fish in his mouth (the following three lines refer to an old
fisherman's superstition)   peerie, little   hannah, the herring gull
bonxie, the great skua   maulie, the Fulmar petrel

There she's again. I see her. I see her.
Toddle up, toddle up. You're far better here.'
I hear the tirricks roarin' astern.
'I'll sing to the herrin' in the mornin', lad.
I'll tell her to shiver her noses then
When she's taen the best cravat ever she's had.'

The fish Christ Jesus and my ain bonnie lass
Flash sidewise in my blood-pool a' the time.
There's twa fish loupin' in my bosem, Jimmy,
Wi' an ever-mair glorious skyme after skyme.

Flickerin' birds fade into the grim rocks where they nest
As the starry hosts in the sunrise fade.
My body may swing on the fishin' grunds here
But my spirit in the light o' her love is stayed.

Let the night darken. They'll brighten the mair,
My een and the Aeschiness Light and them.
And *them*, I say—but in the howe o' the night
Guid kens they shine like a single flame.

Borin' its way through the hert o' the dark
And bearin' me wi't—till we come aince mair,
Tackin' up the Soond to the Biorgs again
And I see her standin' in the guttin ranks there
Wi' a wreath o' gulls like wavin' white lilies
Plaited aboot her bonnie broon hair
—Sae I'll see her again in the first o' the day
Till she and I blend in yae flame tae,
Fairer than yon that's erst seemed sae fair!

Certes if she* rises to soom the night
There'll be something to meet her afore her face!
Mair than sixty vessels shootin' their nets
In the light o' the sunset a' roond oor place.
Yet aiblins the morn I'll hae white in my net
Purer than ony the ocean's gien yet.

---

tirricks, Arctic terns   skyme, gleam   howe, valley   Guid kens, God knows
yae, one   yon, that   certes, certainly

* 'She' here, also 'her' in verses 16 and 17 refers, of course, to the herring.

White as driven snaw and warmin' as wine
And mine, my sweethert, mine—mine!
Witch that I burn in my hert ilka night,★
The *Valkyrie's* luck and my pride and delight!

Nae lass in the crews† at the Shetland stations
Can gut herrin' mair deftly and quickly than you.
But, certes, you've put the guts *into* me,
And I'd sail for you into Hell's reid mou'.

It's a fine clear trusty sky the night,
The fires o' the sunset are playin' reid yet
Roond the Blue Mull, Valleyfield and the Pobie astern
—Like the fires o' my hert roond you, my pet.

An' I'll sail Earth's seas as lang as I maun
Mixin' my blood wi' the bitterest brine
If that is the only airt I can win
At last to mixin' my blood wi' thine.

For a workin' lad and a workin' lass
Can lo'e each ither juist at least as weel
As Royalty or the wealthiest folk
Or onybody trained in a public skeel.

It's a perfect miracle, lassie, hoo near
You can seem to me whiles even awa' oot here
On the edge o' the main deep. It was ill to ken
It was only a dream I had o' you then.

When the kaim o' Foula lifts on the Smew
My peerie lass I'm aye thinkin' o' you,
And aye I'd leifer see yours instead
O' even the finest dry weather heid,
And when there's nocht else in the warld in sight
You're aye in view.

O Love that pours oot through the welterin' sea
In a constant inviolable muckle moonpath to me
Frae my lass at North Roe, I'se warrant that current
'll find a' life's troubles, and Death itsel', nae deterrent!

---

maun, must   airt, way   skeel, school   kaim, comb   leifer, rather

★ Refers to another old fisherman's superstition.
† Three girls constitute a gutting crew.

Grain o' wind now, boys, and the auld boat
In through its blasts like a greyh'und coorses
Doon the tricky tideways o' Yell Soond, fu'
O' sunshine noo—on white horses!

Three reefs and nae comfort up or doon
Where I'm still thinkin', my love, o' you
While we play Lant in an air smoke, steam,
And sweaty socks mak' like an Irish stew.

Lant, an old and complicated card game much favoured by Shetland fishermen.

From *Poetry Scotland* No. 4
(1949)

Crystals Like Blood

I remember how, long ago, I found
Crystals like blood in a broken stone.

I picked up a broken chunk of bed-rock
And turned it this way and that,
It was heavier than one would have expected
From its size. One face was caked
With brown limestone. But the rest
Was a hard greenish-grey quartz-like stone
Faintly dappled with darker shadows,
And in this quartz ran veins and beads
Of bright magenta.

And I remember how later on I saw
How mercury is extracted from cinnebar
—The double ring of iron piledrivers
Like the multiple legs of a fantastically symmetrical spider
Rising and falling with monotonous precision,
Marching round in an endless circle
And pounding up and down with a tireless, thunderous force,
While, beyond, another conveyor drew the crumbled ore
From the bottom and raised it to an opening high
In the side of a gigantic grey-white kiln.

So I remember how mercury is got
When I contrast my living memory of you
And your dear body rotting here in the clay
—And feel once again released in me
The bright torrents of felicity, naturalness, and faith
My treadmill memory draws from you yet.

From *In Memoriam James Joyce*
(1955)

In the Fall

Let the only consistency
In the course of my poetry
Be like that of the hawthorn tree
Which in early Spring breaks
Fresh emerald, then by nature's law
Darkens and deepens and takes
Tints of purple-maroon, rose-madder and straw.

Sometimes these hues are found
Together, in pleasing harmony bound.
Sometimes they succeed each other. But through
All the changes in which the hawthorn is dight,
No matter in what order, one thing is sure
—The haws shine ever the more ruddily bright!

And when the leaves have passed
Or only in a few tatters remain
The tree to the winter condemned
        Stands forth at last
        Not bare and drab and pitiful,
But a candelabrum of oxidised silver gemmed
By innumerable points of ruby
Which dominate the whole and are visible
Even at considerable distance
As flame-points of living fire.
That so it may be
With my poems too at last glance
Is my only desire.

All else must be sacrificed to this great cause.
I fear no hardships. I have counted the cost.
I with my heart's blood as the hawthorn with its haws
Which are sweetened and polished by the frost!

See how these haws burn, there down the drive,
In this autumn air that feels like cotton wool,
When the earth has the gelatinous limpness of a body
    dead as a whole
While its tissues are still alive!

Poetry is human existence come to life,
The glorious energy that once employed
Turns all else in creation null and void,
The flower and fruit, the meaning and goal,
Which won all else is needs removed by the knife
Even as a man who rises high
Kicks away the ladder he has come up by.

This single-minded zeal, this fanatic devotion to art
Is alien to the English poetic temperament no doubt,
'This narrowing intensity' as the English say,
But I have it even as you had it, Yeats, my friend,
And would have it with me as with you at the end,
I who am infinitely more un-English than you
And turn Scotland to poetry like those women who
In their passion secrete and turn to
Musk through and through!

So I think of you, Joyce, and of Yeats and others
    who are dead
As I walk this Autumn and observe
The birch tremulously pendulous in jewels of cairngorm,
The sauch, the osier, and the crack-willow
Of the beaten gold of Australia;
The sycamore in rich straw-gold;
The elm bowered in saffron;
The oak in flecks of salmon gold;
The beeches huge torches of living orange.

Billow upon billow of autumnal foliage
From the sheer high bank glass themselves
Upon the ebon and silver current that floods freely
Past the shingle shelves.
I linger where a crack willow slants across the stream,
Its olive leaves slashed with fine gold.
Beyond the willow a young beech
Blazes almost blood-red,
Vying in intensity with the glowing cloud of crimson
That hangs about the purple bole of a gean
Higher up the brae face.

And yonder, the lithe green-grey bole of an ash,
    with its boughs

Draped in the cinnamon-brown lace of samara.
(And I remember how in April upon its bare twigs
The flowers came in ruffs like the unshorn ridges
Upon a French poodle—like a dull mulberry at first,
Before the first feathery fronds
Of the long-stalked, finely-poised, seven-fingered
    leaves)—
Even the robin hushes his song
In these gold pavilions.

Other masters may conceivably write
Even yet in C major
But we—we take the perhaps 'primrose path'
To the dodecaphonic bonfire.

The Task

Ah, Joyce, this is our task,
Making what a moving, thrilling, mystical, tropical,
Maniacal, magical creation of all these oppositions,
Of good to evil, greed to self-sacrifice,
Selfishness to selflessness, of this all-pervading atmosphere,
Of the seen merging with the unseen,
Of the beautiful sacrificed to the ugly,
Of the ugly transformed to the beautiful,
Of this intricate yet always lucid and clear-sighted
Agglomeration of passions, manias, occult influences,
Historical and classical references
—Sombre, insane, brilliant and sane,
Timeless, a symbol of the reality
That lies beyond and through the apparent,
Written with the sweeping assurance, the inspired beauty,
The intimated truth of genius,
With natures like ours in which a magnetic fluidity
That is neither 'good' nor 'bad' is forever
Taking new shapes under the pressure of circumstances,

Taking new shapes, and then again,
As Kwang makes Confucius complain of Laotze,
'Shooting up like a dragon.'
But, taking my life as a whole,
And hovering with the flight of the hawk
Over its variegated landscape,
I believe I detect certain quite definite 'streams of tendency'
In that unrolling map,
Moving towards the unknown future.
For one thing I fancy the manner I have allowed
My natural impulses towards romance and mysticism
To dominate me has led to the formation
Of a curious gap or 'lacuna'
Between the innate and almost savage realism,
Which is a major element in my nature,
And the imaginative, poetical cult
Whereby I have romanticised and idealized my life.
In this realistic mood I recognise
With a grim animal acceptance
That it is indeed likely enough that the 'soul'
Perishes everlastingly with the death of the body,
But what this realistic mood, into which
My mind falls like a plummet
Through the neutral zone of its balanced doubt,
Never for one single beat of time can shake or disturb
Is my certain knowledge,
Derived from the complex vision of everything in me,
That the whole astronomical universe, however illimitable,
Is only one part and parcel of the mystery of Life;
Of this I am as certain as I am certain that I am I.
The astronomical universe is *not* all there is.

So this is what our lives have been given to find,
A language that can serve our purposes,
A marvellous lucidity, a quality of fiery aery light,
Flowing like clear water, flying like a bird,
Burning like a sunlit landscape.
Conveying with a positively Godlike assurance,
Swiftly, shiningly, exactly, what we want to convey.
This use of words, this peculiar aptness and handiness,
Adapts itself to our every mood, now pathetic, now ironic,

Now full of love, of indignation, of sensuality, of glamour,
   of glory,
With an inevitable richness of remembered detail
And a richness of imagery that is never cloying,
A curious and indescribable quality
Of sensual sensitiveness,
Of very light and very air itself,
—Pliant as a young hazel wand,
Certain as a gull's wings,
Lucid as a mountain stream,
Expressive as the eyes of a woman in the presence of love,—
Expressing the complex vision of everything in one,
Suffering all impressions, all experience, all doctrines
To pass through and taking what seems valuable from each,
No matter in however many directions
These essences seem to lead.

Collecting up all these essences,
These intimations coming willy-nilly from all quarters,
Into a complex conception of all things,
An intricately-cut gem-stone of a myriad facets
That is yet, miraculously, a whole;
Each of which facets serves its individual purpose
In directing the light collected from every side outwards
In a single creative ray.
With each of these many essences culled
From the vast field of life some part of one's own
Complex personality has affinity and resembles
When climbing on to the ice-cap a little south of Cape
   Bismarck
And keeping the nunataks of Dronning Louises Land on
   our left
We travel five days
On tolerable ice in good weather
With few bergs to surmount
And no crevasses to delay us.
Then suddenly our luck turns.
A wind of 120 miles an hour blows from the East,
And the plateau becomes a playground of gales
And the novel light gives us snow-blindness.
We fumble along with partially bandaged eyes

Our reindeer-skin kamiks worn into holes
And no fresh sedge-grass to stump them with.
We come on ice-fields like mammoth ploughlands
And mountainous séracs which would puzzle an Alpine
    climber.
That is what adventuring in dictionaries means,
All the abysses and altitudes of the mind of man,
Every test and trial of the spirit,
Among the debris of all past literature
And raw material of all the literature to be.

From *Collected Poems*
(1962)

Happy on Heimaey

Meanwhile the last of the human faculties
To be touched by the finger of science,
Still unanalysed, still immeasurable,
The sense of smell is the one little refuge
In the human mind still inviolate and unshareable
Because communicable in no known language.
But someday this the most delicate of perceptions
Will be laid bare too—there will be
Chairs of osmology in our universities,
Ardent investigators searching out, recording, measuring,
Preserving in card indexes
The departing smells of the countryside,
Hayfields will be explained in terms of Coumarin,
Beanfields in Ionome, hedge-roses in Phenyl-Ethyl-
    Propionate,
Hawthorn as Di-Methyl-Hydroquinone.
(But will they ever capture the scent of violets
Among the smoke of the shoeing forge, or explain
The clean smell of a road wet with summer-rain?)
Until that day on Heimaey, 400 miles due North-West
Of Rona in the Hebrides, I am content to walk out
Into an unreal country of yellow fields
Lying at the foot of black volcanic cliffs
In the shadow of dead Helgafell,
And watch a few farmers scything
(Careful of the little birds' nests,
Iceland wheatear, snow bunting, white wagtail, meadow
    pipit,
And leaving clumps of grass to protect them)
A sweet but slender hay-crop
And tell its various constituents for myself
. . . White clover, chickenweed, dandelion,
A very large buttercup, silverweed, horsetail
Thrift, sorrel, yellow bedstraw,
Poa, carex, and rushes . . .
Or look out of my bedroom window
In the farmhouse near Kaupstadur
On a garden planted with angelica,
Red currant, rhubarb, and the flower of Venus,
Or at midnight watch the sun

Roll slowly along the northern horizon
To dip behind the great ice-caps
And jokulls of distant Iceland.
'Mellach lem bhith ind acht ailiuin for beind cairrge
Conacind and ar a mheinci feth na fairrci.'
Ah, me! It is a far better thing to be sitting
Alive, on Heimaey, bare as an egg though it were,
Than rolled round willy-nilly with yonder sun.

Esplumeoir

He's chain lightning. Brains count in this business.

It was an amazing discovery, like the inside of your head being painlessly scraped out. There was an amazing clarity, like the brilliant moon falling into it and fitting it neatly.

But shairly, shairly, there maun be
Or sae, of course, it seems to you—
Some instinct o' black waters swirlin'
And dangerous images juist oot o' view
Ettlin' to spoil happiness and pu' apairt
Dreams that ha'e become realities?

I tell you, No! There's naething—naething o' the kind.
Nae ootward things, shapes, colours, soonds, or memories
   o' these
To strike in on and move and muddle the mind;
Nae *sombra do tempo* cast
By comin' events or present or past,
And least o' a' ony *Scheinprobleme* here!
I ken fu' weel for a man like you
To think o' this maun be as when
On the wa' abune your heid
Shiftin' prisms o' licht frae the water
May dance a fandango
Unutterably free and airy
In a squalid wee ship's-cabin

ettlin', trying   pu' apairt, pull apart

While you couldna hit the wa'
If you were locked in a wardrobe, you fool.
But as for me I canna mind a time
When the mere thocht o't didna mak' me
Licht up like a match!

'Aloof as a politician
The first year efter election'
You grumble, 'There's naething to see.
It's a' expressionless as tho' it micht be
Enamelled wi' an airbrush that tawnish grey
Nae-colour sae common on motors—wasn't only yesterday?—
Yet bricht as when the stars were glowin'
Wi' sic a steady radiance that the lift
Seemed filled to overflowin'—I wadna hae't in a gift.
It mak's me feel upon my word
Like a fly on the edge o' a phonograph record.'
(A phrase divertin'ly *vergeistigt* here)

The Leisure State! Fell dreich, you think? Intelligence is
    characterised
By a natural lack o' comprehension o' life
But here intelligence is a', and a'thing devised
To favour 'life' and its expense excised,
Naething left in human nature cybernetics
Can ever delegate to electronic tricks;
Tint, clean tint, as gin it had never been
A' that could be touched or tasted, heard or seen.
Wi' nae mair expression that a china settin' egg.

The utter stillness o' the timeless world!
The haill creation has vanished forever
Wi' nae mair noise or disturbance than a movie fade-out,
The expression o' blankness which sae often
Distinguishes the profound thinker.

Naething to see—you sudna ha'e far to gang
For an analogy frae your Earth experience tho',
Sin' at winter's edge when a' thing's gone sere,
Emptied o' a' Simmer's routh and bare as a bane gey near,

---

fell dreich, extremely dreary   tint, lost   routh, plenty   gey near, almost

Bacteriologists say the soil's teemin' mair thrang
Wi' life than at ony ither time, yet wi' nocht to show.
Like cricket's deceptive impression o' slowness
Tho' the split-second decisions sae often required
Ha'e to be made quicker than in ony ither game;
Or like the sleepy een o' a great detective
Wha misses nocht and canna be fooled
But's aye maist, when he looks least, alert.
Or as a day that was gaen to be
Oppressively het wi' thunder later
Used to stimulate a'thing to live
Brimmin'ly afore the cataclysm
Till a'thing that ran or flew or crawled
Abune or aneth was filled pang-fu' wi' life
Like yon cicada shrillin' piercin'ly
Try'in to stert up the haill chorus.
He'd been underground an 'oor ago
And micht be doon a bird's throat by nicht.
That he was alive richt then was reason eneuch
For singin' wi' a' his micht.
Eternity's like that—a'thing keyed up
To the heichest pitch as if
A cataclysm's comin'—only it's no!

Eternity is like an auld green parrot
I kent aince. Its conversational range was sma'
Yet when it tilted its heid and cocked
A beady eye at you, you got the feelin'
That, if it chose, it could tell you a thing or twa;
That, as the French pit it,
Il connût le dessous des cartes.
Eternity is like an obstinate jellyfish
That comes floatin' back as soon as you've scared it off
But, if you try to seize it, reverses its tactics
And jouks awa' like a muckle dawd o' quicksilver.

Or pit it like this—Eternity's
Twa doors frae the corner a'whaur

---

thrang, busy   pang-fu', crammed full
jouks, dodges   muckle dawd, big lump   a'whaur, everywhere

A sma', demure white biggin'
Wi' shutters and a canopy.
The canopy's royal blue
And it says *Eternity*
In discreet soap-glass letters
On ilka-side. Under the canopy
You walk up and the front door
Is a' mirror wi' a cool strip
O' fluorescent light on top.
You push the pearl button,
And listen to the delicate chimes
And adjust your tie in the mirror
And fix your hat—but the guy
Ahint the bullet-proof mirror
Sees a' that too,
Only you canna see him.
The guy ahint the mirror
Is Tutti-Frutti Forgle,
A muckle nigger wi' fuzzy-white hair
Wha kens his business.
Aince past Tutti, you check your hat
In a quiet soft-lit anteroom,
Syne the haill place is yours.

Sae cool and sculptured in its lack o' detail,
Its quiet reserve, its expensive simplicity,
Sae couthily different frae earth's nerve-frayin' emotionalism,
Coolness, stillness, nae silly vivacity,
Nae spillin' owre and showin' feelin's here,
Like a wumman wha's daurk hair disna reflect the licht,
Tho' her grey een reflect far mair than their share o't.
Yon cauld snake. Yon *nymphoea tuberosa*!
Water-lilies hae sic a strong urge to live
They can get unco teuch wi' obstacles in their way.

Aye, dreich eneuch, at first sicht—I ken fu' weel
Hoo efter pursuin' his quarry furiously
Mony's the keen hunter feels his spirit unaccoontably
Sag when at last it's wi'in easy reach;

---

biggin', building   couthily, cosily   unco teuch, extremely tough

Staleness clamps on him syne like a muckle leech.
Staleness?—the Deil!
Juist as intense desire whiles mak's a man
Impotent at the richt (or wrang) minute!

That's why a poet like Valéry tried
Frae his poetry to haud a' 'life' ootside.
'You're deid. You've nae mair to dae wi' the warld again.'
Its's neist to impossible for onybody to be
Circumcised frae the warld like this,
Hyne away frae its pleasures, sorrows, comforts—free
O' the haill damned thing as a corpse is.
Of course you canna understand, canna grasp the connection,
For *this*, you fool, *this* is to ken the resurrection!

To a Friend and Fellow-Poet*

It is with the poet as with a guinea worm
Who, to accommodate her teeming progeny
Sacrifices nearly every organ of her body, and becomes
(Her vagina obliterated in her all-else-consuming
Process of uterine expansion, and she still faced
With a grave obstetrical dilemma calling for
Most marvellous contrivance to deposit her prodigious swarm
Where they may find the food they need and have a chance in life)
Almost wholly given over to her motherly task,
Little more than one long tube close-packed with young;
Until from the ruptured bulla, the little circular sore,
You see her dauntless head protrude, and presently, slowly,
A beautiful, delicate and pellucid tube
Is projected from her mouth, tenses and suddenly spills
Her countless brood in response to a stimulus applied
Not directly to the worm herself, but the skin of her host
With whom she has no organised connection (and that stimulus
O Poets! but cold water!) . . . The worm's whole
    musculocutaneous coat

hyne, far
* Ruth Pitter.

Thus finally functions as a uterus, forcing the uterine tube
With its contents through her mouth. And when the
   prolapsed uterus ruptures
The protruded and now collapsed portion shrivels to a thread
(Alexander Blok's utter emptiness after creating a poem!)
The rapid drying of which effectually and firmly
Closes the wound for the time being . . . till, later, the
   stimulus being reapplied,
A fresh portion of the uterine tube protrudes, ruptures, and
   collapses,
Once more ejaculating another seething mass of embryos,
And so the process continues until inch by inch
The entire uterus is expelled and parturition concluded.
Is it not precisely thus we poets deliver our store,
Our whole being the instrument of our suicidal art,
And by the skin of our teeth 'flype' ourselves into fame?

Glasgow 1960*

Returning to Glasgow after long exile
Nothing seemed to me to have changed its style.
Buses and trams all labelled 'To Ibrox'
Swung past packed tight as they'd hold with folks.
Football match, I concluded, but just to make sure
I asked; and the man looked at me fell dour,
Then said, 'Where in God's name are *you* frae, sir?
It'll be a record gate, but the cause o' the stir
Is a debate on "la loi de l'effort converti"
Between Professor MacFadyen and a Spanish pairty.'
I gasped. The newsboys came running along,
'Special! Turkish Poet's Abstruse New Song.
Scottish Authors' Opinions'—and, holy snakes,
I saw the edition sell like hot cakes.

flype, turn inside out.

*Written some years earlier than 1960.

Reflections in a Slum

A lot of the old folk here—all that's left
Of them after a lifetime's infernal thrall
Remind me of a Bolshie the 'whites' buried alive
Up to his nose, just able to breathe, that's all.

Watch them. You'll see what I mean. When found
His eyes had lost their former gay twinkle.
Ants had eaten *that* away; but there was still
Some life in him . . . his forehead *would* wrinkle!

And I remember Gide telling
Of Valéry and himself:
'It was a long time ago. We were young.
We had mingled with idlers
Who formed a circle
Round a troupe of wretched mountebanks.
It was on a raised strip of pavement
In the boulevard Saint Germain,
In front of the Statue of Broca.
They were admiring a poor woman,
Thin and gaunt, in pink tights, despite the cold.
Her team-mate had tied her, trussed her up,
Skilfully from head to foot,
With a rope that went round her
I don't know how many times,
And from which, by a sort of wriggling,
She was to manage to free herself.
Sorry image of the fate of the masses!
But no one thought of the symbol.
The audience merely contemplated
In stupid bliss the patient's efforts.
She twisted, she writhed, slowly freed one arm,
Then the other, and when at last
The final cord fell from her
Valéry took me by the arm:
"Let's go now! She has ceased suffering!"'

Oh, if only ceasing to suffer
They were able to become men.
Alas! how many owe their dignity,
Their claim on our sympathy,

Merely to their misfortune.
Likewise, so long as a plant has not blossomed
One can hope that its flowering will be beautiful.
What a mirage surrounds what has not yet blossomed!
What a disappointment when one can no longer
Blame the abjection on the deficiency!
It is good that the voice of the indigent,
Too long stifled, should manage
To make itself heard.
But I cannot consent to listen
To nothing but that voice.
Man does not cease to interest me
When he ceases to be miserable.
Quite the contrary!
That it is important to aid him
In the beginning goes without saying,
Like a plant it is essential
To water at first,
But this is in order to get it to flower
And I *am concerned with the blossom.*

From *Akros No. 3*
(1966)

A Change of Weather

(Scotland: February 1966)

Even the cauld draps o' dew that hing
Hauf-melted on the beard o' the thistle this Februar day
Hae something genial and refreshin' aboot them
And the sun, strugglin' airgh and wan i' the lift,
Hauf-smoored in the grey mist, seems nane the less
   An emblem o' the guid cause.

It's like quality in weather, affectin' a'thing
But aye eludin' touch, sicht, and soond,
Naething o' the Earth sinks deeper noo
Aneth the canny surface o' the mind
Than autumn leaves driftin' on a lochan.

Yet thinkin' o' Scotland syne's like lookin'
Into real deep water whaur the depth
Becomes sae great it seems to move and swell
Withoot the slightest ripple, yet somehoo gie's me
An unco sense o' the sun's stability
And fills me, slowly, wi' a new ardour and elasticity.

It's like having—hashish, is it?

airgh, hesitantly   lift, sky   hauf-smoored, half-smothered
a'thing, everything   canny, comfortable   syne, then
unco, extraordinary

Index of first lines